About this Book an

"With the appearance of *The Buddha Eye* ... [
has been launched."

> **—Taitetsu Unno**, Jill Ker Conway Professor of Religion at Smith
> College

"This anthology serves as an excellent introduction to the Suzuki version
of Zen."

> **—Journal of Asian Studies**

"Dialogues with the spiritual masters of the East show us the possibility of
a universal ecumenism that is rarely experienced."

> **—Matthew Fox**, author of *Original Blessing* and *One River, Many
> Wells*

"For the pilgrim in each of us who would journey into Eastern or Western
spiritual traditions to chart a path in this troubled time.... "

> **—Joanna Macy**, author of *World as Lover, World as Self*

"His words... make us see the world as a place where, with more understanding and tolerance, we could all live together in harmony."

> **—Rhena Schweitzer Miller**, daughter of Albert Schweitzer

"He simply sees things most people do not.... "

> **—Harvey Cox**, author of *The Secular City* and *Many Mansions*

"Frederick Franck's exploration of what it means to be human and his
moving artistic expression have been transnational, transcultural and
transdisciplinary."

> **—Nuclear Age Peace Foundation**, which awarded Franck
> a World Citizenship Award

"The fact that, over ninety and recovering from a near-fatal automobile accident, Franck still finds hope and beauty in the world around him and can convey it with such simple force, is perhaps the most eloquent answer of all."

—**Parabola** magazine

"Frederick Franck is an artist and author who believes in seeing everything around him.... [This] does not mean simply looking at, but instead actively realizing the importance of everything around him, especially other people."

—**The Online Journal of Peace and Conflict Resolution**

"Above all else, Franck is a bridge builder whose spirituality points to a new way of being in the twenty-first century."

—**Spirituality and Health** magazine

World Wisdom
The Library of Perennial Philosophy

The Library of Perennial Philosophy is dedicated to the exposition of the timeless Truth underlying the diverse religions. This Truth, often referred to as the *Sophia Perennis*—or Perennial Wisdom—finds its expression in the revealed Scriptures as well as the writings of the great sages and the artistic creations of the traditional worlds.

The Perennial Philosophy provides the intellectual principles capable of explaining both the formal contradictions and the transcendent unity of the great religions.

Ranging from the writings of the great sages of the past, to the perennialist authors of our time, each series of our Library has a different focus. As a whole, they express the inner unanimity, transforming radiance, and irreplaceable values of the great spiritual traditions.

The Buddha Eye: An Anthology of the Kyoto School and Its Contemporaries appears as one of our selections in the Spiritual Classics series.

Spiritual Classics Series

This series includes seminal, but often neglected, works of unique spiritual insight from leading religious authors of both the East and West. Ranging from books composed in ancient India to forgotten jewels of our time, these important classics feature new introductions which place them in the perennialist context.

World Wisdom wishes to express its gratitude to the Nanzan Institute for Religion and Culture in Nagoya, Japan, and to James W. Heisig, general Editor of their Nanzan Studies in Religion and Culture series, for their cooperation and assistance with this revised edition of *The Buddha Eye*. Please visit their website at http://www.nanzan-u.ac.jp/SHUBUNKEN for more information on their projects and publications.

Cover: Amida Nyorai, 11th century, Japan

The Buddha Eye

An Anthology of the Kyoto School and Its Contemporaries

Edited by
Frederick Franck

Foreword by Joan Stambaugh

World Wisdom

The Buddha Eye:
An Anthology of the Kyoto School and Its Contemporaries
© 2004 World Wisdom, Inc.

The Buddha Eye: An Anthology of the Kyoto School and Its Contemporaries
is a revised edition of the 1982 edition which was originally published as
The Buddha Eye: An Anthology of the Kyoto School, Crossroad, New York, 1982.

Most recent printing indicated by the last digit below:
10 9 8 7 6 5 4 3 2

Library of Congress Cataloging-in-Publication Data

The Buddha eye : an anthology of the Kyoto school and its contemporaries
/ edited by Frederick Franck ; foreword by Joan Stambaugh.
p. cm. – (The spiritual classics series)

Includes bibliographical references and index.
ISBN 0-941532-59-3 (pbk. : alk. paper)

1. Buddhism–Doctrines. 2. Philosophy, Buddhism. 3. Philosophy,
Japanese–20th century. I. Franck, Frederick, 1909- II. Series:
Spiritual classics
(Bloomington, Ind.)
BQ4165.B79 2004
294.3'420427–dc22

2004001541

Printed on acid-free paper in the United States of America

For information address World Wisdom, Inc.
P.O. Box 2682, Bloomington, Indiana 47402-2682

Pluck out the Buddha eye
and sit in its hollow!

DŌGEN

Table of Contents

PART III. What is Shin Buddhism?

IKKYŪ'S SKELETONS

Publisher's Note to the 2004 edition

One of the defining notes in the history of twentieth century philosophical and religious thought is the encounter of East and West; and especially the enormous influence of Buddhism on many Western thinkers, artists, and spiritual seekers. Within the Buddhist tradition, Zen has achieved a level of prominence which has brought it so deeply into the public consciousness that in the last twenty years one has begun to hear this word used in connection with all manner of activity as a kind of mysterious informing intuition which allows us to transcend all "otherness" and harmoniously express the inward nature of things in the face of everyday life.

But what exactly is Zen and why have so many people, across so many ranges of human endeavor, become interested in its teachings? This book, edited by the renowned artist and author Dr. Frederick Franck, offers a multi-faceted jewel of an answer to these questions. First published in 1982, it continues to shed light and provide insights into Zen and is especially well-suited to Western readers. Moreover, we feel that it has achieved the status of a classic work on the subject and that it should thus become required reading for all serious students of the Mahayana Buddhist tradition and its influence upon Western thought. We should also add that the final section of the book—on Shin Buddhism, often outwardly viewed as a perspective at the very antipodes of Zen—could hardly be a better introduction to this little known, but widely practiced, school of Buddhism. The very fact that the editor has chosen to include selections on Shin underlines the important idea of the resolution of opposites, which is key to developing a true understanding of Zen.

The essays in *The Buddha Eye: An Anthology of the Kyoto School* are taken from *The Eastern Buddhist*, certainly one of the most quietly influential journals to have appeared in the twentieth century. Founded in 1921 by the now famous Suzuki Teitaro Daisetz, during the many decades of its life it has been a vehicle for seminal articles by many of the most important philosophers of Zen, including D.T. Suzuki, Nishitani Keiji, Abe Masao, Hisamatsu Shin'ichi and many others who regularly contributed to its pages. Their capacity to explain, both in terms of breadth and depth, the meaning of Zen in a language attuned to the Western ear is remarkable. Many of these authors entered into the broader debate surrounding such characteristically twentieth century concerns as the relationship between science and religion, the rising tide of secularism, and the spiritually erosive influence of the nihilism which cannot but arise from a world suffering under what Frithjof Schuon has called "the contradiction of relativism".

For an excellent outline of the Kyoto School and its particular features the reader can do no better than turn to Dr. Franck's beautiful Prologue, which forms an integral part of the content of this book. Nevertheless, it might be worthwhile to offer a word of explanation as to why a publisher that typically focuses on books relating to the Perennial Philosophy would decide to reprint this work. In his Prologue, Dr. Franck quotes D.T. Suzuki as writing somewhere in his voluminous works that "Zen is not a religion . . . Zen *is* religion". The search for the very nature of religion, for the fundamental meaning of wisdom, and for the heart of reality which is the Eternal Religion—the *Sophia Perennis*, or *Sanatana Dharma*—strikes at the central root of the reason why World Wisdom's books exist. We continue to remain dedicated to publishing works which point to the inner unanimity, transforming radiance, and irreplaceable spiritual values of the great spiritual traditions. As an introduction to the knowledge of some of the most important exponents of Zen in the last one hundred years, we believe that this work will continue to enlighten countless minds for the next century and beyond.

Barry McDonald
World Wisdom
October 2003

Foreword to the 2004 edition

It is not possible within the brief scope of this foreword to do justice to all of the essays—many of which are by among the most important Japanese philosophers and exponents of Zen in the twentieth century—which make up the content of this excellent anthology. We must be content with highlighting a few main themes that surface in the overall three-part structure of the book: Self, Reality, and Shin Buddhism.

In his prologue Frederick Franck cites Nishitani's statement that Zen is not a religion, it *is* religion; Zen is not an art, it *is* art. He refers to Nishitani's series of essays on Religion and Nothingness appearing in *The Eastern Buddhist*, which has since been published in book form.[1] Nishitani's "analysis of modern nihilism as the dominant pseudo-religion of contemporary society" strikes Franck as "of vital importance in the most literal sense of the word."

To turn to the three major themes of the book, the first, Self, stands in contradistinction to the Hindu doctrine of *Atman* (Self). Buddhism proclaims the doctrine of *anatman* (no-self), which means that there is no permanent, unchangeable psychological substratum, or individual ego, underlying our experience. But this no-self, not completely unlike the *advaitic* doctrine of *Brahma-nirguna* (attributeless, devoid of qualities) which can only be described as *neti, neti* ("not this, not this"), is not a mere inert nothing or emptiness. It is alive in our sense of freedom and authenticity. It is a nothingness unattainable by the intellect. Finally, to know reality one must *be* it.

Satori (enlightenment) is described as nothing seeing itself as such. This is a seeing that transcends subject and object, or a seeing where subject and object disappear as separative, distinct entities. The true Self or Buddha-nature is precisely this nothingness or emptiness (*sunyata*). It entails overcoming the self-attachment that is rooted in ignorance (*avidya*) which lies in what Buddhism denotes as the eighth "storehouse consciousness." This highly enigmatic concept of the storehouse consciousness, which some

---

[1] Nishitani Keiji, *Religion and Nothingness*, trans. Jan Van Bragt (University of California, 1983).

Western scholars have aptly or inaptly tried to liken to Jung's collective unconscious, is embodied in our fleshly body. Basically it is neutral and can either freeze into the blindness of ego or it can flash up into Suchness (*tathata*) or the Buddha-nature, which is—as Abe Masao points out in his essay on "God, Emptiness, and the True Self"—"strikingly similar" to the concept of *theosis* (deification) found in the writings of Pseudo-Dionysius. It is important to point out, however, that this *mysterium magnum*, so often referred to as "Him" or "Thou" in many mystical traditions of both East and West, in Zen must be, as Abe Masao states, viewed not as an "other" but as one's "true Self."

Ultimate reality for Buddhism is *sunyata*, emptiness, or rather a fullness containing all possibilities. It takes place on a dimension higher than that of science (or scientism) or common sense. This dimension lies beyond both the mechanistically viewed world and the teleologically viewed world. It is the dimension of bottomlessness opened up by the Great Death, described by Nishitani Keiji in the following way: "It is something that presents itself as real from the one ground of the self and all things. It is the true reality of the self and all things, in which everything is present just as it is, in its *suchness*."[2]

"Naturalness" or *jinen* has been defined by the Shin scholar Taitetsu Unno as "the power of each being (*ji*) realizing itself, becoming what it was meant to become (*nen*)."[3] As Abe Masao writes in his essay on "Man and Nature in Christianity and Buddhism," *jinen* is "thought to underlie both the natural and the supernatural, creature and creator, man and God, sentient beings and so-called Buddhas, as their original common basis. In the *jinen* all things, including man, nature, and even the supernatural, are themselves, and as they are." On the human plane, this involves the insight of "likewise," the fact that I am and *likewise* I am not. In the formulation of the *Diamond Sutra*: A and likewise not-A. This can also be expressed as "nature naturing," a phrase that occurs in Spinoza and Nietzsche. Or again, the sacred in man is affirmed by realizing that the realm of the transcendent and the realm of the immanent, sacred object and sacred subject, known and knower, are not essentially different in the very ground of being.

---

[2] *Religion and Nothingness*, p. 21.

[3] Taitetsu Unno, *River of Fire, River of Water* (Doubleday, 1998), p. 234.

Finally, we turn to the chapters on Shin Buddhism. The distinction between *tariki* (other-power) which is emphasized by Shin and *jiriki* (self-power) emphasized by Zen dissolves when one realizes that it is from the same deep reality that the concepts of "other" and "self" arise. The Pure Land of the Shin Buddhists may be understood as a place where enlightened beings dwell, in this life or the next, and in this sense it is the realm of enlightenment as such. The emphasis on other-power as opposed to self-power entails the idea that what is achieved (enlightenment, *satori*) cannot be forced by an act of will. On the other hand, if we do not at least exert ourselves, nothing at all will happen.

Joan Stambaugh

Prologue

Serenades and nocturnes, clearly intended to be played after dark, I found out, may be enjoyed even before lunch and without serious disadvantage. Antipastos, on the other hand, if served as a dessert, prove to be a culinary disaster.

Most of the introductions which authors add as appetizers to their *pièce de résistance*, however, seem to become more profitable and palatable when read as epilogues, if at all.

In this particular case, I hope that what I called "Prologue" will be perused before the texts that follow. Less because these essays are in need of the compiler's directions for use, than to grant his wish to make a few remarks about the history of the project, his motivations in shouldering the perilous task of selecting and editing, and in the hope of adding a few elucidations which may help to make the contents of the book more accessible.

In connection with this accessibility, I hope it will be realized that these essays are expressions of the oriental mind, and more particularly of the Japanese Buddhist spirit, at its best. They were invariably translated by men of erudition, linguistic sensitivity, and philosophical sophistication, who in their commitment to be faithful to the originals often had to make the painful choice between graceful English usage and authenticity. This was bound to result in peculiarities of style, and even ways of reasoning and exposition, that may strike the unforewarned Western reader as infelicitous, even odd. I only became aware of these linguistic hurdles when I started to edit these essays, which through the years I had read and reread, apparently making automatic allowances for stylistic peculiarities which it would be foolhardy to expect the average reader of English to make quite as automatically. Hence, as editor I tried here and there to do some polishing, streamlining, touching up, as much in consultation with author or translator as possible, in order to avoid misinterpretation. This was one of the perilous complications of my task, and made it into a high-tightrope act between Content and Form, without any safety device in case of vertigo.

I can only hope that the female reader will be forgiving: trying to replace *man* in the original by *person* wrought intolerable confusion; to complicate sentences by *his or her* would have compounded the trouble. To cure what is essentially a deficiency disease of the English language will require more than this one editor's despair.

Since the subtitle of the book mentions the Kyoto School, let me attempt a brief explanation.

With very few exceptions the essays in this book have appeared in the highly esteemed, but all too little known journal *The Eastern Buddhist.* It was founded in 1921 by Suzuki Teitarō Daisetz, that Francis Xavier of Zen to the Western world, and published by Otani University, Kyoto, which is a Buddhist but not a Zen institution. Otani is the highly reputed university sponsored by the Higashi Honganji branch of Jōdo-Shinshū Buddhism. D. T. Suzuki, who taught at Otani University, edited *The Eastern Buddhist,* and it was not until after World War II that he was joined by Nishitani Keiji as coeditor. The latter was then a professor at Kyoto University, which—along with Tokyo University—is generally regarded as Japan's most prestigious institution of higher learning.

What was to become known as the Kyoto School of philosophy, is the school of thought, the way of practicing philosophy, of which the main characteristics are: its staunch faithfulness to, and rootedness in, the Mahāyāna Buddhist tradition, coupled with a complete openness to Western thought and a commitment to bring about a meeting of East and West, a "unity beyond differences." The Kyoto School has initiated an existential dialogue with the modern world in its aspects of science, secularization, and its operational, be it not usually formal, atheism.

The foundation of the Kyoto School was laid by Nishida Kitarō (1870-1945), who is generally regarded as the father of modern Japanese philosophy. To quote Professor Takeuchi Yoshinori, one of the highly respected protagonists of the Kyoto School: "It is no exaggeration to say that in him Japan had the philosophical genius who was the first to know how to build a system permeated with the spirit of Buddhist meditation by fully employing Western methods of thinking." Nishida took up the challenge of seeking a synthesis between traditional oriental, especially Japanese, modes of thought, first with French positivism, later with German idealism. His life-work as a philosopher consisted of the continuous struggle with the relationship between religion and philosophy, East and West, a struggle in which his Zen insights remained the unwavering basis. His labors were to be continued by his disciples at Kyoto University and this became known as the Kyoto School. Its principal exponents are such thinkers as Tanabe Hajime, Nishitani Keiji, Hisamatsu Shin'ichi, Takeuchi Yoshinori, Abe Masao, and Ueda Shizuteru. Its influence has far exceeded the borders of Japan, for it has provided the solid ground on which the dialogue between Mahāyāna Buddhism and the other world religions became possible.

D. T. Suzuki's creation, *The Eastern Buddhist*, was to offer for more than half a century a panorama of the most vital, contemporary Buddhist thought and scholarship, often in its confrontation with Western culture. As such it also became the vital link between the Kyoto School and the English-speaking world. Nevertheless Suzuki, however highly revered, is not regarded by the Kyoto School as belonging to its inner circle, for he was never connected with Kyoto University and, moreover, was not a disciple of Nishida. These men considered one another as complementary: Nishida as the philosopher, Suzuki as the man of religion.

Suzuki Daisetz and Nishida Kitarō had been schoolmates in the provincial city of Kanazawa. The third one in the trio of friends was Ataka Yōkichi. Early in life the three discussed their future. Nishida opted for philosophy; Suzuki chose religion; and Ataka resolved to make money so he could support his friends: he became the millionaire whose collection of antique ceramics was to become world famous.

Suzuki left in 1893 for America to attend the First Parliament of World Religions at the Chicago world's fair. It would be his first step on the way to becoming Zen's great prophet in the West, where Nishida himself is still almost unknown.

The field of Buddhist studies is a well-fenced-in preserve, and the readership of a scholarly journal like *The Eastern Buddhist* was bound to remain all too exclusively limited to a handful of specialists. I, in no sense a denizen of the fenced-in field, and not a Buddhist scholar but an artist and writer, happened on it by pure chance. But a first shy peek through the fence made me espy some veritable treasures. One of the first of these was the essay by D. T. Suzuki, "Self the Unattainable," written at the ripe age of ninety, perhaps his noblest statement, and summary of a lifetime of distilling and redistilling the very essences of Mahāyāna to limpid clarity.

I had first read Suzuki's *Introduction to Zen Buddhism* some fifty-five years ago, and I avow that it affected the course of my life profoundly. Not that it told me so much that was new. It was a revelation, but not in the sense that it disclosed new facts. On the contrary, I have elsewhere described what happened and could not do so more clearly: "It was as if I entered a landscape I had never visited before, and in which I recognized every hillock, tree, and bush. . . ."

As I went on reading everything Dr. Suzuki had written, all that was available in translation, I felt that throughout his life he wrote variations on themes he had laid down in this little book, variations that would shed new light on these central themes from every possible angle. It was as if he led one by the hand, urging one to look again, closer, deeper, with greater openness and relaxed concentration. He did not always make sense, for his English was sometimes turgid. One simply had to read him with the third eye—Saint Bonaventure's "eye of contemplation that sees unto liberation"—for that was the eye with which he himself saw the world. All that I had known forever, deep within, but that had become confused, barnacled with all the nonsense of my conditioning, became ordered and structured in the magnetic field he seemed to set up. "Zen is not a religion," he writes somewhere, "Zen *is* religion."

Indeed, Zen clarifies what makes religion—or rather one's own religiousness—religious. "Zen is not an art, it is art," he might have added. For Zen clarified to me, as an artist—an image-making animal—what art is, and is definitely not. It changed my attitude towards the work of my hands radically. It was very moving to see this confirmed in a note K. Nishida wrote in 1905: "1 am neither psychologist nor sociologist; I am a researcher of life itself. . . . Zen is music, Zen is art, Zen is movement . . . apart from this there is nothing in which one can find peace of soul."

I must have read Dr. Suzuki's *Essence of Buddhism*, those two lectures he gave for the emperor of Japan immediately after the war, a few hundred times, without ever exhausting their wealth. It was the book I read aloud to Claske, my wife, a few days after we first met in 1955. My first present to her was R. H. Blyth's masterly *Zen in English Literature and Oriental Classics*. Both these gifts and this meeting have lost none of their freshness, have been tested again and again by the buffetings of life.

I met Dr. Suzuki, who had become my "pocket guru," only once, in New York, but not too briefly and quite unforgettably.

I may have made it clear by now that my interest in Zen, and that in the learned journal from which I gleaned the essays that form this book, is quite unscholarly. It is purely existential, it is merely a matter of life and death. Although I am awaiting each new issue of *The Eastern Buddhist* with keen anticipation, I shall not pretend having read them all from cover to cover. Yet, apart from contributions of a too technical nature, all too far over my unscholarly head, I have always found others which for this layman—and possibly not only for this particular one—proved to be extremely enlightening, or in view of the rather flippant use of this term in recent years, let me rather say enriching and clarifying.

I found many other splendid posthumous essays by Suzuki in *The Eastern Buddhist*. Sometimes in Japan, the prophet's homeground, he has been shrugged off as a "popularizer." But the one who the cold, and especially the envious, intellect presumes to dismiss so cavalierly, the heart may recognize as the figure in the last of the ox-herding pictures, the Awakened One, the Bodhisattva who returns to the market place to bestow blessings, to awaken the ones still mired in delusion.

In Arnold Toynbee's estimation, the introduction of Zen to the West—the gigantic feat Suzuki achieved singlehandedly—may in later centuries be compared in importance to the discovery of nuclear energy. Let us hope that the latter will not prevent the comparison to be made.

How was it possible that since his death in 1966, and with every single one of his works in English a perennial bestseller—to use this vulgar term for the legacy of an almost century-long life—hardly anything new of his had been published in English? In the thirty-seven years since he left us, only *The Eastern Buddhist* has regularly offered items of the still untranslated communications of this exceptional spirit, as if to celebrate his abiding presence among us. But I also found a rich lode of illuminating contributions in this journal by the protagonists of the Kyoto School: K. Nishitani, S. Hisamatsu, M. Abe, and those translations of Zen classics, as for instance of Dōgen and Bankei, without which life would have remained so much the poorer. Glancing through my pile of back issues, I find essays black with the underlinings and annotations made through the years, during the repeated readings which these writings not only demand but richly reward. I think here particularly of those chapters of Nishitani's *Religion and Nothingness* which appeared serially in *The Eastern Buddhist* as their meticulous translation slowly progressed, and which especially in their analysis of modern nihilism as the dominant pseudoreligion of contemporary society struck me as of vital importance in the most literal sense of the word.[1]

I also remember among the outstanding essays Abe Masao's lucid exposition and interpretation of the Buddha-nature in his "Dōgen and Buddha-Nature," a long essay for which we unfortunately lack space here and have therefore substituted the shorter "Man and Nature in Christianity and Buddhism."

In the work just completed, as compiler of these texts, I am struck how this Buddhist "theologizing" seems singularly unconcerned with scoring intellectual or doctrinal points. Rather its purpose seems to be the clarification, the transmission between author and reader of the stimulus towards deeper contemplation. The presentation is *upāya*, skillful means or stratagems, rather than argumentation. To attempt a concrete example: the use of an indefinable term like *śūnyatā* is not so much delineated theoretically as disclosed as a contemplative tool to guide and reach deeper insight. I also realized how *The Eastern Buddhist* represents one of various currents in Japanese Buddhist thought, albeit an extremely important one, for it is the by now more than half-a-century-old tradition of patient bridge building between Japanese Buddhism and Western philosophy consistently pursued by a limited number of distinguished scholars and thinkers.

Some thirty years ago I visited Kyoto for the first time on a round-the-world trip which at the same time was the inward journey which I described in *Pilgrimage to Now/Here*.[2] After some hesitation I decided to visit *The Eastern Buddhist* in its quaint old-fashioned office at Otani University. This led to long talks with Professors Nishitani, Abe, and others. I was surprised to find them so pleasantly unprofessorial, although I had already noticed in their writings and those of other exponents of the Kyoto School that whereas their brilliant scholarship cannot fail to impress one, it is not coldly academic. For scholarship here is conjoined by an element that transcends it,

---

1. *Religion and Nothingness* was published as a first book-length work of K. Nishitani in the English translation of Professor Jan Van Bragt, by the University of California Press in 1983.

2. *Pilgrimage to Now/Here: Christ-Buddha and the True Self of Man. Confrontations and Meditations on an Inward Journey to India, Sri Lanka, the Himalayas and Japan* (Maryknoll, N.Y.: Orbis Books, 1974).

probably due to the long years of meditational training each one of these men has gone through, and which tends to destroy the isolationism of the intellect. A master like Hisamatsu, for instance, was proficient in tea ceremony, calligraphy, poetry, sumie, and even wrote a standard work on Zen art.

Whether by Providence, good karma, or perhaps a felicitous mixture of both, I have since returned to Japan almost a dozen times, and each time I have visited *The Eastern Buddhist* and spoken to its editorial board about the crying need for an anthology. I argued that it would be all too sad if what had such rich meaning for me would be withheld from others, gathering dust on some library shelf, to be consulted once in a long while by a student writing a thesis.

In the recent flood of literature on Buddhism of very unequal merit I argued, it would be simply tragic if all this noble material should go unnoticed instead of fulfilling its function. Here was a fount of *Mahāprajñā*, transcendental insight, waiting for the *Mahākaruṇā*, the great Compassion, that would offer it to all who needed it. In the end the Kyoto School not only gave its blessings to the project but charged me with its editorship.

I assumed and executed my task in gratitude for bounties received, and with profound humility. According to my private glossary, however, humility is simply the realistic assessment of one's place in the fabric of the cosmic whole. It does not imply some feeling of inferiority for not having the proper academic credentials.

Mozart and Bach after all—the examples are not taken lightly but as a measure of my reverence for some of the authors presented— may be presumed not to have written D Minor Quintet or Suite for Unaccompanied Cello with an audience of musicologists in mind. They must have written these miraculous works as they welled up from the depths, thereby bestowing rapture, consolation, blessing on generations of us mortals. To share these summits of the human spirit all one needs is the ear to hear, the heart to respond. The recipient of these inestimable gifts does not require training in either harmonics or orchestration, does not even have to know how to distinguish "adagio" from "vibrato." All one needs is to be neither closed off, coarsened, or tone-deaf.

Similarly, worthwhile religious thinkers and theologians must be presumed to be innocent of writing merely to impress their colleagues, but to be moved to address their fellow *homo religiosus*, heart to heart. To qualify as *homo religiosus*, of course, one does not need the erudition to annotate Chinese or Aramaic texts, nor to have patristic or Vedic footnotes at the ready. To qualify it is enough not to be spiritually colorblind. Academic erudition does not confer on us the dynamic which propels us on our search for meaning, nor that specifically human potentiality which is our birthright: humans from the northern bank of the river are no less gifted with the Buddha-nature than the ones from the southern shore, we are told. Saint Paul got by nicely without a Ph.D., and old Hui Neng is claimed to have been quite illiterate.

Whether recent theories about the contrasting functions of left and right brain are apposite or not, one of these halves is supposed to specialize in processing intellectual data, conceptualizations, and logic, and to abound in analytical prowess. The other half is said to be endowed with intuitive, esthetic, poetic, synthesizing qualities.

The rather characteristically twentieth-century specimen of *homo religiosus* who writes this, suspects that in him the analytical hemisphere, so overwhelmingly dominant in the scholar, is decidedly recessive. Yet he consoles himself by wondering whether it might not be the intuitive side of our caput with its poetic, esthetic flair that is precisely the locus of what makes a *homo* so incurably *religiosus*. Could it not be that symbol and myth yield their life-giving meaning here, and might this not be the reason that doctrines and dogmas which clash so violently in the too isolated logical hemisphere can be pondered, may even fuse with a minimum of fuss in the poetic half? Might that intuitive hemisphere perhaps be what was traditionally spoken of as the heart? And was the isolated and specialized analytical hemisphere perhaps never intended or even equipped to handle symbol and myth? Has it simply, brutally, and ironically usurped these to concoct its "systematic" theologies that are so out of touch with the human need for spiritual nourishment?

The structure of this book is based on personal preference: I thought it desirable to start with a number of essays dealing with the nature of the self in the light of contemporary Buddhist thought, and with the penetrating view of the relationships between self and other, of I and Thou, as exemplified in Professor Nishitani's essay "The I-Thou Relation in Zen Buddhism." The second part concerns itself with the Kyoto School's conception of the structure of reality. Between these two sections I inserted R. H. Blyth's presentation of Ikkyū's "Skeletons" because of its beauty, as an homage to that great fourteenth-century Zen master and poet, whose name Ikkyū in itself implies "a break" or "a rest." I hope it may serve indeed as a refreshing pause in this rather demanding sequence of essays; it is also added in loving memory of Reginald Horace Blyth, for whose work I have such admiration.[3]

So much has been written about Zen that it is not surprising that in the minds of many people the words *Buddhism* and *Zen* have somehow become synonymous. Some may have a vague notion of the division between Theravāda, Mahāyāna, and perhaps—since Tibetan Buddhism became popular—Vajrayāna. But even then, the impression may prevail that Zen and Mahāyāna are more or less the same. It is rarely realized that according to a recent census in Japan of the eighty-one million who described themselves as Buddhists, ten million claimed adherence to Zen and fifty million to other Mahāyāna Buddhist sects, of whom twenty-one million mentioned Shin Buddhism. After it was introduced in Japan in the sixth century, Buddhism adapted itself to widely varying historical and social situations and became differentiated into many schools. Of these survive Tendai, Shingon, the Rinzai School of Zen introduced by Eisai (1141-1251), and the Sōtō School of Zen, founded by Dōgen (1200-1253). But there is also the numerically stronger Jōdo School of Pure Land Buddhism founded by Hōnen (1133-1212) and Jōdo-Shinshū, which originated with Hōnen's disciple Shinran (1173-1262), as well as the activist Nichiren School founded by Nichiren (1222-1282), with its various subschools, of which contemporary Sōka Gakkai has recently exerted considerable influence in Japanese society and has come to play a powerful role in national politics.

Since Shin is practically unknown as compared to Zen, yet is deeply rooted in Japanese religiosity and to a great extent integrated in the world of ideas presented by the Kyoto School, I have added an article on Shin by D. T. Suzuki and another one by a distinguished thinker of the Shin faith, Soga Ryōjin, which I found not only exceptionally informative, but a movingly personal witness to the Shin faith.

---

3. *Zen and Zen Classics: Selections from R. H. Blyth,* compiled and with drawings by Frederick Franck (New York: Vintage Books, 1978).

May this book fulfill its function to add to, and strengthen, the many profound contacts in which East and West have recently become awakened to their complementarity. May it give some delight to those who rejoice in the treasure-house they share and in which the roots of all religions and cultures fuse.

Frederick Franck

Acknowledgments

It is impossible to express adequate gratitude to the editor of *The Eastern Buddhist*, Professor Nishitani Keiji, and to the members of its Editorial Board, not only for the honor of being allowed to present this book to Western readers, but for their generous and patient assistance and advice. I am especially grateful to Norman Waddell for his loyal, enthusiastic, and warm support for this project.

To the translators, especially my friends Jan Van Bragt, James W. Heisig, and Norman Waddell my heartfelt thanks.

To Nanzan University, Nagoya, Japan, its president, Professor Johannes Hirschmeier, S.V.D., and especially to the Nanzan Institute for Religion and Culture and its director, Professor Jan Van Bragt, I owe sincere and heartfelt gratitude for offering me a Research Fellowship and for the months of exquisite hospitality and friendship which my wife and I enjoyed.

I am particularly grateful to Jan Van Bragt and James W. Heisig, general editor of the Nanzan Series of Studies in Religion and Culture of which this book is part, for their constant advice and constructive counseling. Dr. Heisig's part in performing the subtle feats of plastic surgery that resulted in a text which for the English-speaking reader is reasonably accessible is a major one.

To Professor Doi Masatoshi, editor of *Japanese Religions*, my thanks for allowing me to use Professor Abe's "Man and Nature in Christianity and Buddhism" and Professor Takeuchi's "The Philosophy of Nishida," and to Mr. and Mrs. Wayne Yokoyama for their assistance with the biographical material and other matters.

To the Crossroad Publishing Company and especially to Richard Payne, my editor, goes the credit of having recognized the importance of the Kyoto School and of this particular project, which, but for the labors and encouragement of Claske, my wife, who typed and retyped the manuscripts, would have remained a fascinating idea and no more.

Frederick Franck
Nanzan Institute for Religion and Culture
Nagoya, Japan

Pacem in Terris
Warwick, New York

I

Essays
on the
Self

1

SUZUKI TEITARŌ DAISETZ

Self the Unattainable*

Dr. Suzuki wrote this essay in 1960. He was then ninety years old and had spent almost three score and ten years in his continuous efforts to make Zen known to the West. The often glib and superficial appropriations of Zennish slogans in the years that "Beat Zen" had become somewhat of a fad, the gross misinterpretations of Zen offered by enthusiasts who had only the most frivolous acquaintance with it, the flippant use of misunderstood *mondō* and *kōan* used to cover hedonistic self-indulgence and antinomianism, must have saddened Suzuki. For he prefaced this essay, in which he recapitulates certain of the essences of the Zen view of life, with a note of warning that Zen is not an easy subject matter, and that if one intends to write about it responsibly, it is not only necessary to have several years of experiencing Zen, but also to be thoroughly acquainted with a wide range of Zen literature. And he reminds his readers that in spite of their claim that Zen is beyond expressions and explanations, the Zen masters of ancient China, where Zen originated, and in Japan, where it is still flourishing, have written voluminously on the subject. Moreover, their sayings, sermons, and *mondō*, as recorded by their disciples—especially in the T'ang and Sung periods—are both historically and doctrinally highly significant. Meanwhile, in the last forty years that have elapsed since this essay was written, a considerable number of such important writings have fortunately become available in reliable translations.

The essential discipline of Zen consists in emptying the self of all its psychological contents, in stripping the self of all those trappings, moral, philosophical, and spiritual, with which it has continued to adorn itself ever since the first awakening of consciousness. When the self thus stands in its native nakedness, it defies all description. The only means we have to make it more approachable and communicable is to resort to figures of speech. The self in its is-ness,

---

* "Self the Unattainable," *The Eastern Buddhist* III/2 (1970): 1-8.

pure and simple, is comparable to a circle without circumference and, therefore, with its center nowhere—which is everywhere. Or it is like a zero that is equal to, or rather identical with, infinity. Infinity is not to be conceived here serially as an infinite continuum of natural numbers; it is rather a group whose infinitely multitudinous contents are taken as a totality. I formulate it in this way: 0 = Infinity. Of course, this identification transcends mathematical speculation. It yields a kind of metaphysical formula: self = zero, and zero = Infinity; hence self = Infinity.

This self, therefore, emptied of all its so-called psychological contents is not an "emptiness," as that word is generally understood. No such empty self exists. The emptied self is simply the psychological self cleansed of its egocentric imagination. It is just as rich in content as before; indeed it is richer than before, because it now contains the whole world in itself instead of having the world stand opposed to it. Not only that, it enjoys the state of being true to itself. It is free in the real sense of the word because it is master of itself, absolutely independent, self-reliant, authentic, and autonomous. This Self—with a capital S—is the Buddha who declared at his birth: "I alone am the most honored one in heaven and on earth."

This way of understanding the self, that is, the Self, requires a great deal of explanation. When left to itself, Zen explains itself and no words are needed. But I have already committed myself to talking about it and hence have to do my best, however briefly, to make my description more comprehensible for the reader.

We all know that the self we ordinarily talk about is psychological, or rather logical and dualistic. It is set against a not-self; it is a subject opposing an object or objects. It is full of contents and very complex. Therefore, when this complexity is dissected and its component factors are set aside as not belonging to it, it is reduced, we think, to a nothing or an emptiness. And it is for this reason that Buddhism upholds the doctrine of *anātman*, egolessness, which means that there is no psychological substratum corresponding to the word *self* (*ātman*), as there is, for example, when we say "table" and have something substantial answering to this sound, "table." "Ego," in other words, useful as it may be for our daily intercourse as social beings, is an empty phonetic symbol.

We refer to the ego or self by using the pronoun *I* when we are introspective and bifurcate ourselves into subject and object. But this process of self-introspective bifurcation, which is part of our attempt to orient the self, is endless and can never lead us to a terminating abode where "the self" comes comfortably to rest. The "self," we may conclude, is after all nonexistent. But at the same time we can never get rid of this self—we somehow always stumble over it—which is very annoying, as it interferes with our sense of freedom. The annoyance we feel, consciously or unconsciously, is in fact the cause of our mental uneasiness. How does or how can this nonexistent "self"—that which can never be taken hold of on the rationalistic, dualistic plane of our existence—interfere in various ways with our innate feeling of freedom and authenticity? Can this ego be really such a ghostly existence, an empty nothing, a zero like the shadow of the moon in the water? If it is really such a nonexistent existence, how does it ever get into our consciousness or imagination? Even an airy nothing has something substantial behind. A memory always has some real basis, be it in some unknown and altogether forgotten past, or even beyond our individual experience.

The self then is not a nothing or an emptiness incapable of producing work. It is very much alive in our innate sense of freedom and authenticity. When it is stripped of all its trappings, moral and psychological, and when we imagine it to be a void, it is not really so; it is not "negativistic." There must be something absolute in it. It must not be a mere zero symbolizing the negation of all dualistically conceived objects. It is, on the contrary, an absolute existence that exists in its own right. Relatively or dualistically, it is true, the self is "the unattainable" (*anupalabdha*), but this "unattainable" is not to be understood at the level of our ordinary dichotomous thinking.

The Unattainable, so termed, subsists in its absolute right and must now be taken hold of in a way hitherto unsuspected in our intellectual pursuit of reality. The intellect is to be left aside for a while, in spite of a certain sense of intellectual discomfort, so that we may plunge into that nothingness beyond the intellect, as if into a threatening abyss opening up at our feet. The Unattainable is attained as such in its just-so-ness, and the strange thing is that when this takes place the intellectual doubts that made us so uncomfortable are dissolved. One feels free, independent, one's own master. Experiences at the level of intellection are restrictive and conditioning, but the "inner" self feels the way God felt when he uttered, "Let there be light." This is where zero identifies itself with infinity and infinity with zero—if we recall that both zero and infinity are not negative concepts, but utterly positive.

As a positive concept, infinity is not, as I said before, to be conceived serially as something taking place in time where things succeed or precede one another endlessly in all directions. It is the idea of a wholeness that can never be totalized or summed up as a whole. It is a circle whose circumference knows no boundaries. It is what makes us sense or feel that the world in which we live is limited and finite, and yet does not allow us to be taken as limited and finite. From our ordinary point of view, such a conception is inadmissible, impossible, and irrational. And yet there is something there that compels us to accept it. And once we accept it, all impossibilities and irrationalities vanish, regardless of the intellectual discomfort we may feel. In fact, this kind of discomfort arises out of our failure to accept the ultimate "irrationality" totally and unconditionally.

This failure on our part is precisely what Zen tries to do away with. To understand Zen, therefore, means to be "comfortable" in every possible way. This state of mind is known as the "pacification of mind" or "making mind restful and comfortable" (*anjin* or *an-hsin*). It takes place when the impossible—or, in Zen terminology, "the Unattainable" is experienced as such. The word *experience* is used here in its most specific sense as a sort of inner sense that becomes manifest on the individualized plane of sense-experience as a totalistic response of one's being. It is an *immediate* and altogether personal response, one that makes the total experience appear like a sense perception; but in actuality the total experience takes place simultaneously with the sense experience. The sense experience is partitive and stops at the periphery of consciousness, whereas the total experience springs from the being itself and makes one feel or perceive that it has come to the Unattainable itself.

When the senses are thus backed up by the total being, Zen "irrationalities" or "absurdities" become intelligible. The one trouble we have with language, and which frequently misleads us to commit a gross error—and this especially when we encounter metaphysical questions—is that our language does not truthfully and exactly represent what it is supposed to represent. Language is a product of intellection and intellection is what our intellect adds to, or rather, subtracts from, reality. Reality is not in language as it is in itself. To understand reality one must grasp it in one's own hands, or, better, one must *be* it. Otherwise, as the Buddhist saying goes, we shall be taking the finger for the moon; the finger is the pointer and not the moon itself. Similarly, money is a convenient medium exchanged for real substance, but in a time of crisis we let money go and hold on to bread. Let us not get confused: language is only the finger, only the money.

The reason Zen distrusts language should now be plain enough. Those who find Zen foolish are still under the spell of linguistic magic. To cite from a poem of the National Teacher of Japan, Daitō (1282-1337):

> When one sees with ears
> and hears with eyes,
> one cherishes no doubts.
> How naturally the raindrops
> fall from the leaves!

It is not really the ears or eyes that hear or see. Were it so, then, as the Buddha asks, do not the dead see and hear just as well as the living? What hears and sees is not the sense organ, but Self the Unattainable. The sense organs are instruments the self uses for itself. And when it hears, its hearing reaches the end of the universe. This applies also to the rest of the senses. It is not the particular sense alone that hears or sees. When it hears I hear, you hear, everybody, every being hears. It is for this reason that when I attain enlightenment the whole universe attains enlightenment. The Unattainable is attained *as unattainable*—this is the experience not of the psychological or logical self, but of the Unattainable Self.

A monk in China asked an ancient master, "What made Bodhidharma come from the West to our country?"

Surprised, the master countered with a question of his own, "Why do you ask about Bodhidharma instead of about yourself?"

For those who have never studied Zen, this may require a little explanation. Bodhidharma of India is supposed to have brought Zen to China early in the sixth century, though the historical fact is that Zen as we have it today actually started in China early in the T'ang with a native master known as Enō (Chin.: Hui Neng, 683-713 C.E.). The traditional story of Zen's Indian origin, however, raised the question about Bodhidharma's motive in trying to propagate

Zen in China. But the real meaning of this question is concerned with the source of human will or with the awakening of human consciousness: What makes us will this or that? What is the meaning of life? Therefore, the monk's question about Bodhidharma really has to do with the being of the monk himself. The master pointed this out when he challenged the monk by asking, "Why do you not ask about yourself?" The challenge is meant to make the monk think about himself, about his own being, his own destiny.

Hence the monk followed with another question, "What then is my self?"

And the master told him, "There is something deeply hidden within yourself and you must be acquainted with its hidden activity." When the monk begged to be told about this hidden activity, the master opened his eyes and closed them. No words came from him.

Butsugen (1067-1120), who quotes the above story in one of his sermons, adds:

> In other places they give a *kōan* to solve, but here with me the present is the problem. Do you not remember? It was Ummon [d. 949} who said that one's self is mountains and rivers and the great earth. This was Ummon's answer when a monk asked him about the monk's self. My question is: Are these—mountains and rivers and the great earth—really existent or nonexistent? If they maintain their existence, where among them are we to see the self? If we say they are nonexistent, how can we deny that they are actually existent? Here is where we need an awakening [*satori*]. Otherwise, the teaching of the ancient masters means nothing. (*Kosonshuku Goroku*, "Sayings of the Elder Masters," fasc. 31)

What Butsugen tries to present through this allusion to the ancient master is an objective presentation of the self. The self, far from being an empty notion of nothingness, is here right before us in full revelation. The great earth with its mountains and rivers, plants and animals, rains and winds—are they not all revealing themselves in front of us, for us to see, and to hear, what they are? They are just waiting to make us become conscious of "the sense of nondiscrimination" (*avikalpa-jñāna*) that is dormant within us this very moment. This *jñāna* (cognition) is to be distinguished from intellection: intellection helps us discriminate, dichotomize, dissect, and finally kill the objects it attempts to understand. The *jñāna* is inborn, indefinable, unattainable, but ultimately leads us to the self in its just-so-ness. Until this time comes upon us, we would do better to refrain from talk about freedom, independence, authenticity, and self-determination. These things do not belong in the realm of intellectual relativity.

Avikalpa-jñāna is also called "*jñāna* not learned from a teacher," that is, a kind of inborn sense not acquired by means of learning or experience. It has nothing to do with accumulated knowledge. It comes out of one's innermost being all at once, when the zero-self becomes identified with the totality of infinity. Hō-kōji once asked his master Baso (Chin.: Ma-tsu, d. 780), "What kind of person is he who has no companion among the ten thousand things [*dharma*]?" Baso replied, "I will tell you when you have swallowed up the Western River at one gulp." This is a most illuminating answer on the self. For the self emptied of all its relative contents and standing in its nakedness knows no companion like the Buddha, "who alone is the most honored one" in the whole universe; he at this very moment drinks up not only the Western River but all the rivers in the world, no, all the oceans surrounding Mount Sumeru, at one gulp. This then enables the formula 0 = Infinity.

This *jñāna* or *prajñā* cannot be included under any category. It is not knowledge, or wisdom, or mere cleverness, or intelligence of any order, but something we find buried deeply in our inmost being. To awaken it and become conscious of its presence within ourselves requires a great deal of self-discipline, moral, intellectual, and spiritual.

Zen is decidedly not latitudinarian, not antinomian. The masters are always very emphatic on this point of self-discipline, and Jōshū (Chin.: Chao-chou, 778-897) is even reported to have said: "If you cannot get it [*satori*] in twenty or thirty years of hard study you may cut off my head."

What Zen emphasizes most strongly in its disciplinary practice is the attainment of spiritual freedom, not the revolt against conventionalism. The freedom may sometimes consist merely in eating when one is hungry and resting when one is tired; at other times, and probably frequently, in *not* eating when one is hungry and *not* resting when one is tired. So it is, that Zen may find more of its great followers among the "conformists" than among the rebellious and boisterous nonconformists.

2

NISHITANI KEIJI

The Awakening of Self in Buddhism*

Nishitani Keiji (1900-1990) graduated from Kyoto University in 1924, where he was later appointed assistant professor. From 1943 he held the Chair of Philosophy until he reached emeritus status in 1964. Thereafter he taught philosophy and religion at Otani University. He was one of Nishida's most brilliant students and also studied under Tanabe Hajime. Among his books published in Japanese are: *Philosophy of Fundamental Subjectivity* (1940), *Studies in Aristotle* (1948), *God and Absolute Nothingness* (1948), *Nihilism* (1949), *Religion and the Social Problems of Modern Times* (1951), and *Religion and Nothingness* (1956).

Professor Nishitani was widely regarded as the most significant philosopher of contemporary Japan and the most authoritative representative of the Kyoto School.

Starting from Nishida's philosophy, Nishitani studied Plato, Aristotle, Saint Augustine, and the Western mystics, especially Plotinus, Eckhart, and Jakob Böhme. His refusal to separate philosophy as an intellectual endeavor from religion as an attitude to life made him characteristic for the Kyoto School, and an heir to Nishida's thought. He was particularly preoccupied with the phenomenon of nihilism as the inevitable direction Western culture has taken after the loss of its absolute center, namely, God, and hence was particularly interested in the philosophies of Hegel, Kierkegaard, and Nietzsche. The conquest of nihilism by the adoption of the Buddhist viewpoint of *śūnyatā* ("emptiness," "absolute nothingness") as reinterpreted by Nishitani may prove to be his most challenging and epoch-making contribution to Western thought. The difficulty of translation has delayed his becoming sufficiently known in the West. Hence the publication of one of his major works, *Religion and Nothingness*—in the translation of Professor Jan Van Bragt of the Nanzan Institute for Religion and Culture—may well turn out to be a significant event in the development of Western thought.

* "The Awakening of Self in Buddhism," trans. Bandō Shōjun, *The Eastern Buddhist* I/2 (1966): 1-11.

Professor Nishitani contributed to numberless symposia on philosophi-cal and religious subjects in Japan. As president of The Eastern Buddhist Society, editor of its journal *The Eastern Buddhist*, and president of the Institute of Japan Studies, he was particularly active in Buddhist-Christian dialogue. He held visiting professorships in the United States and Europe and was honored with the prestigious Goethe Prize.

As an introduction to Nishitani's thought, see Hans Waldenfels: *Absolute Nothingness: Foundations for a Christian-Buddhist Dialogue*, trans. James W. Heisig, Nanzan Studies in Religion and Culture, vol. 1 (New York: Paulist Press, 1980).

I

Japanese Buddhism is having little influence upon people's lives in our time, and this is taken as proof of the decline of Buddhism. The impact of Buddhism upon society has become weak because it has penetrated too pervasively into our daily life itself; it has changed into a sort of social custom, and has stagnated. The major reason for this may perhaps be traced back to the religious policy of the Tokugawa Shogunate.

Some people say that the cause of the decline of Buddhist influ-ence lies in its negative doctrine of resignation, but looking back on its past history, we find that Buddhism has been as great a force for moving society as Christianity and Muhammadanism have been. Of course, "moving society" does not imply that Buddhism has a social theory of its own, or that it proposes some social revolution, for it is not a "social movement." Rather it transforms man's innermost mind radically, and develops man's most basic being to an unprece-dented flowering. In short, it has acted as a moving force in society by opening up ways to transform man himself. As far as its religious function is concerned, Buddhism has exerted a really deep and last-ing influence on society, be it to all appearances an indirect influ-ence.

Nowadays people are inclined to think that to transform society is one thing and to transform man is another, and that the former takes precedence over the latter. In reality, however, these two aspects cannot be separated so simply.

Many "progressives" in this country, for instance, hold that the present crisis surrounding atomic warfare is a result of modern capitalism, which obstructs the inevitable course of history, or especially, of international monopoly capitalism's imperialism. They believe that the only way to overcome the crisis lies in a social revolution. But is this really so? Is it not rather that the crisis is not to be blamed on capitalist society alone, but is caused equally by the very thought that the crisis must be blamed exclusively on the capitalist system? The very viewpoint from which the conflict of social ideologies is seen as ultimate, and social revolution as necessarily having priority over anything else, constitutes one of the major factors in the very crisis that it is attempting to overcome. The very idea that social revolution should take precedence over man's inner transformation is a not insignificant part of the crisis itself. In this context it is interesting to recall, for instance, that Georgi Malenkov, when still prime minister of Soviet Russia, once declared that the use of the latest weapons might result in the destruction of both the Soviets and its enemies, even of civilization as a whole. The following years, after his resignation, he was severely criticized in *Pravda*. What he had declared before, the Communist press reproached him, was ideologically untenable: only the West would be destroyed while the Soviets would survive!

Behind such an incident one perceives a way of thinking we might call with Nikolai Berdyaev a "pseudomessianism," according to which the direction of history leads inevitably to an entirely communist world wherein all the problems of mankind would automatically be solved. It is that fanatical attitude, that black-and-white vision by which special revolution and the transformation of man are naively seen as two unconnected problems, while, in truth, the one presupposes the other. Without this simplistic presupposition the conflict of ideologies would not have to be considered as an insolvable one, and ways could open up towards mutual understanding between both camps.

Matters concerning man's inner life are indeed not as remote and abstruse as they appear to be at first sight.

II

Since Buddhism opens up an altogether revolutionary view of the essential nature of man, it is not surprising that it should offer a more fundamental and permanent principle of social transformation than could ever be offered by a mere ideology. From its very beginning, Buddhism was a religion that showed a way to transcend the "world." According to Buddhism, all that is needed is to become emancipated from the innumerable attachments that arise spontaneously from within ourselves and tie us to things of this world. Hence it speaks of *nirvāna* as the extinguishing of the fire. The Buddhist way of transcending the "world" as well as the "self-in-the-world," is not a mere "otherworldliness," but an awakening in which we become aware of our original and authentic nature (our *Dharma*-nature) and may thus live in accord with it. The possibility of attaining this enlightenment depends upon ourselves alone. That is to say, the ability to attain it lies deeply hidden in the *Dharma*-nature of each one of us. All that is required from us is that we cut the threads of attachment and so become "homeless" in the world. It was for this reason that the community of Buddhists, the *samgha*, was from the beginning based on an absolute negation of all "worldly" differentiations, social as well as psychological, of the differentiation between the rich and the poor, the learned and the unlearned, and so forth, and in particular of distinction between castes, that "primal distinction that Brahmanism presumed to have originated in the mystical depths."[1]

As is well known, the first disciples who gathered around the Buddha came from various castes. They must have been fully conscious of the fact that their establishment of a "brotherhood" was a historical event of revolutionary character, and that it was made possible only by a wholly new basis of human relationship being initiated beyond the rigid Brahmanic framework of caste—a basis on which men, freed of all bondage, are ultimately independent and truly equal.

> As the great streams, O disciples, however many they be, the Gangā, Yamunā, Aciravatî, Sarabhū, Mahî, when they reach the great ocean, lose their old name and their old descent, and bear only one name, "the great ocean," so also, my disciples, these four castes, Brahmans, Nobles, Vaicya, and Cudra, when they, in accordance with the law and doctrine which the Perfect One has preached, forsake their

home and go into homelessness, lose their old name and old paternity, and bear only the one designation, "Ascetics who follow the son of the Sakya house."[2]

This way of awakening to one's self on a plane beyond the world, and this absolute denunciation of caste distinctions, have been maintained throughout the development of Buddhism. For example, in the *Tripitaka* there is a short tract entitled *Kongō Shin Ron* ("Diamond Needle Tract"), supposedly written by Ashvaghosha, a thinker and poet who lived at the end of the first century and beginning of the second century C.E. In this tract he disapproved, from a Buddhist standpoint, of all class distinctions and established an entirely new universal and religious norm for the nobility of the fundamental character of man based upon morality. We find here a revolutionary shift in human viewpoint from the external to the internal, and an example of the religious reformation that transformed the concept of man as a social being.

Needless to say, the establishment of the caste system in India was due to historical circumstances in which the aboriginal Dravidians were conquered and enslaved by the invading Aryans. The enslaved aborigines became the Sudras (*Śūdra*), upon which the other three castes (Brahmans, Ksatriyas, and Vaisyas) were superimposed according to occupation. This caste system was so strict as to prevent anyone born in one caste from climbing to a higher one, and also to prevent marriage outside of one's caste. This *idée fixe* of caste has been justified in a variety of ways by the Brahmans.

The "Diamond Needle Tract" mentions seven items—life, blood, body, knowledge, custom, practice, and Veda—as grounds for this justification. Since it is not necessary here to dwell upon each one of them, we shall take only the first of them by way of example.

The Brahman justification grounded on "life" is that those who die in the Human Realm are reborn in the Human Realm. The same applies to the animal realm. According to this way of thinking, heavenly beings, humans, and animals are reborn in the same realm as before and seem to be predestined to be reborn in the same realm eternally, and this forms the basis for class distinctions derived from Brahmanic canons.

Ashvaghosha repudiates this ideology by quoting from the same canons to the effect that Indra himself was originally a kind of creature. He questions what could be meant by "life" as such, and shows that in spite of the Brahmans' insistence that their superiority is maintained by "blood," there are obviously among Brahman families many whose ancestors are identified with some mythological figures other than Brahman. He further observes that in spite of the Brahmans' insistence upon their superiority by "knowledge," there are, among Sudras, some whose knowledge equals that of even the most erudite Brahman. He concludes that, after all, not one of their arguments is grounded "in accordance with right reason." His positive arguments are even more convincing.

According to Ashvaghosha, what determines man's position is "virtue." Only "virtue" is the essential norm for classifying man as man *per se*. A man's nobility is determined only by whether or not he is possessed of virtue. In his words: "Therefore, it is to be known that one is called a Brahman, not according to his lineage, conduct, practice, or blood, but according to his virtue." "Virtue," as he called it, is that which can be developed in the Buddhist life. He declares: "Those who have mastered their senses and extinguished their defilements, who are detached from the differentiation of 'self' and 'other,' and are altogether free from craving, anger, and ignorance, are the ones worthy of the name of Brahmans in the true sense of the word." Elsewhere he asserts that those who are endowed with the five characteristics of perseverance, endeavor, contemplation (*dhyāna*), wisdom (*prajñā*), and compassion, are Brahmans; others who, being devoid of these five characteristics, are attached to the differentiation of "self" and "others," are all Sudras. He thus asserts persuasively that on these grounds a Brahman can be called a Sudra, and a Sudra can be called a true Brahman.

III

The revolutionary shift expressed in the "Diamond Needle Tract" by Ashvaghosha is that human existence has emerged from behind the fortified caste system which it had inherited over a long period of history and which it had regarded as fixed, as if it defined man himself *a priori*. Through this change, the realization of man as "man" emerged for the first time. Especially noteworthy here is the fact that the realization of the human was grounded precisely on the Buddhist standpoint of non-ego. This marks a fundamental difference from its Western counterpart occurring at the dawn of the modern era, where man's realization of himself took the form of the realization of ego.

In the West, the realization of "man" came into being mainly through the process of the "secularization" of culture, in which man became separated from his religious view of self. The result was that man came to see himself as an independent, self-centered, self-motivated being, rather than as a God-centered being, subservient to the Will of God. The "self" thus became aware of itself as an autonomous being whose independent existence is sustained only in relation to itself, not as a "created" being whose existence is grounded on its relationship to God. This is why I go so far as to say that the self-realization of man took the form of the realization of "ego."

The opinion often advanced by historians, that this realization of man, despite its radical deviation from Christianity, nevertheless had its origin in the Christian view of man, seems justified. This Christian view encompasses the *personal* relationship of man with God, the essential equality among men as related to God and man's freedom attained in the faith of being a son of God, and so forth. Man's autonomous existence, however, could only be based on the process of social and cultural "secularization" if its religious roots were first severed. Hence this self-realization is from the beginning beset with contradictions. It means that as man came to realize himself as "autonomous man," he left out the most essential component of his being, namely the factor of "love," which is inseparable from freedom and equality in the existence of religious man. To say the least, love ceased to be an essential ingredient of man's self-realization. This was indeed unavoidable, for whereas freedom and equality can maintain their identity (although in the rather paltry guise of "liberty" and "equal rights") in spite of the transition from the religious to the irreligious or secular way of living, this is not the case with love.

For in this transition, love undergoes a qualitative change. In Christian terms *agape* is transformed into *eros*. Religious love (*agape*) is so particular to religion that the separation of the self-realization of man from his religious background required a motive apart from love. Thus, liberty and equality without the ingredient of love came to be claimed as the "rights" of man inherent *a priori* in his being a man. Liberty and equality were insisted upon as "human rights." With man's grasp of himself having taken the form of the realization of "self" as *ego*, love became manifest as the *fraternité* of the French Revolution, as the "love of humanity" of Ludwig Feuerbach, as the "spirit of service" of modern America, and in any number of other disguises. But this love never assumed the essential dynamism to break through the boundaries and enclosures of the ego; it did not succeed in becoming—as did the assertions of liberty and equality—a driving force in the formation of societies and individuals. This points to the phenomenon which underlies one of the critical problems that besets the modern world: *man's self-realization as the self-realization of ego.*

The reason why the self-realization of man in the modern West took this particular form is that, before this event, the religious (in this case Christian) outlook of man had been dogmatically God-centered in such a manner as to make it impossible for human autonomy to function fully. Because of this deep-seated self-contradiction, it was inevitable that the realization of "man" would eventually detach itself from his religious background. In this respect the realization of man as discussed in the "Diamond Needle Tract" made possible by the evolution of the religious standpoint of the "nondifferentiation of self and others"—as expounded in Buddhism— assumes real significance in contemporary life.

IV

If one phase of the revolutionary shift appearing in the "Diamond Needle Tract" is that its realization of "man" succeeded in overcoming a caste system previously regarded as virtually predestined, another phase is the subsequent disclosure of a new standard for determining the essential value of man. As Ashvaghosha says, "For that reason" [i.e., because of the presence or the absence of the Buddhist virtues], "a Brahman can be called a Sudra, and a Sudra can be called a true Brahman." This is the complete reversal of a value system brought about by completely new norms. Sudras, who had been regarded as the lowest in rank of man, could be true Brahmans provided they possessed the Buddhist virtue; and Brahmans, regarded as the highest of men, were in reality Sudras if they lacked it.

Here we see a revolutionary change in the evaluation of what is truly human, which negates the Brahman's claims to moral and spiritual superiority. The new idea of the meaning of what it is to be "Brahman" radically overturns conventional caste practices. It is even stated, "If those Candalas but possess the characteristics of a king, they deserve to be called true Brahmans." (Candalas are an especially low grouping among the Sudras.) The kingly characteristics referred to here are the "Buddhist virtues." Anyone who possesses those virtues is said to be kinglike in his essential being as a man. What it means to be a "true" Brahman is clear: where the truly essential things in man are concerned, even the lowly can possess the traits of a king. In this we find revealed the core of Buddhism as a religion.

In this connection it becomes understandable why Buddhist monks would voluntarily take up the mendicant way of life and have no private property except for an alms bowl and a robe that was no more than a bundle of rags. They were following their Master, who was reputed to have rejected the throne of *Cakravarti-rāja,* the world ruler, and to have chosen instead the life of a beggar. "The begging bowl was the Buddha's badge of sovereignty. . . . He received it as the reward of rejecting the position of world ruler. Teachers often gave their begging bowl to their successor as a sign of the transmission of authority."[3] The tract also states that there is no essential distinction among human beings belonging to any of the four castes, as children born of the same parents: "Having been born of the one same father, why the conceited attachment to the differences of the four castes?"

The "lowly" in the modern West, the modern "proletariat," are said to have become estranged from their humanity in the capitalistic society. Modern revolutionary ideology preaches that in order to recover a lost humanity, which has been exploited so thoroughly that nothing remains to be lost, the proletariat should in turn exploit their exploiters; and that this would constitute the recovery of its human rights. At the same time it would constitute the actualization, the realization of self. The "humanity" whose recovery is being sought, however, is the humanity of the "ego," not the realization of "man" as non-ego, as referred to in the passage on the possession of "kingly characteristics," not the realization of man in terms of the Buddhist virtues.

However materially enriched and culturally elevated this restoration of humanity, so long as its self-realization is limited to the realization of "ego," one may say, from the standpoint of the realization of man as "non-ego," "those Brahmans can also be called Sudras . . ." Even when the proletariat has reached the highest possible standard of living, has ceased to be a proletariat, it may, from a more essential viewpoint, still remain proletarian. Needless to say, aristocracy and bourgeois are equally proletarian from this point of view, whereas the lowliest remain ever capable of possessing the kingly characteristics of the true man.

Not only Marxism, but all other modern social ideologies have failed to recognize this paradox. They may have reached the concept of "nothing" in a material sense, as implied in the very idea of a "proletariat," but they remain ignorant of nothingness as the religious self-realization of "being human." They have no inkling that even those who possess nothing materially can be possessed of kingly characteristics in the "nothingness" of religious realization. Their interpretation of religion, derived as it is from various ideologies, in whose perspective man appears only as "ego," and for which human self-realization can only take place on the level of "ego," not that of "non-ego," inevitably leads them to call it an opiate. Wherever social revolution is advocated without at the same time advocating the transformation of man, such blindness prevails.

In the contemporary West, conflict among the theocentric standpoint of Christianity, the anthropocentric realization of "ego," and a variety of atheisms seem to be *sui generis*. Might not the Buddhist realization of man have something of value to contribute towards the solution of these dilemmas?

NOTES

1. Hermann Oldenberg, *Buddha*, 5th ed. (Stuttgart and Berlin: J. G. Cotta, 1906), p. 176, note.
2. Hermann Oldenberg, *Buddha*, trans. W. Hoey (London and Edinburgh: William and Norgate, 1882).
3. Edward Conze, *Buddhism: Its Essence and Development* (New York: Harper, 1959), p. 55.

3

SUZUKI TEITARŌ DAISETZ

What is the "I"?*

By way of introduction for this essay by D. T. Suzuki I would like to quote from Thomas Merton's brief "In Memoriam," written shortly before his own untimely death in Bangkok in 1968, for *The Eastern Buddhist*.

After quoting Albert Camus: "One may feel proud to be the contemporary of a certain number of human beings of our time," he goes on to say that "on meeting Suzuki one seems to meet that 'True Man of No Title or Rank' ancient Zen speaks about—the only man one really wants to meet."

"Speaking for myself," Merton continues, "I can venture to say that in Dr. Suzuki Buddhism became for me finally completely comprehensible, whereas before it had been a very mysterious and confusing jumble of words, images, doctrines, legends, rituals, buildings, and so forth. . . . One cannot understand Buddhism until one meets it in this existential manner, in a person in whom it is alive."

He speaks of the part of Suzuki's oeuvre translated into English as "without question the most complete and most authentic presentation of an Asian tradition and experience by any one man in terms accessible to the Westerner. I do not think Dr. Suzuki was the kind of person to be bothered with any concern about whether or not he was sufficiently 'modern.' The True Man of No Title is not concerned about such labels, since he knows no time but the present, and knows he cannot apprehend either the past or the future except in the present.

"It may be said that all Dr. Suzuki's books are pretty much about the same thing. Occasionally he will draw back and view Zen from the standpoint of culture, or psychoanalysis, or from the viewpoint of Christian mysticism (in Eckhart), but even then he does not really move out of Zen into some other field, or take a radically new look at his subject. He says very much the same things, tells the same wonderful Zen stories perhaps in slightly different words, and ends with the same conclusion: Zero equals infinity. Yet there is no monotony in his works and one does not feel he is repeating himself, because in fact each book is brand new. Each book is a

---

* "What Is the 'I'?" *The Eastern Buddhist* IV/1 (1971): 13-27.

whole new experience. Those of us who have written a great deal can well admire this quality in Dr. Suzuki's work: its remarkable consistency, its unity. Pseudo-Dionysius says that the wisdom of the contemplative moves in a *motus orbicularis*—a circling and hovering motion like that of the eagle above some invisible quarry, or the turning of a planet around an invisible sun. The work of Dr. Suzuki bears witness of the silent orbiting of *prajñā*, which is (in the language of the same Western tradition of the Areopagite and Erigena) a 'circle whose circumference is nowhere and whose center is everywhere.' The rest of us travel in linear flight. We go far, take up distant positions, abandon them, fight battles and then wonder what we got so excited about, construct systems and then junk them, and wander all over continents looking for something new. Dr. Suzuki stayed right where he was, in his own Zen, and found it inexhaustibly new with each new book. Surely this is an indication of a special gift, a special quality of spiritual genius.

"In any event, his work remains with us as a great gift, as one of the unique spiritual and intellectual achievements of our time. It is above all precious to us in the way it has moved East and West closer together, bringing Japan and America into agreement on a deep level, when everything seems to conspire to breed conflict, division, incomprehension, confusion, and war. Our time has not always excelled in the works of peace. We can be proud of a contemporary who has devoted his life to those works, and done so with such success."

The full meaning of what Merton derived from his contact with Zen through Dr. Suzuki's work are the words he spoke to John Moffit, author of "The Road to Ghandara," on the very eve of the tragic accident that ended his life: "Zen and Christianity are the future."

What is known nowadays as Zen is simply the name for a school of Buddhism that originated in China about one thousand three hundred years ago.

The Buddhist teachings of whatever school, Southern or Northern or Eastern, Theravāda or Mahāyāna, Tibetan or Japanese, Indian, Chinese, or South-Asian, all center around the question: What is the "I"? What is the true self, apart from what we ordinarily understand when we speak of the "psychological or empirical ego"?

To answer this most significant question Zen has developed its own methodology, which has proved quite effective in convincing its questioners of the validity of Buddhism. The method is known as *mondō*, "question and answer." It is the simplest form of dialogue, in sharp contrast with the lengthy, even book-length dialogues of which the Platonic dialogues are an example. The Zen *mondō* is epigrammatic. It may often seem cryptic or enigmatic. This is because Zen does not intend to explain anything intellectually or conceptually, but rather strives to the fullest extent to elicit the answer from within the mind of the questioner himself, since the answer lies— potentially, as it were—in the question itself.

When a man asks, "What is the 'I'?" only the answer that comes out of himself can be completely satisfactory to him. Any answer that might come from the teacher is the teacher's own and not the questioner's. What is not your own is something borrowed, and does not belong to you. You cannot use it freely or creatively as you wish. You cannot go about with the plumage you get from another bird. However superficially beautiful, it bears the mask of its alien origins and you do not feel at home with it. If we are to be sincere to ourselves, we cannot go around with such a mask on. Zen wants us to be real, genuine, and thus utterly free, uninhibited, and creative.

A number of historical examples may be given from a work known as *The Transmission of the Lamp*, which records answers given by the Zen masters to such questions as: What is "I"? What is the essence of Buddhist teachings? What is transmitted from one master to another as embodying the ultimate truth? What is the mind? What is the meaning of birth and death? What constitutes Buddhahood? The *mondō* which follow these questions illustrate in a practical way what Zen is and what Zen proposes to give us. The examples that follow are given more or less in historical order.

I

Nangaku Ejō (677-744) first went to see E-an of Sūzan (582-709) in order to learn what it was that brought Bodhidharma to China from India. His idea was to find out what was the special message of Zen that proposes to point directly to the mind or self at the basis of all Buddhist teachings. So his questioning started with, "What was in the mind of Bodhidharma when he came from India to China?"

E-an answered, "Why not ask about your own mind?" In other words: What is the use of asking about another's mind? The main thing is to know what your own mind is, for once you know it, you know everything. When the subject appears, subject and object stand opposed to each other. When this is understood, the rest follows naturally. Hence the master's counterquestion.

Then Ejō asked, "What is my own mind?" But this is really a stupid question, for what does it profit you to ask others about yourself?

Nevertheless, we are in fact all groping for ourselves, we are like the man who dreamed he had no head of his own and spent all night searching for it outside himself. The master gave Ejō a very subtle answer: "Look within, for something inscrutable is at work there."

"What is that, master?"

The master gave him no further verbal answer. He simply opened his eyes and then closed them. Ejō thought he understood what the master meant by this.

Later when Ejō went to visit Enō (Chin.: Hui Neng, 683-713 C. E.) in the hope of getting further enlightened on the matter, Enō asked first, "Where do you come from?"

"I come from Sūzan."

Enō's counterquestion followed immediately: "Who is it that thus comes here?"

According to the story it took Ejō eight years to answer this question satisfactorily for himself. His answer was, "When one defines it as being a something, one has already missed the mark."

Enō asked further, "Does one require any specific discipline?"

"As to a discipline, one cannot say it is unnecessary, but as to this being definable (when not disciplined), I say it remains absolutely free."

This would mean that the something inscrutable, absolutely beyond any form of verbal description or conceptual discrimination, something that remains always pure and free, unconditioned by anything, is the Zen object of discipline. To see it in its original state of suchness, of being-so-ness, is what the Zen masters strive for. In fact we all have it, but, since awakening from the "innocence" of our primal naiveté, we have the strange feeling that we have lost it altogether. We somehow no longer recognize it, because it has become buried deep in the unconscious.

Once Ejō came to the realization of this fact, he fearlessly asserted that the thing buried in the unconscious is absolutely free from contamination of any sort. Enō confirmed it and told Ejō to guard himself well against committing the fault of seeking it outside himself.

I would caution the reader in this connection not to fall into the grave error of taking this "something inscrutable" for a concrete entity that lies secretly and securely hidden deep down in the mind.

It is the nature of the intellect to butt in when statements like these are made and to criticize them as being absurd, irrational, and impossible. But we must accept the fact that the intellect has its limitations, and that things or facts belonging to our innermost experience are altogether beyond its domain. The intellect wants to see everything physical or psychological analyzed, determined, and defined so that it can place its fingers right on these defined objects and pick them up for demonstration. But it utterly fails when it tries to dispose in this manner of experiences that take place in our inmost being.

"What is it that thus comes here?" To answer this question to the full satisfaction of a questioner whose insight has penetrated to the deepest levels of being, one must shed all the superficialities that have been piled up in one's mind. The answer as it comes out of the depths of being or self or mind, necessarily lacks logical precision, because logic has here to abandon its probing tools and confess its inability to go any further. Ejō's answer—"When one has defined it to be a something, one has already missed the mark"—is negative and can mean many things. But from the point of view of one who has gone through the same experience, it is clear at once that this answer is genuine and does hit the mark. The experience would permit many other answers to the question, "What is it that thus comes here?" But the one who knows can distinguish at once a correct answer from a wrong one. A "self" knows another "self" without any difficulty.

II

When Daishu Ekai came to Baso Dōichi (Chin.: Ma-tsu, 709-788), Baso asked, "Where do you come from?" This is one of the most common questions a master would ask a newcomer. The question is an ordinary form of salutation like "How do you do?" or "How are you?" and at the same time a crucial metaphysical question. When one knows the "whence" one knows also the "whither," and hence everything about one's self, so there is no need of asking anything further and the pilgrim's progress has come to an end; he has reached his objective. "The mind is pacified." Generally, however, the newcomer to the Zen monastery gives a worldly answer on the plane of relativity. For instance, from a geographical point of view he might say, "From London" or "From New York," or from anywhere else on the globe. In its way this answer is correct and straightforward. But it misses the point.

Daishu answered in this ordinary, worldly manner, "I come from the Daiun-ji Temple in the district of Eshū."

Baso then asked, "What are you here for?"

"I wish to take hold of the Buddha-Dharma,"[1] was the reply.

But Baso said, "How stupid you are! You leave your own precious treasure behind and go around asking for things that don't belong to you! What do you think to gain by this? I have here not a thing to give you! What Buddha-Dharma are you after?"

Daishu then made a profound bow and asked, "Please, tell me, master, what is my precious treasure?"

Baso said, "That which makes you ask the question at this moment is your treasure. Everything is stored in your own precious treasure house. It is at your disposal, you can use it as you wish, nothing is wanting. You are the master of everything. Why do you run away from yourself and search outside for it?"

This at once opened up Daishu's mind to its primary state altogether beyond the reach of mere intellection. Overjoyed, he expressed his deepest gratitude and stayed for six years with Baso until he had to return to his native province.

One of the sermons Daishu Ekai later gave goes as follows:

You are fortunate that you are all men of no-business [that is, you have from the very first nothing to worry about]. Just because you are unnecessarily afraid of death, you run around and put your own cangues around your necks, imprisoning yourselves. What does it profit you? Every day you tire yourselves out by exerting your minds and bodies and complain of your hard Zen disciplines in your efforts to realize the Buddha-Dharma. All this is much ado for nothing. As long as you keep on pursuing sense objects, there will be no time for you to rest.

Since being told by the master west of the river that I am in full possession of the precious treasure belonging to me, and ready for my use at any moment, and that there is no need for me to seek anywhere outside myself, I began to feel at once quiet in mind. I am now using my own treasure as I wish, and how refreshingly delighted I am!

There is no Dharma that is to be apprehended, there is no Dharma that is to be abandoned, there is no Dharma that goes through the process of birth and death, there is no Dharma that undergoes the phases of coming and going. The mind pervades the world filling the ten quarters, and there is not a particle of dust that is not included in my treasure. We must simply carefully contemplate our own mind, which, being one in substance, manifests itself in a triple mode without being urged by any outside agency. These manifestations are at all times present before us; there is no room here for doubt. Once assured of this, you need not argue about it, nor search for it. The mind is primarily pure.

Thus we read in the *Avatamsaka Sutra* that all dharmas [i.e., all things] are neither born nor pass away. When your understanding rises to this stage, you are always in the presence of Buddhas. The *Vimalakīrti Sutra* says that seeing the substantiality of your person is like seeing Buddha.

When you are not affected by objects of the senses in your comprehension of Reality, when you are not pursuing appearance in your understanding of the Truth, you will naturally enjoy a life of no-business, that is, a life of peace and freedom.

Do not tire yourselves out by standing so long. I take leave of you now. Farewell.

We come across terms like *a man of no-business, one who has experienced the emptiness,* or *a man of satori* ("the enlightened one," "the Buddha") throughout Zen literature. Confronted with these expressions for the first time, one wonders what they actually mean. The idea of emptiness is particularly puzzling; it smacks of nihilism or the highest degree of abstraction.

But what Zen teaches is neither nihilism, nor its opposite. What Zen speaks of as the *satori* experience, as enlightenment, is this immediate seeing into the reality or suchness of things. This suchness is nothing other than emptiness, which is, after all, no-emptiness. The reality is beyond intellection, and that which lies beyond intellection we call emptiness. "Look into it profoundly," Daishu has told us repeatedly, for here the transcendental field of suchness, of being-so-ness is revealed.

Satori is the "looking into" or "seeing into" whereby the veil of finitude or relativity is penetrated thoroughly and we are ushered into a world where we have never been before. A disciple asked Daishu, "We are often told of the ultimate truth, but, master, who is the one who sees it?"

The master answered, "The one who is endowed with the *prajñā* eye sees into all this."

Prajñā is a Sanskrit term often used by Buddhist thinkers. It is sometimes translated as "transcendental wisdom," but I prefer "transcendental vision." In the Chinese versions of the Sanskrit texts the original *prajñā* is frequently given in Chinese reading as *pan-jo* (Jap.: *hannya*). It is evident that the Chinese scholars of these early days could not find an appropriate character for it, though we have generally *hui* or *chih-hui*. When they find it inadequate, they even go so far as to combine Sanskrit and Chinese together, as in *pan-jo shih chih-hui*, thereby showing that *prajñā* is that activity or function used by the human mind in order to go beyond the ordinary domain of relative or logical analytical knowledge. *Prajñā* cannot be specifically categorized as will, affect, or intellect; it is something absolutely fundamental and altogether undifferentiated, or better, absolutely "unattainable," "ungraspable," "inscrutable."

The terminology we cannot help resorting to in this case has nothing to do with the subject itself as unattainable or ungraspable or incomprehensible. The subject is as real as the stone or the mountain I see before me now. Indeed, the reality of the unattainable is more real, more essential than any of the objects of our sense-intellect because, although the entire system of galaxies may someday collapse, the unattainable remains forever just as it is. All Buddhist teachings are built upon this rock of unattainability which they designate as suchness or emptiness of mind (*hsin*) or dharma (*fu*) or essence (*hsing*). *Satori* is the term given to the experience we have when this unattainable is attained as such, namely, as unattainable, as ungraspable. Thus *satori* as spoken of in Zen is *prajñā* in action.

III

The questioner goes on to ask master Daishu, "How do we then proceed to study Mahāyāna?" (Mahāyāna is the Buddhist teaching dealing extensively with the subject under discussion and in this case may be identified with Zen.) The question then amounts to, "What is Zen?"

> DAISHU: When you have *satori* you have it; without *satori*, there is no understanding at all of Zen.
> DISCIPLE: How do we attain *satori?*
> DAISHU: Have a clear look inside.
> DISCIPLE: What does it look like?
> DAISHU: No resemblance at all to anything.
> DISCIPLE: Then, ultimately, all is emptiness?
> DAISHU: Emptiness has nothing to do with ultimacy.
> DISCIPLE: Is it then just "is"?
> DAISHU: It "is," but it has no tangible form.
> DISCIPLE: How about when one has no *"satori"*?
> DAISHU: You may have no *satori*, but nobody hinders your having it.

The most difficult thing we as finite beings have to experience is that whenever a name is given to something, we take it to be something that has a form, and hence we make puppets of ourselves with the tools of our own making. We are afraid and anxious, and finally we turn into schizophrenics. Not only individually, but collectively, modern man is not of sound mind, he trembles before the symbolic phantoms of his own imagination.

The old masters were conscientious in this respect, though they did not use highly abstract concepts. A monk asked, "Is speech the mind or not?" By this the monk meant that the mind is no more, no less than a word, an empty concept.

Daishu the master answered, "Speech is symbolic, but not the mind itself."

> MONK: Outside the symbolic, what is the mind?
> DAISHU: Outside the symbolic, there is no mind.
> MONK: If there is no mind outside the symbolic, what can it be?
> DAISHU: Being formless, the mind is neither separated from speech nor is it unseparated from speech. The mind remains always serene and acts autonomously without being controlled by any outside agency. The patriarch said, "When it is understood that mind is no mind, one for the first time understands what is designated as mind."

The Emperor, Shuk So of the T'ang, asked Chū the National

Teacher:

> EMPEROR: What is the Dharma you attained?
> TEACHER: Your Majesty, do you see a floating cloud in the sky?
> EMPEROR: Yes, I see.
> TEACHER: Is it nailed to the sky? Or just hung there?

> EMPEROR: What is the great Buddha endowed with all the marks of superman?

Chū the National Teacher stood up and said:

> TEACHER: Do you understand?
> EMPEROR: No, sir, I do not.
> TEACHER: Please be good enough to bring up that water pitcher over here.
> EMPEROR: What is meant by the *samādhi* of absolute affirmation?
> TEACHER: Your Majesty, walk over the head of Vairocana Buddha.
> EMPEROR: What is the meaning of this?
> TEACHER: Commit no mistake of regarding yourself as the Dharma Body of absolute purity.

The Emperor went on asking other questions, but the Teacher seemed to pay no further attention. The Emperor was incensed:

> EMPEROR: I am the supreme one governing this empire of the T'ang. Why do you refuse to pay me due respect?
> TEACHER: Do you see the emptiness of the great Void [space]?
> EMPEROR: Yes, I see.
> TEACHER: Does it face Your Majesty with its eyes down?

IV

Shi, an abbot and scholar in the philosophy of Kegon, asked Daishu: "Why do you not agree with the statement that the green bamboos are of the *Dharmakāya* and the luxuriantly blooming yellow flowers are of *prajñā*?" This kind of pantheistic interpretation of Kegon philosophy is held by some Buddhist scholars even now. The idea is that if the *Dharmakāya* ("Ultimate Being") pervades all over the world, everything partakes of it. So with *prajñā*. *Prajñā* is an epistemological term, one might say, but when understood psychologically it refers to the mind. This being so, if all things have their origins in the mind (a sort of Cittamātra philosophy), is it not true to declare all things to be of the mind? This is the contention of the Kegon abbot and scholar Shi.

> DAISHU: The *Dharmakāya* is formless, whereas green bamboos have form; *prajñā* is nonsentient, whereas yellow flowers are manifest; *prajñā* and the *Dharmakāya* remain existent though the yellow flowers and green bamboos may vanish. So we have in the sutra: The true *Dharmakāya* of Buddha is like the Void and manifests itself in form according to the varying conditions, as the moon reflects itself in water. If the yellow flowers are of *prajñā*, *prajñā* is nonsentient; if the green bamboo are of the *Dharmakāya*, the green bamboos must be able to function in accordance with the conditions. Do you understand, O Abbot?
> SHI THE ABBOT: No, I fail to comprehend.
> DAISHU: It all depends on whether or not a man has experienced what is known as *kenshō*. *Kenshō* literally means "to see into the nature," i.e., the ultimate Reality. An enlightened man (*kenshō no hito*) may respond to the question either affirmatively or negatively. Whichever statement he makes is right. In the case of the unenlightened man, when he makes an affirmative statement in regard to the green bamboo he is attached to it. So with the yellow flowers, he attaches himself to what he affirms. He knows neither the *Dharmakāya* nor *prajñā*, and therefore anything he can say about them is all wrong. The result is, he is caught in the meshes of vain argumentation.

Kenshō (Chin.: *chien-hsing*) is an important Zen term, especially in Japan. It requires a thorough understanding as far as its literal significance is concerned. When this is achieved, what Zen purports to accomplish will be clearly brought to light.

Ken (*chien*) is "to see," "to sight," "to open one's eye to," "to have a direct view of," etc. *Shō* (*hsing*) is "nature," "essence," "that which makes a thing what it is," "the suchness of a thing." *Shō* thus is often indiscriminately identified, psychologically, with mind, and ontologically with Reality, or Being.

Kenshō thus is seeing into what makes man a man, his essence, what is behind the mind, supporting it, moving it, making it respond to the outside world. And this seeing is not a knowledge of the mind, analytically arrived at, but a direct, immediate view of it as when the eye perceives an object before it. However, it is most important to remember that the seeing in the experience of *kenshō is* not dualistic or dichotomous, because there is no separation here between the object of sight and the seeing subject, because the seer is the seen and the seen is the seer, the two are completely identical. It is our logic or intellection that dichotomizes the *kenshō*, because we are used to this way of talking about our ordinary experiences in the realm of sense and intellect. When, however, we come to the realm that lies beyond limited and finite experiences, or rather which envelops and permeates them, we must abandon all we usually take to be most useful, most valuable, and most necessary. For as long as we are attached to this, we cannot hope to solve those problems, which are not only annoying and upsetting to the intellect, but actually threaten our existence itself. Hence the emphasis Zen thinkers put on an altogether new experience, and their use of terms and expressions whose meaning cannot be subsumed under logical categories.

For this reason Zen is full of contradictions and irrationalities. To the disciple of Zen who has experienced *kenshō*, or *satori*, right may be wrong, wrong may be right, true may be false and vice versa. When this is interpreted as we generally do according to the principle of the excluded middle, we must say that the realm of Zen is absolutely chaotic, and as the values we so prize in our ordinary life are utterly ignored, we cannot live in such a world. But we must remember that the eyes of the disciple of Zen are fixed upon things "before the foundation of the world" or before God uttered his *fiat*: "Let there be light." And we must never forget that the realm of transcendence is neither physically nor literally separate from the one where we are living our everyday life. The greatest error is to assume that there are two worlds, one within the limits and the other beyond them. If the latter is separate from the former, it limits itself by this fact of separation and cannot be the one transcending them. The world of the Zen disciple is at once beyond and within the limit. When this logical contradiction ceases in our everyday life as we live it, we really and truly understand what Zen is.

We can talk of limits because there is something that is not limited, that is beyond these limits and at the same time limiting itself within them. This something is not really a "something" as understood on the level of ratiocination. It is therefore a "nothing," a strange, irrational kind of nothing—a nothing that is not a nothing.

The seeing in the *kenshō* experience therefore is not the ordinary kind of seeing, in which we confront an object: no object, no seeing! In *kenshō*, *ken* is *shō* and *shō* is *ken*. Seeing is always there, no matter whether there is an object or not. The *shō* which transcends all limits is only attained when this mode of seeing becomes possible. It is a seeing in which there is no more bifurcation of subject and object. Subject and object are done away with, the limits or the between have been wiped away. The logician may think this impossible, for he stays within the limits and assumes that beyond these limits he confronts nothing. Or else, afraid of stepping out of the limits, he tries to hold on to the between. To this logician the experience of *kenshō* will never come. For *kenshō* is an experience, an event that simply comes to one, not something to be argued about according to rules of dialectics. When you have it, you have it, and no argument will undo it. It is something final.

The seeing in the experience of *kenshō* can therefore not be classified as a sense category; it is not the seeing of any object before the eye. *Kenshō* is the *shō's* seeing itself. There is no dualism here. Daishu explains it in this way: "The Essence in itself is from the beginning pure and undefiled, it is serene and altogether empty, and in this body of absolute emptiness, the seeing takes place."

V

When the questioner asks, "The body of absolute purity is in itself something unattainable, and could any kind of seeing take place here?" Daishu answers:

> It is like a brightly polished mirror; it has no image itself, but every kind of image appears on it. Why? Because the mirror itself is no-minded. When your mind is free from taints, when no form of illusive thought arises in it, and all ideas based on the ego-consciousness are cleared away, the mind will be naturally pure and undefiled. And because of its being pure and undefiled, the seeing we spoke about can occur. In the *Dharmapada* [Chinese version] we read, "In the midst of Ultimate Emptiness there arises [the seeing] in the manner of a flame, which characterizes a good wise man!"

QUESTIONER: In the chapter of the *Nirvāna Sutra* on "The Vajra Body," we come across such phrases as "impossible to see," "most clearly

33

seen," "no knower," "yet nothing unknown." What do they mean? [They are apparently related to the experience of seeing in *kenshō*.] DAISHU: "Impossible to see" means that the Essence in itself is form-less and altogether impossible to grasp, and therefore impossible to see. "It is seen but not graspable," and because of this it is "the see-ing in the highest degree of clarity." This means that the Essence is absolutely tranquil and serene, showing no signs of becoming and yet always going along with the current of worldly events, though the current is unable to carry it away. Calm yet freely moving—this is see-ing in the highest degree of clarity. "No knower" means that because of its being formless the Essence-in-itself is not at all discriminating. And "yet nothing unknown" means that the Essence-in-itself, in which there is no discriminating agent present, functions in every possible mode and is able to discriminate everything; there is noth-ing it does not know. This is the meaning of "nothing unknown." The "Gāthā on *Prajñā*" reads: "*Prajñā* is not the knower, and yet there is no event it does not know. *Prajñā* is not the seer, and yet there is no event it does not see."

That is to say, *prajñā* does not discriminate between "to be" and "not to be," it is above relative knowledge. Just because of this "igno-rance" it knows everything in the sense that *prajñā*'s knowledge is not to be subsumed under logic categories. The knowledge ascrib-able to *prajñā* is absolute, an omniscience that underlies all our knowledge of particulars. The knowledge of this kind is the seeing in the experience of *kenshō*.

Daishu also quotes from the *Śūramgama Sutra*: "To recognize knowing in the experience of the knowing-seeing is the origin of ignorance [*avidyā*]; when there is no seeing in it, it is *nirvāna*—which is called emancipation [*moksa*]."

This may require some explanation. In *satori* there is the experi-ence of seeing, which corresponds to a sense perception: both are immediate, with nothing between the seer and the seen. But in the case of a sense perception the seer is conscious of the object, there is a discrimination between "I" and "not-I." In the *satori* kind of see-ing there is no such "knowing," nor is there any seeing that gener-ally takes place in the domain of our ordinary life. Because in the *satori* seeing there is neither subject nor object, it is a nothing see-ing itself as such.

VI

QUESTIONER: When we confront objects of all kinds we see them; when we have nothing before us, can that be called seeing?
DAISHU: Yes.
QUESTIONER: The confronting is the seeing. How can we say "we see" when there is nothing before us?
DAISHU: Our seeing takes place regardless of whether we confront something or nothing. Why? Because *kenshō* is constant in nature. The seeing is not a momentary phenomenon. The objects may come and go, but the seeing nature of *kenshō* is not subject to such changes. The same applies to all other sense activities.
QUESTIONER: When the *kenshō* seeing takes place, does it see anything?
DAISHU: No, there is no-thing in the seeing.

If there is a "no-thing" confronting the seeing experience of *kenshō*, this will be a momentary psychological event. In the *kenshō* there is not even a "no-thing." The same applies to "hearing." The Essence-in-itself (*shō*) hears without hearing, just as it goes without seeing. It is in this sense that the disciple of Zen speaks of the Mind or no-mind or emptiness or suchness.

When Tokusan was challenged by the old lady of the roadside tea house where he stopped to take a refreshment (*tien-hsin*, literally "punctuating the mind"), he failed to answer her and hence had to go on his way without getting anything to eat. The famous challenge was: "According to the sutra, the past mind is unattainable, the future mind is unattainable, and the present mind is unattainable. Which mind do you wish to 'punctuate' here?" Daishu adds:

> Let the mind reside in emptiness but do not let it harbor the thought of residing in emptiness. If it does, it attaches itself to the thought and it is no more "empty" or "pure."

> If you wish to attain to this state of mind where it is free from all forms of attachment, even to the thought of emptiness, that is, if you wish to keep the mind in the state of no-abiding, you should practice the right meditation, keep the mind free from thoughts, and not let it dwell on any definite object, good or evil. Let not things of the past possess your mind. The past is past, do not pursue it, and the past mind ceases by itself. This is said to be cutting off all past affairs. The things of the future are not yet here. Have no anticipation of whatever nature for them, and the future mind ceases by itself and you are

35

shut out from affairs of the future. As to the present, it is already here, and you are it; have no attachments whatever. When you have no attachment you are free from hate and love. And the present mind ceases by itself, and affairs of the present are nonexistent.

When thus the past, future, and present are not taken hold of, they are nonexistent. [You are in the absolute present. You are the Here-Now.]

When the mind rises and passes away, do not follow it, and no thought will bind you. The same with the abiding mind: do not cherish the thought of abiding. When the mind is not following it, it is in the state of no-abiding. When there is self-knowing in the highest stage of clarity, the mind abides; when it is abiding it just abides, is just at rest, not at all cognizant of where it is abiding or where it is not abiding. When one realizes this state of mind thus altogether free from all form of attachment, one sees one's own mind with the highest degree of clarity. The seeing experience of *kenshō* has here reached the highest point of clarity.

All is possible when the Essence-in-itself is liberated from attachments, encumbrances, delusive thought, and affects, and abides in suchness or emptiness or no-mind-ness. In *kenshō*, the seeing is the Essence-in-itself and the Essence-in-itself is the seeing. They are not two separate events. To understand all this, the disciple of Zen tells you that you are once to go through the experience and be a man of *kenshō*. When you have it all, you say yes or no according to the situation you are in, and you are always in the right. Then you may see the green bamboos or the yellow flowers and assert that they are yellow or green, or neither green nor yellow, and you will not be contradicting your experience.

QUESTIONER: Is *prajñā* large?
DAISHU: Yes, it is.
QUESTIONER: How large?
DAISHU: It is of infinite magnitude.
QUESTIONER: Is *prajñā* small?
DAISHU: Yes, it is.
QUESTIONER: How small?
DAISHU: It is invisible.
QUESTIONER: Which is right? Large or small?
DAISHU: Is there anything wrong in my statements?

This kind of *mondō* is characteristic of Zen. Daishu is great in this kind of repartee and he insists that it can never be understood by those who have not experienced *satori* or *kenshō* (seeing the Essence-in-itself).

In his *mondō* with the scholar of the *Vimalakīrti Sutra,* Daishu is more explicatory and tries to make his point clear for the questioner.

NOTES

1. "The Buddha-Dharma," or simply "the Dharma," means the ultimate reality, the absolute truth, the self pure and simple, the person, the godhead, the one mind, suchness, emptiness, being (*sat*), pure reason (*prajñā*), nature, the uncreated, etc. It is variously designated in Buddhism. Briefly, it is the most primary and at the same time the last real thing the human mind can only grasp "immediately," "directly," "from within," and "holistically." And when this experience takes place, a man feels at last at home with himself and with the whole world, and does not have to ask any more questions, for now he *is* the way, the truth, and the life.

4

NISHITANI KEIJI

The I-Thou Relation in Zen Buddhism*

This essay, which in my opinion contains not only the very quintessence of Zen but also insights into the unplumbed depths of interhuman relationships, seems particularly characteristic of the workings of Nishitani's creative thought processes. Similar characteristics in structure may be discerned in other essays of this series, and perhaps even in oriental ways of thinking as such. They seem, for instance, clearly discernible in those of Nishida Kitarō and Soga Ryōjin.

But especially in Nishitani's essay which we present here, I am constantly reminded of its almost musical, even fugal structure. For a fugue is a composition in counterpoint based on a general theme, in which different voices enter successively in "imitation," as if in pursuit of one another, yet preserving a clear unity of form. Fugues of two or three voices are most frequent. Here the subject or theme, stated by the first voice alone, then taken up by the others, will in the course of the fugue's development appear and reappear in different form, slightly modified or even inverted. It is as if the voices answer one another's questionings, but in such a way that tonal unity is preserved, and hence the answers have to undergo mutations. The part of the fugue which includes the successive entrance of the voices in subject-answer alternation is known as the "exposition." It is the progressive enrichment of the polyphonic web so characteristic of the fugue that carries us along and enchants us.

I hope that this musical digression may add to the reader's delight in the essay that follows, in which one may listen to the *mondō* as if it were the fugue's subject stated by the first voice, and to the countersubject as sounded by Daitō's stirring poem, followed by the involved mutations and enrichments of the essay's development until it reaches a majestic resolution in "Kyōzan's roar of laughter."

* "The I-Thou Relation in Zen Buddhism," trans. N. A. Waddell, *The Eastern Buddhist* II/2 (1969): 71-87.

I

Kyōzan Ejaku asked Sanshō Enen, "What is your name?"
Sanshō said, "Ejaku!"
"Ejaku!" replied Kyōzan, "that's *my* name."
"Well then," said Sanshō, "my name is Enen."
Kyōzan roared with laughter.

Daitō Kokushi comments on the passage: Where does it go?

The sun shines warmly, the spring snow clears;
The jaws of the plum and the face of the willow vie
    with their fragrant freshness.
The occasion for poetry and spiritual divertissement
    holds boundless meaning.
Permitted only to the man who wanders in the fields
    and arduously composes poetry.[1]

This encounter between Kyōzan and Sanshō is an old and well-known Zen kōan included in the collection entitled the "Blue Cliff Records" (Jap.: *Hekiganroku*; Chin.: *Pi-yen-lu*),[2] where it bears the title "Kyōzan Roars with Laughter." It shows the true significance contained in the encounter of one man with another.

We are constantly meeting others—wives, children, family, colleagues at work, people in the street and in buses, total strangers. Reading history we encounter people who lived hundreds of thousands of years ago. Oddly enough, we see nothing extraordinary in these encounters, or even question what makes these contacts possible, what infinite beauty, what boundless terror may be hidden below the surface of all such confrontations.

This question cannot be answered at a distance, from somewhere outside of the encounter itself. Nor can it be answered with the tools of biology, anthropology, sociology, or ethics, which cannot fathom its depth dimension. One can argue about human rights in such terms *ad infinitum* without ever facing the problem of what might be involved in meeting another being, and so end up as defenseless as ever against images like Hobbes's *homo homini lupus*, or the German mystic Heinrich Seuse's "manwolf." Nor is Kant's approach of the mutual affirmation of men as persons much help in solving the riddlesome, mysterious depths of the human encounter. Philosophical and theological probings seem wont to recoil from looking into this bottomless pit. I cannot help feeling that looking at the relationship of man to man from within, let us say, the *communia sanctorum* of the church is—as the Chinese saying has it—like scratching an itchy foot without taking off one's shoe: a rather inefficient solution, given those layers of leather in the way. . . .

With Martin Buber the interhuman encounter has come to be seen as a personal relationship between an "I" and a "Thou." Although the approach no doubt has its own validity, it is far from exhausting the hidden depths of the person-to-person, I-and-Thou, relationship. Where it stops is the very point at which Zen exploration begins. Two factors need to be kept firmly in mind. First, the I and the Thou are absolutes, each in its own respective subjectivity. And second, both I and Thou are, because of their relationship to one another, at the same time absolutely relative. The subject in its absolute subjectivity has been spoken of in various ways. One of these, already alluded to above, is that men are like wolves to one another. Another, the Kantian concept of personality, sees the moral will of man as autonomous and does not allow of any outside determination, not even from God. From the usual religious point of view, the I stands in relation to God as to an Absolute Thou, an Absolute Other. In all three cases, the absoluteness of individual subjectivity means that nothing can take its place. And yet in each case we see something, either in man as an individual or above him, of a universal quality, something lawlike. By means of this universal, the relationship of one individual to another is both established and at the same time partly relativized. That is, the universal acts as a kind of obstruction to absolute individuality.

This universal may take a variety of forms. Where men encounter each other as wolves, the state or its laws might serve to check their individuality. For the ethical man, this function may be performed by practical reason or by moral law. For the religious person, an Absolute Other or divine law may act as a universal ground for the relationships between human beings. But in each case, the general structure of those relationships is conditioned by the universal, and so takes on a kind of halfway quality. The problems this presents is that on the one hand the individual has an irreplaceable subjectivity and hence complete freedom, while on the other, he is simultaneously subordinated to some universal or other. Insofar as all individuals are so subordinated, this would seem to imply that any one individual could take the place of any other.

It is a bit like a neighborhood funeral, which the head of a household should attend to offer condolences in the name of his family. Let us assume that he is too busy and sends his wife instead, or even that they are both unable to attend and have their oldest son substitute for them. In this case, it hardly matters who represents the family. Any one of its members can take the place of any other, thereby demonstrating the principle of substitution or surrogation. Now, whereas equality implies the possibility of such substitution, freedom implies its impossibility. A mixture of equality with freedom implies that this freedom is imperfect. As soon as the individual is subject to a universal, he is relativized and loses his absoluteness. All problems concerning correlations between freedom and equality are of this sort.

Looked at from another angle, this imperfect freedom implies as well an imperfect sameness or equality. Subordination to a universal cannot totally absorb or destroy the freedom of the individual as individual. To recover that freedom, unimpeded by law, he may have to escape from the prison of the universal. The power of the state and its laws can never fully succeed in transforming the wolf into a sheep, and from time to time the wolf will act as a wolf. Usually this takes place only on a limited scale, but should an individual so act on a grand scale, he could become the very incarnation of the Will to Power. Similarly, the rigor of moral law can never extinguish completely a man's self-love. In fact, that self-love may lead him to stoop to the "radical evil" that Kant speaks of. The sanctity of divine law cannot curb a man's obstinate appetites nor prevent him from ever turning his back on God, and falling happily into Satan's blandishments. Once his duty is over, the good householder who has just represented his respectable family at the neighborhood funeral might hail a taxi and rush to his mistress. Or the son who takes his father's place may turn around later and go to the movies with the money pilfered from his mother's purse. In short, for the individual relativized by some universal, both equality and freedom are imperfect. This means that where interhuman relationships are subordinate to such universals, with the result that equality and freedom accompany one another in their incompleteness, no authentic encounter between human beings is possible. In the "natural state" of the man-wolf, the original character of man's encounter with man is hidden by laws, be they civil, moral, or divine.

When subordination to a universal proves incapable of absorbing the totality of the freedom of the private, individual self, we may find the very breath being squeezed out of individual freedom in an irate attempt to enforce equality. This is what happens, for instance, where socialism turns into totalitarianism. Of course an equality enforced in this way cannot be genuine and absolute. To be sure, for such equality to succeed the universal must swallow both private and individual freedom totally. But then, with nothing left of the individuality of the individual, there is also nothing left to which a common sameness could relate, with the result that the concept of equality or sameness becomes meaningless. Somehow an emancipation, a reinvention of the individual with some personal freedom would become necessary, and a way would have to be found by which the absolute negation of the individual and his freedom would at the same time be an absolute affirmation, and vice versa. In other words, what is required is an equality in which the negation of the individual and his freedom would become the absolute affirmation of the individual and his freedom. This is of course quite inconceivable, unless seen from the point of view of absolute nothingness, *śūnyatā*—nonbeing in the Buddhist sense of the term.

For a universal to posit itself in relation to the individual and thus become a universal that actually *exists*—whether as state, as practical reason, as God, or whatever—it has to mediate, one way or another, between individual and individual, and thereby bring them to unity. It is within this unity through law that the universal manifests itself as *being*, as something with self-identity, as "substance." The relation between man and man is then such that the individual forfeits half of itself in the relation. It is no longer an absolute individuality, standing as an independent totality. Meanwhile the universal remains to a certain extent inherent in individuals and radiates their capacity for relationship. Because of this immanence the universal cannot, however, completely pass over the individual and, as it were, deprive him of his roots. Therefore, as subsequently the freedom of the individual becomes more and more emphasized, unity through law is gradually weakened and in the end dissolves altogether. This tendency is demonstrated in the lapse from liberalism into anarchy. Anarchy might be called a "natural state" raised to a higher plane, though no true freedom can ever be achieved through it. There is only one situation in which complete freedom can be attained without falling into anarchy, namely, the situation in which freedom and equality—which are essentially contradictory—can coexist in a paradoxical way. And this can only take place where the locus of *śūnyatā* becomes the locus of freedom. This locus of *śūnyatā* is attained when equality, which tends to negate freedom, is broken through to its unmoving ground of absolute negation or nothingness. True freedom can only be consummated where its absolute negation is absolute affirmation. Anything else would only mean a wobbling between the poles of totalitarianism and anarchy. I am not using totalitarianism and anarchy only in a political sense here, but as means to extend them to all categories of human relations. Totalitarianism is always capable of changing into anarchy and vice versa. The road to anarchy and the road to totalitarianism often run parallel.

II

The reader may have wondered what this long discourse on reality that belongs to our everyday experience might have to do with the strange Zen *mondō* between two ancient Chinese Zen monks we started with. The fact is, this *mondō* encompasses everything we have been dealing with. Let us go back to that original problem then, to face squarely, without compromise, the twofold conditions that affect I and Thou as subjects: namely, that they are each absolutes and at the same time absolutely relative. Unless we go back to this point we will be unable to realize either true individual freedom or true universal equality.

The fact that I and Thou are both thoroughly and absolutely absolute means that both of them in relation to one another are absolutely relative. This sounds like pure nonsense, an outright contradiction. It would imply a total hostility, an absolute animosity of one to the other, where each one would find it impossible to live under the same sky with the other, to use a Chinese expression. And where two cannot share the same sky, the one must kill the other. This is precisely the relationship of *homo homini lupus*—eat or be eaten. In such conditions, relativity would be eliminated altogether. (That is, we should have to refuse to allow for relative, respective absolutes. Moreover, no basis would exist for accepting one and rejecting another; both are entirely equal.) For this reason, arch-enemies unable to live under the same sky nevertheless coexist quite efficiently. Should this be out of the question, they will have to resign themselves to a compromise by means of a universal and its law. This compromise will always be full of contradictions and conflicts and ever in danger of collapse, as is confirmed by events throughout history. It is that boundless suffering that, according to the Buddha, marks the way of the world. The ground of this suffering can be located in the relation of human beings one to another, in the simple fact that human beings do exist side by side, notwithstanding the theoretical impossibility of two absolutes coexisting alongside one another. That impossibility—which from time immemorial has proven to be possible and is still our day-to-day reality—has been the source of innumerable entanglements and boundless suffering. How does Zen see this situation? How does it succeed in proving the possibility of the absurd notion that absolute enmity is at the same time absolute harmony?

Kyōzan asked Sanshō, "What is your name?" Going back into the history of mankind we find that at one time the name had profound significance. It symbolized the bearer of the name, it revealed who he was, it became one with him. This view played an important role in magic, religion, and social life itself. If a woman disclosed her name to a man, it meant that she had disclosed herself to him, had already given herself to him. Later in history, expressions like "the name of Amida" and "in the name of Jesus Christ" implied that Buddha and God had revealed and proclaimed themselves and had given themselves to mankind. As we approach our own time, the name becomes ever more "just a name." Here we arrive at the point where man begins to boast about his own awakening intellect; here is the beginning of the modern scientific spirit and the appearance of nominalism and empiricism. It remains to be seen, however, whether considering the name as one with existence can simply be shrugged off as belonging to some mythological age prior to the emancipation of the intellect.

The opposite might well prove to be true: that men were once, long ago, in contact with reality in a very real way, and indeed experienced themselves as having their being within that reality. Perhaps the name was perceived *realiter* because reality was intimately felt, concretely lived, directly realized. This would indicate that the interpretation of the name as being "just a name" shows up the intellect in its isolation from reality. Might not, then, the "awakened intellect" conceal a fall into a greater blindness? Might not our pride in the so-called scientific age be an expression of folly, of our lack of awareness of our own utter blindness?

Be this as it may, Kyōzan and Sanshō are not men of some mythological age. Zen is a radically demythologized religion, as typified in its injunction to "kill the Buddha and the Patriarchs." In our *mondō*, we might assume at first that it is a question about "just a name." But since Sanshō was a great Zen master and Kyōzan no doubt knew his name, it should be clear that Kyōzan's question is not simply an inquiry in Sanshō's name on the level of intellect. The question is, on the contrary, the opening gambit of a Zen happening—that of a simple encounter between two people—in order to penetrate, and to explore at its depths what happens every day between ordinary human beings. Sanshō and Kyōzan are here acting out the situation of two men whose natures make it impossible for them to live under the same sky, and who nevertheless must live under the same sky: the impossibility that we spoke of as becoming a possibility, or rather a fact, in our everyday reality. For here the exploration of reality in our everyday reality begins.

Commenting on Kyōzan's query, "What is your name?" Engo (Chin.: Yüan-wu, 1062-1135) says: "He robs at one time the name and the being." To ask someone for his name means also to take over his being. The eighteenth-century Zen master Hakuin remarked of this question that "it is like a policeman interrogating some suspicious fellow he has found loitering in the dark."

This does not necessarily mean that Kyōzan himself would so express the meaning of his question; it only points to the tone of the question. When that which has the nature of an absolute operates in the relative world, its operation, of itself, shuts out all relativity. That which opposes the self as "other" must be stopped short in its tracks, pulled over alongside the self, and swallowed up by it. Insofar as the self is its own master and maintains its full subjectivity—which is to say, insofar as it is in a true sense a "self"—this will take place naturally. This means that Kyōzan is Kyōzan. But now, from the standpoint of the Thou as subject, the same could be said to hold true. The essence of the I-Thou relationship is still characterized by the problem of eating or being eaten. Engo adds a further comment to this dialogue: "Kyōzan had trapped him. He thought he had Sanshō firmly, but then to his astonishment discovered that he had caught a thief, a thief who turned the tables on him and robbed him of everything he owned."

When asked his name, Sanshō answered that it was Ejaku, which was in fact Kyōzan's own name: with that answer, therefore, Sanshō actually took over for himself, as it were, Kyōzan's absolute nature—the nature of Kyōzan as Kyōzan himself, the one who will not allow any Thou to stand in opposition to him, and who would take all others to himself. Skirting Kyōzan's defenses and attacking him from behind under the banner of his own self, Sanshō pulls the rug from under Kyōzan's feet, and seizes his very existence.

Besides, since it is all done in terms of Sanshō's genuine self, Engo observes that by his answer Sanshō cuts off Kyōzan's tongue: "He snatches flag and drum away from him." He also cuts short the contest and cuts off the self that put the question to him, snatching away the signs of victory. Sanshō is revealed as Sanshō.

Turning now to that aspect of Kyōzan's self that asked the question in the first place, we note that it arose from the same elemental ground. Kyōzan tries to rob Sanshō of his name and being, to steal Sanshō's self. This means that they remain in a relation of absolute enmity to one another. But the essential point is that the subjective relation of man to man is no longer that of I and Thou in the universal sense. When Sanshō calls himself by Kyōzan's name (Ejaku) Sanshō *is* Kyōzan and the I *is* the Thou, even as the Thou *is* the I. It is precisely the same from Kyōzan's standpoint. The I is no longer an ordinary I, it is the I (Sanshō) that is at the same time the Thou (Kyōzan). The Thou, too, is no simple Thou. It is now the Thou that is simultaneously I, so that I and Thou blend completely into one another.

Here one might think of absolute nondifferentiation, absolute oneness, absolute sameness. We find this expressed in Western thought, in such things as the Oneness of Plotinus and the Absolute Identity of Schelling. It is the point at which all relationship ceases to exist, with nothing to call it back. *There is neither self nor other; hence there is no person and no personal relationship left.*

Our *mondō* would seem to imply that the reality of the I-Thou relationship is simply a return to the problem of nondiscrimination, but in fact it demonstrates just the opposite. Although every simple nondiscrimination is separated from reality, the problem here is surely one that actually involves the reality of I and Thou, and actually includes the reality of the encounter between man and man and the absolute opposition that belongs to it. Only in this case the I and the Thou are not simply I and Thou. Since the I is the Thou, and the Thou is the I, both are absolutely nondifferentiated. For the I, this absolute nondifferentiation belongs to the I itself, and it is the same for the Thou. In this way the I is a true I, and the Thou a true Thou. This is the genuine I-Thou relation.

We might formulate this paradox after the manner of the *Diamond Sutra* as follows: "The I-Thou relation is an I-Thou relation because it is not an I-Thou relation." This brings out the necessity for an absolute opposition as well. The I and the Thou that contend with one another for the ground of absolute nondifferentiation— each asserting that it belongs to itself (which it essentially does)— are thus really absolutely related to one another and therefore relative. They are an I and a Thou that, as genuine subjects, are absolutely different from each other. Here there is no relationship at all between I and Thou, and yet it is not a nonrelation as a mere nondifferentiation. *It is nonrelation as absolute opposition, and as a relative on the plane where all relations have been utterly transcended.* In fact, the reality of the I-Thou encounter in everyday life is one in which just such an absolute relativity and just such an absolute opposition exist. At the ground of such an encounter there lies unbounded horror.

Looked at from the other side, the absoluteness in absolute relativity is due to the fact that the absolute nondiscrimination belongs to both the I and the Thou; I can be I, and Thou can be Thou as absolute individuals because each of them is grounded on the absolute identity in which I am Thou and Thou are I, and every form of relation and relativity is superseded. Here, I *am* with you in no way discriminated from you, and you *are* with me, equally undiscriminated from me.

Sanshō's calling himself by Kyōzan's name means, then, that he is emptying himself and putting Kyōzan in his place. Where the other is at the center of the individual, and where the existence of each one is "other-centered," absolute harmony reigns. This might be called "love" in the religious sense. I stress "in a religious sense," because it is a case of "void" or "*muga*" (non-self) that has absolutely severed self-and-other from self-and-other in their relative sense.

Thus, absolute opposition is at the same time absolute harmony. Both are the same. Here, absolute opposition is, as it is, a sport, and absolute harmony is not simply nondifferentiation. *Self and other are not one, and not two.* To be not one and not two means that each self retains its absoluteness while still being relative, and that in this relativity the two are never for a moment separated. While the I to be the I acknowledges the Thou in relation to the Thou's own absolute non-differentiation, and thus permits itself to become absolutely the Thou, at the same time it takes the Thou to itself. Situated within this absolute nondifferentiation which opens up in the I, the I is the I itself—I am I. Even if we refer to the harmony of this absolute nonrelation as love, it is still different from love in the sense of *eros*, or in the sense of *agape*.

In any case, when Sanshō said he was Ejaku, Kyōzan answered, "Ejaku, that's my name!" whereupon Sanshō gave his own name, Enen. Commenting on this answer Hakuin says: "He has changed himself from head to foot. The old fox, with advanced age grown more and more cunning, has various tricks of transformation up his sleeve." And Engo notes: "They are both back to holding their original positions. After several changes of form, each has returned to his home ground."

This happening is indeed harmony and concord alluded to earlier—a harmony possessed of infinite beauty. Hakuin compares this encounter to the fight between a dragon and an elephant "stepping on and kicking each other," and says that "this is no place for lame horses and blind asses." But then he adds, "Their singing together and handclapping, their drumming and dancing—it is as if the spring blossoms had their reds and purples competing against one another in the new warmth." Here each self returns to its original position, where each is itself. Although each of us needs, in the midst of everyday encounters, to find a place where we can maintain our original position in spite of ourselves, we do not in fact explore and realize such a place thoroughly. The only way this can be done is to break through to the ground of the encounter. It is there that the condition of eat or be eaten is penetrated to the condition of at once eating *and* being eaten, until the little self of each one dissolves. It is the point where self and other are not two different things, where strife is transformed into sport. There it is like flowers competing with their reds and purples in the spring warmth. Unless the relations between individual and individual, between nation and nation, between all factions, all groups, return to this condition, there remains only the battle between wolves in the wild.

III

In the light of what has been said, let us once more return to the poem by the Japanese Zen master Daitō Kokushi (1282-1337) written as a commentary on our *mondō*. It is included together with the *mondō* in the *Kwaiankoku-go*, a work in which Hakuin (1685-1768) comments upon Daitō's sayings and poems.

Of the first two lines Hakuin says: "If you trample on and kick over the dark valley of the eighth consciousness, the sun of the Great Mirror Wisdom will suddenly flash and immediately dissolve the piled-up snow drifts of the abiding aspect of all phenomena." And "He breaks away the solid-frozen all-sameness of the *Tathatā*, he melts away the ice of the one Dharma nature."

We might simply call this the transcendence of attachment, the attachment to self and all other attachments, including attachment to the dharma. The standpoint of the "man-wolf," as well as the source of the conflicts that cut mankind in two, will be found to have their roots in self-attachment which puts one's "self" at the center and so discriminates between "self" and "other."

Ultimately, however, this self-attachment itself is rooted in that *Ignorance* (*avidyā*), to be found in the eighth, or "store" consciousness (*ālayavijñāna*), the foundation on which all human consciousness is based. I was referring to this Ignorance when I said previously that there is a layer of profound blindness at the very root of the human intellect. Illusion and suffering have their sources there. To master them, all kinds of theories and ideologies have been contrived, and numberless "laws"—civil, moral, and divine—have been formulated. But all these laws are incapable of cutting through the powerful roots of self-attachment; self-attachment continues under the very cover of these laws. One falls into pride in one's country, into moral pride, pride in one's gods or buddhas. To justify these "attachments to law" is merely self-attachment on a higher plane. The same is true for theories and ideologies.

Not that law is bad. What is bad is to fix one's self on some universal as "being," to become attached to law—in its heteronomous, autonomous, or "theonomous" form. The mode of all such law attachments is precisely the "abiding aspect of all phenomena." All the laws involved in these attachments are the snowpile that hides them. Transcend the plane of the universal, as the nonduality of self and other, the void, or *muga* (non-self), and for the first time the sunlight of the Great Mirror Wisdom will shine on ignorance and break it asunder. It is the Light of Great Wisdom, the Light of Mahāprajñā. But if this nonduality of self and other were taken simply as nondiscrimination, it would become the *concept* of nondiscrimination, which is just another attachment to law. The "solid-frozen all-sameness of the *Tatahatā,*" the "ice of the one Dharma nature," the "ice-covered absolute one or absolute identity," etc. refer to those higher attachments to self and law that lie hidden at a level beyond ordinary attachments to self and law. When this place too is broken through, true reality is attained for the first time, where a contest of "fragrant freshness" goes on between the self as the self, the other as the other, and the law as the law. There the everyday encounters between all men are something of infinite freshness, pervaded with an infinite fragrance.

In the third line we meet the words *poetry* and *spiritual divertissement.* Here, of course, the encounter between man and man, just as the fine scenery with its plums and willows, becomes an occasion for poetry. This "poetry" does not consist in images imagined by human consciousness, nor is it composition made up of human language. Here the poem uses as its images actual things themselves; it is composed of the words that all things themselves recite.

The "spiritual divertissement" spoken of is not a spiritual divertissement staged in our consciousness, but one that arises from the very depths of our being and the being of all things. This is not a poetry of Romanticism, but of radical realism. By radically penetrating into reality as it actually is, reality itself becomes sheer poetry. It is the same as when the struggles in the ultimate ground of hostility become sport or play. The "poetry" that appears in the place that transcends what is ordinarily referred to as the realm of poetry—*that poetry not created by man, but in which man participates and which becomes part of man himself as well*—to what realm would that belong? When man casts off his small self and devoutly enters reality, the Great Wisdom (*prajñā*) opens up as the native place of all things, as the place where they emerge and realize themselves as they are—the place of reality itself. This opening up is indeed the realization of reality in its suchness. The light of Wisdom, in which reality shines and is seen in its suchness, is reality's own light. The light of this "Sun of Wisdom" as it is, is also the insight in which man sees his "primary and original face." The poetry that arises spontaneously from *prajñā* is what we here call poetry. In this *prajñā* the reality of each and every real thing becomes, as it is, the "occasion for poetry and spiritual divertissement," which contains "boundless meaning."

Hakuin uses the following well-known passage from the *Analects* to comment on the third line:

> At the end of spring, when the making of the spring clothes has been completed, I go with five times six newly-capped youths and six times seven uncapped boys, perform the lustration in the river, I take the air at the Rain Dance altars, and then go home singing.[3]

Prajñā is the place where not only poetry, but also religion, philosophy, and morality originate—the place where all of these are perhaps united in such a way as makes it difficult to separate them, since it is prior to them all. If this is so, the poetry I refer to here may well be the realm from which all man-made poetry originates, and to where it returns as to its own wellspring. It is almost impossible to speak about such secret areas of our existence. We must be satisfied simply to raise the questions.

The tale of this encounter, which comes to a close with Kyōzan giving his name and Sanshō giving his, ends with Kyōzan's roaring laughter. The sound of this laughter is the essence of the whole tale. It is at this point that the struggle—which is really a "sportive *samādhi*"—and with it all the singing and clapping, drumming and dancing, comes to an end. What was both battleground and the place where men sang in unison has now turned back to the place of origin. It is like the ancient battlefield spoken of by the haiku poet Bashō:

> Ah! Summer grasses!
> All that remains
> Of the warriors' dreams.[4]

The men who fought here, the men who sang together here, the men who stood face to face, have long since vanished. Kyōzan and Sanshō, too, are gone. But Kyōzan's roaring laughter still resounds in the air. Daitō Kokushi "caps" this with "where does it go?" Of course, he is not merely after information. He is pointing to the place where Kyōzan hides in laughter. In this "place of laughter" the reality of the encounter between one man and another may be transformed *as it is* into a superreality. That is to say, here reality manifests itself in its original aspect of superreality. Such is the implication of the words "the occasion for poetry and spiritual divertissement holds boundless meaning." More about it we cannot say. To understand the boundless meaning here is possible only for "the man who wanders in the fields and arduously composes poetry." The figure of the poet struggling to write poetry in order to transmit to others this meaning—which he has understood—suggests the conjunction of *Mahāprajñā* and *Mahākarunā* contained in Kyōzan's great laughter. This third line, together with the comment "Where does it go?" may be said to be the *ecce homo* of Daitō Kokushi himself.

NOTES

1. *Daitō-roku* ("The Sayings of Daitō Kokushi"), Book 3, fasc. 11, under "Juko"; also *Kwaiankoku-go*, Book 5, under "Juko."

2. A somewhat different translation appears in Katsuki Sekida, *Two Zen Classics* (New York: Weatherhill, 1977), p. 328.

3. The *Analects of Confucius*, trans. Arthur Waley (New York: Random House, 1938), XI. 25, p. 160.

4. Translation by R. H. Blyth.

5

ABE MASAO

God, Emptiness, and the True Self*

Abe Masao (b. 1915) is a disciple of both Hisamatsu Shin'ichi and
Nishitani Keiji, and maintained a close contact with D. T. Suzuki during
the last ten years of his life.

After studying law, philosophy, and comparative religion at Japanese
universities, Abe attended Columbia University and Union Theological
Seminary on a Rockefeller Research Fellowship. He was lecturer at Otani
University, Kyoto University, and Hanazono Zen College and a full profes-
sor of philosophy at Nara University of Education. He has held numerous
visiting professorships, among others at Columbia University, the
University of Chicago, Carleton College, Claremont Graduate School,
Princeton University, etc., and was appointed full professor at Claremont
College. He has lectured with exceptional frequency in Japan and the
United States, including such important lectureships as the Berry Lecture
at the University of Hawaii and the Stewart Lecture in World Religion at
Princeton University.

The Japan Foundation sponsored his study trips to England, the
European continent, India, etc., where he also presented noted papers at
innumerable conferences and symposia. Professor Abe is a prolific writer
whose essays appear frequently in such learned journals as *The Eastern
Buddhist, Japanese Religions, Japan Studies, Indian Philosophy and Culture,
Young Buddhist, International Philosophical Quarterly, Religious Studies, Journal
of Chinese Philosophy, Theologische Zeitschrift*, etc., and he contributed chapters to many books as well as articles in Japanese.

Abe Masao has also translated classics like Dōgen and works by Nishida
and Hisamatsu into English.

His professorship at Claremont College may well be seen as a first
bridgehead of the Kyoto School on the American continent.

A Zen master said, "Wash out your mouth after you utter the word
'Buddha.'" Another master said, "There is one word I do not like to

* "God, Emptiness, and the True Self," *The Eastern Buddhist* II/2 (1969): 15-30.

55

hear, and that is 'Buddha.'" Wu-tsu Fa-yen (Jap.: Hōen, d. 1104), a Chinese Zen master of the Sung dynasty, said, "Buddhas and Patriarchs are your deadly enemies; *satori* is nothing but dust on the mind. Rather be a man who does nothing, just leisurely passing the time. Be like a deaf-mute in the world of sounds and colors." At the close of his life, Daitō (1282-1338) of the Kamakura era of Japan left the following death verse:

> I have cut off Buddhas and Patriarchs;
> The Blown Hair (Sword) is always burnished;
> When the wheel turns,
> The empty void gnashes its teeth.

Or in Kobori Nanrei's translation:

> Kill Buddhas and Patriarchs;
> I have been sharpening the sword Suimo;
> When the wheel turns [the moment of death],
> Śūnyatā gnashes its teeth.

Chao-chou (Jap.: Jōshū, 778-897), a distinguished Zen master of T'ang China, while passing through the main hall of his temple, saw a monk who was bowing reverently before Buddha. Chao-chou immediately slapped the monk. The latter said, "Is it not a laudable thing to pay respect to Buddha?"

"Yes," answered the master, "but it is better to go without even a laudable thing."

What is the reason for this antagonistic attitude toward Buddhas and Patriarchs among the followers of Zen? Are not Buddhas enlightened ones? Is not Sakyamuni Buddha their Lord? Are not the Patriarchs great masters who awakened to Buddhist truth? What do Zen followers mean by "doing nothing" and "empty void"?

There is even the following severe statement in the *Lin-chi lu* (Jap.: *Rinzairoku*), one of the most famous Zen records of China.

> Encountering a Buddha, killing the Buddha;
> Encountering a Patriarch, killing the Patriarch;
> Encountering an Arhat, killing the Arhat;
> Encountering mother or father, killing mother or father;
> Encountering a relative, killing the relative,
> Only thus does one attain liberation and disentanglement

from all things, thereby becoming completely unfettered and free.

These words may remind some readers of the madman described in Nietzsche's *Die Fröhliche Wissenschaft* who shouts, "God is dead! God stays dead! And we have killed Him." Are Zen followers who kill Buddhas to attain liberation madmen such as Nietzsche described? Are they radical nihilists in Nietzsche's sense? Are they atheists who not only reject Scriptures but also deny the existence of God? What do they mean by the "liberation" that is attained only by killing Buddhas and Patriarchs?

To answer these questions properly and to understand Zen's position precisely, let me call your attention to some more Zen sayings.

A Zen master once said: "Let a man's ideal rise as high as the crown of Vairocana Buddha (highest divinity), but let his life be so full of humility as to be prostrate even at the feet of a baby."

In the "Verses of the Ten Ox-Herding Pictures," Kuo-an Chi-yuan (Jap.: Kakuan), a Zen master of the Sung dynasty, said:

> Worldly passions fallen away,
> Empty of all holy intent
> I linger not where Buddha is, and
> Hasten by where there is no Buddha.

What do all these examples mean? When a Zen master said, "Cleanse the mouth thoroughly after you utter the *word* 'Buddha,'" or "There is one *word* I do not like to hear, and that is 'Buddha,'" he sounds like a recent Christian theologian who, by means of linguistic analysis, insists that the *word* "God" is theologically meaningless. The ancient Chinese Zen master, though unfamiliar with the discipline of linguistic analysis, must have found something odious about the *word* "Buddha." The Christian theologian who emphasizes the inadequacy of the *word* "God" still points to the ultimate meaning realized in the Gospel. In other words, he seems to conclude that not God but the *word* "God" is dead. Zen's position, however, is more radical. Statements such as "Buddhas and Patriarchs are your deadly enemies" and "I have cut off Buddhas and Patriarchs," and emphasis on "doing nothing" and the "empty void" take us beyond the Death-of-God theologians. This seems especially to be true of Lin-chi's above-mentioned saying: "Encountering a Buddha, killing the Buddha."

What is the real meaning of these frightful words? The fourth and fifth lines of Lin-chi's saying, about encountering mother or father or a relative and killing them, remind me of Jesus' words:

> If any one comes to me and does not hate his own father and mother and wife and children and brothers and sisters, yes, and even his own life, he cannot be my disciple (Luke 14:26).

With these words Jesus asked his followers to follow him even if this meant opposing earthly obligations.

Lin-chi's words ("Encountering mother or father or relative, kill them") mean much the same as Jesus' words—though Lin-chi's expression is more extreme. The renunciation of the worldly life and the hatred for even one's own life are necessary conditions among all the higher religions for entering into the religious life. Thus Jesus said:

> Truly, I say to you, there is no man who has left house or wife or brothers or parents or children, for the sake of the kingdom of God, who will not receive manifold more in this time, and in the age to come eternal life (Luke 18:29, 30).

In contrast to Jesus' emphasis on doing things "for the sake of the kingdom of God," Lin-chi says that by "encountering a Buddha, killing the Buddha," and so on, "only thus does one attain liberation." This is simply because for Lin-chi to attain real liberation it is necessary not only to transcend worldly morality but also to rid oneself of religious pietism. Zen does not teach that we come to the Ultimate Reality through encountering and believing in Buddha. For even then we are not altogether liberated from a dichotomy between the object and the subject of faith. In other words, if we believed in Buddha, Buddha would become more or less objectified. And an objectified Buddha cannot be the Ultimate Reality. To attain Ultimate Reality and liberation, Zen insists, one must transcend even religious transcendent realities such as Buddhas, Patriarchs, and so forth. Only when both worldly morality and religious pietism, both the secular and the holy, both immanence and transcendence, are completely left behind, does one come to Ultimate Reality and attain real liberation.

The fundamental aim of Buddhism is to attain emancipation from all bondage arising from the duality of birth and death.

Another word for this is *samsāra,* which is also linked with the dualities of right and wrong, good and evil, etc. Emancipation from *samsāra* by transcending the duality of birth and death is called *nirvāna,* the goal of the Buddhist life.

Throughout its long history, Mahāyāna Buddhism has emphasized: "Do not abide in *samsāra,* nor abide in *nirvāna.*" If one abides in so-called *nirvāna* by transcending *samsāra,* one is not yet free from attachment, namely, attachment to *nirvāna* itself. Being confined by the discrimination between *nirvāna* and *samsāra,* one is still selfishly concerned with his own salvation, forgetting the suffering of others in *samsāra.* In *nirvāna* one may be liberated from the dualities of birth and death, right and wrong, good and evil, etc. But even then one is not liberated from a higher-level duality, i.e., the duality of *samsāra* and *nirvāna,* or the duality of the secular and the sacred. To attain thorough emancipation one must also be liberated from this higher-level duality. The Bodhisattva idea is essential to Mahāyāna Buddhism. Not clinging to his own salvation, the Bodhisattva is one who devotes himself to saving others who suffer from various attachments—attachments to *nirvāna* as well as to *samsāra*—by negating or transcending the so-called *nirvāna* which is attained simply by transcending *samsāra.*

Therefore, *nirvāna* in the Mahāyāna sense, while transcending *samsāra,* is simply the realization of *samsāra* as really *samsāra,* no more, no less, by a thoroughgoing return to *samsāra* itself. This is why, in Mahāyāna Buddhism, it is often said of true *nirvāna* that "*samsāra*-as-it-is is *nirvāna.*" This paradoxical statement is based on the dialectical character of the true *nirvāna,* which is, logically speaking, the negation of negation; that is, absolute affirmation, or the transcendence of transcendence; that is, absolute immanence. This negation of negation is no less than the affirmation of affirmation. The transcendence of transcendence is nothing other than the immanence of immanence. These are verbal expressions of Ultimate Reality, because Ultimate Reality is neither negative nor affirmative, neither immanent nor transcendent in the relative sense of those terms. It is beyond these dualities. *Nirvāna* in Mahāyāna Buddhism is expressed as "*samsāra*-as-it-is is *nirvāna,*" and "*nirvāna*-as-it-is is *samsāra.*" This is simply the Buddhist way of expressing Ultimate Reality. Since *nirvāna* is nothing but Ultimate Reality, to attain *nirvāna* in the above sense means to attain liberation from every sort of duality.

Zen takes this Mahāyāna position in its characteristically radical way. "Killing a Buddha" and "killing a Patriarch" are Zen expressions for "not abiding in *nirvāna.*"

Now we can see what Lin-chi meant when he said, "Encountering a Buddha, killing the Buddha; encountering a Patriarch, killing the Patriarch. . . . *Only thus* does one attain liberation and disentanglement from all things." In this way, Zen radically tries to transcend religious transcendence itself to attain thoroughgoing freedom. Therefore the words and acts of the Zen masters mentioned earlier, though they seem to be extremely antireligious and blasphemous, are rather to be regarded as paradoxical expressions of the ultimate truth of religion.

Since the ultimate truth of religion for Zen is entirely beyond duality, Zen prefers to express it in a negative way. When Emperor Wu of the Liang dynasty asked Bodhidharma, "What is the ultimate principle of the holy truth?" the First Patriarch replied: "Emptiness, no holiness."

In his "Song of Enlightenment" Yung-chia (Jap.: Yōka, 665-713) said:

> In clear seeing, there is not one single thing:
> There is neither man nor Buddha.

On the other hand, in Christianity, when Jesus emphasized action for the sake of the kingdom of God, the kingdom of God is not simply transcendent. Being asked by the Pharisees when the kingdom of God was coming, Jesus answered them, "Behold, the kingdom of God is within you." With this answer Jesus declared that God's rule is a new spiritual principle already operative in the lives of men, and perhaps referred to his own presence in the midst of his followers. We might say, therefore, that the kingdom of God is both immanent and transcendent.

This may be especially true when we remind ourselves of the Christian belief that the kingdom is within only because it has first entered this world in Jesus, who was the incarnation of God. Jesus Christ as the incarnation of God may be said to be a symbol of "transcending even the religious transcendence." In the well-known passage of the Letter to the Philippians, Saint Paul said:

> Have this mind among yourselves, which was in Christ Jesus, who,
> though he was in the form of God, did not count equality with God

a thing to be grasped, but *emptied* himself, taking the form of a ser-
vant, being born in the likeness of men. And being found in human
form he humbled himself and became obedient unto death, even
death on a cross (2:5-8).

As clearly shown in this passage, Jesus Christ is God who became
flesh by emptying or abnegating himself, even unto death. It is really through this *kenotic* negation that flesh and spirit, the secular and
the sacred, the immanent and the transcendent became identical in
Jesus Christ. Indeed, Jesus Christ may be said to be the Christian
symbol of Ultimate Reality. So far, this Christian idea of the *kenotic*
Christ is close to Zen's idea of "neither man nor Buddha." At least
it may be said that Christianity and Zen equally represent Ultimate
Reality, where the immanent and the transcendent, the secular and
the sacred, are paradoxically one.

In Christianity, however, Ultimate Reality as paradoxical oneness
was realized in history only in Jesus Christ as the incarnation of
God. Indeed, Jesus Christ is the Mediator between God and man,
the Redeemer of man's sin against God, and the only historical
event through which man encounters God. Accordingly, it is
through faith in Jesus as the Christ that one can participate in
Ultimate Reality.

In this sense, being the Ultimate Reality, Jesus Christ is somewhat
transcendent to man. He is the object, not the subject, of faith.
Therefore, the relation between Christ and his believer is dualistic.
A kind of objectification still remains. In this respect Zen parts company with Christianity.

Of course, as Paul admirably stated: "I have been crucified with
Christ; it is no longer I who live, but Christ who lives in me; and the
life I now live in the flesh I live by faith in the Son of God, who loved
me and gave himself for me" (Gal. 2:20). Christian faith has a mystical aspect which emphasizes the identification of the faithful with
Christ.

Further, as Paul said, "we are . . . always carrying in the body the
death of Jesus, so that the life of Jesus may also be manifested in our
bodies" (2 Cor. 4:10). Paul died Jesus' death and lived Jesus' life.
And this, for Paul, meant being "baptized into Christ," "putting on
Christ" (Gal. 3:27), and "being changed into his likeness" through
the Spirit (2 Cor. 3:18).

Being "in Christ" in this way, i.e., identifying with Christ as
Ultimate Reality is, if I am not wrong, the quintessence of Christian

faith. The essence of Zen, however, is not identification with Christ or with Buddha, but identification with emptiness. For Zen, identification—to use this term—with an Ultimate Reality that is substantial is not the true realization of Ultimate Reality. Hence Zen's emphasis on "emptiness, no holiness," and "neither man nor Buddha."

So far Zen is much closer to the *via negativa* or negative theology of Medieval Christianity than to the more orthodox form of the Christian faith. For instance, in his *Mystical Theology*, Pseudo-Dionysius the Areopagite wrote about God as follows:

> Ascending higher, we say . . .
> not definable,
> not nameable,
> not knowable,
> not dark, not light,
> not untrue, not true,
> not affirmable, not deniable,
>   for
> while we affirm or deny of those orders of beings
>   that are akin to Him
> we neither affirm nor deny Him
>   that is beyond
> all affirmation as unique universal Cause and
> all negation as simple preeminent Cause,
> free of all and
> to all transcendent.[1]

This is strikingly similar to Zen's expressions of the Buddha-nature or mind.

In Pseudo-Dionysius, identification or *union* with God means that man enters the godhead by getting rid of what is man—a process called *theosis*, i.e., deification. This position of Pseudo-Dionysius became the basis of subsequent Christian mysticism. It may not be wrong to say that for him the Godhead in which one is united is the "emptiness" of the indefinable One. The words "nothing, nothing, nothing" fill the pages of *The Dark Night of the Soul*, written by Saint John of the Cross. For him nothingness meant "sweeping away of images and thoughts of God to meet Him in the darkness and obscurity of pure faith which is above all concepts."[2]

Despite the great similarity between Zen and Christian mysticism we should not overlook an essential difference between them. In the above-quoted passage, Pseudo-Dionysius calls that which is beyond all affirmation and all negation by the term *him*. Many Christian mystics call God "Thou." In Zen, however, what is beyond all affirmation and all negation—that is, Ultimate Reality—should not be "him" or "thou" but "self" or one's "true self."

I am not concerned here with verbal expressions but with the reality behind the words. If Ultimate Reality, while being taken as nothingness or emptiness, should be called "him" or "thou," it is, from the Zen point of view, no longer ultimate.

For in this case "nothingness" or "emptiness" is still taken as something *outside* of oneself; in other words, it is still more or less objectified. "Nothingness" or "emptiness" therefore becomes *something* merely named "nothingness" or "emptiness." It is not true nothingness or true emptiness. True emptiness is never an object found outside of oneself. It is what is really *nonobjectifiable*. Precisely for this reason, it is the ground of true subjectivity. In Christian mysticism, it is true that God is often called nothingness or the unknowable. However, if this is taken as the ultimate, or the object of the soul's longing, it is not the same as true nothingness in Zen. In Zen, this is found only by negating "nothingness" as the end, and "emptiness" as the object of one's spiritual quest.

To reach the Zen position, one must be reconverted or turned back from "nothingness" as the end to "nothingness" as the ground, from "emptiness" as the object to "emptiness" as the true subject. Ultimate Reality is not something far away, over there. It is right here, right now. *Everything starts from the here and now.* Otherwise everything loses its reality.

Consequently, while Zen emphasizes emptiness, it rejects mere attachment to emptiness. While Zen insists on killing the Buddha, it does not cling to what is non-Buddha. As quoted earlier, Kuo-an said in his "Verses of the Ten Ox-Herding Pictures":

> Worldly passions fallen away,
> Empty of all holy intent.
> Here both worldly passions and holy intent are left behind.
> I linger not where Buddha is, and
> Hasten by where there is no Buddha.

With these words Kuo-an tried to show that if one takes what is non-Buddha as the ultimate, what is non-Buddha turns into a

Buddha. Real emptiness, which is called in Buddhism *śūnyatā*, is not a nihilistic position that simply negates religious values. Overcoming nihilism within itself, it is the existential ground of liberation or freedom in which one finds for himself liberation even from what is non-Buddha, liberation even from a rigid view of emptiness.

Zen's strong criticism of attachment to emptiness or non-Buddhaness is seen in the following stories:

A monk asked Chao-chou, "When I bring nothing at all with me, what do you say?"

Chao-chou said, "Throw it away!"

"But," protested the monk, "I said I bring nothing at all; what do you say I should throw away?"

"Then carry it off," was the retort of Chao-chou.

In commenting on this D. T. Suzuki says: "Jōshū (Chao-chou) has thus plainly exposed the fruitlessness of a nihilistic philosophy. To reach the goal of Zen, even the idea of 'having nothing' ought to be done away with. Buddha reveals himself when he is no more asserted; that is, for Buddha's sake, Buddha is to be given up. This is the only way to come to the realization of the truth of Zen."[3]

Huang-po (Jap.: Ōbaku, d. 850) was bowing low before a figure of Buddha in the sanctuary, when a fellow disciple saw him and asked: "It is said in Zen 'Seek nothing from the Buddha, nor from the *Dharma*, nor from the *samgha*.' What do you seek by bowing?"

"Seeking nothing from the Buddha, the *Dharma*, or the *samgha* is the way in which I always bow," replied Huang-po.

But his fellow disciple persisted: "For what purpose do you bow?" Huang-po slapped his face. "Rude fellow!" exclaimed the other.

To this Huang-po said, "Where do you think you are, talking of rudeness and politeness!" and slapped him again.

In this way, Huang-po tried to make his companion get rid of his negative view of non-Buddhaness. He was anxious to communicate the truth of Zen in spite of his apparent brusqueness. While behaving and speaking in a rude and negative way, the spirit of what he says is affirmative.[4]

As these stories clearly show, the standpoint of emptiness or *śūnyatā* in Zen is not a negative but an affirmative one. Zen affirms the ground of complete liberation—liberation from both the secular and the holy, from both morality and religion, from both theistic religion and atheistic nihilism.

Since the Zen position regarding true emptiness (*śūnyatā*) transcends both the secular and the sacred (through a negation of negation), it is itself neither secular nor sacred. And yet, *at the same time*, it is both secular and sacred. The secular and the sacred are paradoxically identical, coming together as a dynamic whole outside of which there is nothing.

I, myself, who am now writing about the dynamic whole as the true emptiness, do not stand outside of, but within this dynamic whole. Of course, the same is true of those who read what I am writing.

When you see a Zen master, he may ask you, "Where are you from?" "I am from Chicago," you may reply. "From where did you come to Chicago?" the master may ask.

"I was born in Chicago. Chicago is my hometown," may be your answer.

"Where did you come from, to your birth in Chicago?" the master may still ask. Then what will you answer?

Some of you may reply, "I was born of my parents. And their background is Scotland," and so forth.

Others, falling back upon the theory of evolution, may answer, "My origin may be traced back to the anthropoid apes and from them back to the amoeba, or a single cell of some sort."

At this point, I do hope the master is not so unkind as *not* to slap your face. Anyhow, he will not be satisfied with your answers.

Science can answer the question, "How did I get here?" but it cannot answer the question "Why am I here?" It can explain the cause of a fact but not the meaning, or ground of a fact.

Socrates' philosophy started from the oracle's admonition: "Know thyself?" and King David once asked, "But who am I, and what is my people?" (1 Chron. 29:14)

Zen is also deeply concerned with the question, "What am I?" asking it in a way peculiar to Zen, that is: "What is your original face before you were born?" Science seeks for the origins of our existence in a temporal and horizontal sense—a dimension which can be pushed back endlessly. To find a definite answer to the question of our origin we must go beyond the *horizontal* dimension and turn to the *vertical* dimension, i.e., the eternal and religious dimension.

Saint Paul once said, "For in him [the Son of God] all things were created . . . and in him all things hold together" (Col. 1:16-17). In

Christianity it is through creation, as the eternal work of the only God, that all things hold together. Zen, however, raises a further question. It asks, "After all things are reduced to oneness, to what must the One be reduced?" *Śūnyatā* or nothingness in Zen is not a "nothing" out of which all things were created by God, but a "nothing" from which God himself emerged. According to Zen, we are not creatures of God, but manifestations of emptiness. The ground of my existence can and should not be found in the temporal dimension, nor even in God. Although this groundlessness is deep enough to include even God, it is by no means something objectively observable. On the contrary, groundlessness, realized subjectively, is the only real ground of our existence. It is the ground to which we are "reconverted" or turned back by a negation of negation.

In the *Lin-chi lu*, the story is told of Yajñadatta, a very handsome young man who used to look in a mirror every morning and smile at his image. One morning, for some reason, his face was not reflected in the mirror. In his surprise, he thought his head was lost. Thrown into consternation, he searched about everywhere for it, but with no success. Finally, he came to realize that the head for which he was searching was the very thing that was doing the searching. The fact was that being a careless fellow, he had looked at the back of the mirror. Since his head had never been lost, the more he searched for it outside of himself, the more frustrated he became. The point of this story is that that which is sought is simply that which is seeking. Yajñadatta had searched for his head with his head. Our real head, however, is by no means something to be sought for in front of us, but is something that always exists for each of us here and now. Being at the center of one's searching, it can never be objectified.

You can see my head. When you see my head from where you are, it has a particular form and color; it is indeed *something*. But can you see your own head? Unless you objectify your head in a mirror you cannot see it by yourself. So, to you, your head has no particular form and color. It is not *something* which can be seen objectively by you. It is in this sense formless and colorless to yourselves. We call such a thing *mu* or "nothing" because it is not something objective. It is called "nothing" not because, in the present case, our heads are missing, but because our heads are now functioning as the *living* heads. As such they are *nonobjectifiable*.

The same is true of our "self." We often ask ourselves, "What am I?" and get used to searching for an answer somewhere outside of ourselves. Yet the answer to the question, "What am I?" lies in the question itself. The answer to the question can only be found in this *here and now* where I am—and which I am fundamentally.

The ground of our existence is nothingness, *śūnyatā*, because it can never be objectified. This *śūnyatā* is deep enough to encompass even God, the "object" of mystical union as well as the object of faith. For *śūnyatā* is the nothingness from which God himself emerged. *Śūnyatā* is the very ground of the self and thereby the ground of everything to which we are related. The realization of *Śūnyatā*-as-such is precisely what is meant by the self-awakening of *Dharma*. *Śūnyatā* as the nonobjectifiable ground of our existence *expands endlessly into all directions*. The same is true of "awakening in the *Dharma*." Can we talk about the relationship between ourselves and the world without being, ourselves, in the expanding awakening of the self which embraces the relationship itself? Can we even talk about the divine-human relationship without a still deeper ground which makes this relationship possible? And is not the still deeper ground for the divine-human relationship the endlessly expanding *śūnyatā* or self-awakening?

All I-Thou relationships among men and between man and God are possible only within an endlessly expanding self-awakening. Zen calls this our "Original Face," the face we have before we are born. "Before we are born" does not refer to "before" in its temporal sense, but in its ontological sense. The discovery of one's prenatal face—in its ontological sense—places us within an endlessly expanding self-awakening.

To the extent that we are men, whether from the East or from the West, this is equally true of all of us. We should not think that we will come to our awakening at some future time and place and will then *be* awakened. On the contrary, we *are* originally—right here and now—in the expanding of self-awakening that spreads endlessly into all directions. This is why we can talk about relationships with the world and about an I-Thou relationship with God. Nevertheless, just as Yajñadatta looked for his head outside of himself, we are used to looking for our true self outside of ourselves. This is our basic illusion, which Buddhism calls *māyā* or *avidyā*, i.e., ignorance. When we realize this basic illusion for what it is, we immediately find that, in our depths, we are grounded in endlessly expanding self-awakening.

The "Song of Zazen" by Hakuin, an outstanding Zen master of the middle Tokugawa era of Japan, expresses the point well:

> Sentient beings are really Buddha.
> Like water and ice—
> Apart from water, no ice;
> Outside of sentient beings, no Buddha.
> Not knowing it is near
> They seek for it afar!
> Just like being in water—
> But crying for thirst!
>
> Taking as form the formless form
> Going or coming you are always there
> Taking as thought the thoughtless thought
> Singing and dancing are *Dharma*'s voice.
> How vast the boundless sky of *samādhi*,
> How bright the moon of Fourfold Wisdom.
> What now is there to seek?
> With *nirvāna* revealed before you,
> This very place is the Lotus Land,
> This very body is Buddha.

NOTES

1. Elmer O'Brien, *Varieties of Mystical Experience* (New York: Holt, Rinehart, and Winston, 1964), pp. 86-88.

2. William Johnston, "Zen and Christian Mysticism," *The Japanese Missionary Bulletin* XX (1966): 612-13.

3. D. T. Suzuki, *An Introduction to Zen Buddhism* (London: Rider, 1969), pp. 54-55.

4. *Ibid.*, pp. 52-53.

6

Ikkyū's Skeletons*

The late R. H. Blyth called Ikkyū (1394-1481) "the most remarkable monk in the history of Japanese Buddhism, the only Japanese comparable to the great Chinese Zen masters." This makes it all the more regrettable he did not live to translate more of Ikkyū's writings for Western readers beyond the brief glimpse afforded in the Buddhist verse, the *dōka* or "Way poems," which appeared in the fifth volume of his *Zen and Zen Classics*. When Dr. Blyth died in 1962, he left fragmentary translations of several of Ikkyū's *kana hōgo* (easy Buddhist sermons in the vernacular) and a nearly complete manuscript translation of the *Skeletons*, perhaps for a book he had planned. The manuscript of the *Skeletons* is the basis for the present translation. It is probably the first of Ikkyū's prose writings to be published when he was already in his sixties, just a few years before the great love affair of his life was to scandalize Kyoto's clerical world, and almost two decades before he would end his career as abbot of Daitokuji.

The few facts of Ikkyū Zenji's life that need to be recalled in introducing this translation may be found in Blyth's essay on Ikkyū in *Zen and Zen Classics*.

The editor of this section, Professor N. A. Waddell, lecturer in International Studies, Otani University, writes:

> Ikkyū's *Skeletons*, timeless as they are, will be more easily understood when placed in the historical context in which they belong.
>
> A hundred and fifty years prior to Ikkyū's birth, the priest Nichiren (1222-82) in his *Risshō ankoku ron* painted a picture of the social unrest of Kamakura times in which he tells of earthquakes, fires, famines, and epidemics, and describes streets cluttered with corpses, skeletons, and the carcasses of animals. Ikkyū's times were not any better. The records show that throughout the Muromachi period such horrors were quite common, often aggravated by riots and feudal warfare. During the frightful Ōnin civil war, Kyoto with its palaces and temples was reduced to ashes. In the uncertainties

* "Ikkyū's Skeletons," trans. N. A. Waddell, *The Eastern Buddhist* VI/1 (1973): 111-25.

and catastrophes of the fifteenth century, the upper classes often had to flee to the countryside for shelter. The remaining towns-people lived constantly on the brink of anarchy: governmental and religious authority had broken down. This was the environment in which Ikkyū passed his entire life. The Ōnin war began in 1467 and ended in 1477, four years before his death.

Strangely, vigorous cultural activity continued during the Ashikaga Shōguns' rule, notwithstanding all the turmoil. It reached new heights after 1450, in the period of the Higashiayama culture, which centered around the Silver Pavilion, built by Ashikaga Yoshimasa (1435-90), a lavish patron of the arts.

The *Skeletons* seems to have been first printed in 1457 when Ikkyū was sixty-three years old, and became in the course of time known by the popular title *Ikkyū's Gaikotsu*. It is written partly in prose and partly in verse, and falls naturally into three sections. The first is mainly prose, with a few poems scattered at intervals, the middle portion a series of poems (*dōka*, Buddhist *waka*) with illustrations, and the third, once more, is mostly prose. The illustrations of skeletons and groups of skeletons engaged in various human occupations which illuminate the central section are imaginative, humorous, but at the same time allegorical and didactic.

The earliest extant edition of the work is undated, but it is believed to belong to the Muromachi period (1338-1573). Whether it was actually published during Ikkyū's lifetime is unknown. It is presumed to be a reproduction of an illustrated manuscript by Ikkyū himself. Both the calligraphy and the illustrations strongly suggest it is indeed his creation. Another printing, from the original woodblocks, or perhaps a facsimile, was apparently made in the early seventeenth century. A photo-facsimile of an undated edition ascribed to the Muromachi period was published in a reduced-size, limited edition by Ryukoku University, Kyoto, in 1924. During the Tokugawa period (1603-1867) two or three other editions appeared, all showing important textual variations from earlier ones. Their illustrations are similar in format but different in artistic conception, and not to be compared to the delightful drawings which are reputedly Ikkyū's own.

The translator used the text of a modern edition for his translation, based on the later woodblock versions that show considerable variance from the earlier text. I have not indicated these variants, but merely want to draw attention to them.

Dr. Blyth's manuscript dates from the mid-1950s or earlier. A portion of the prose text and a few of the poems scattered throughout the work are missing. In preparing it for publication, editorial revisions and footnotes have been kept to a minimum. In order to present a complete translation I have translated the portions of the text left unfinished by Dr. Blyth. Notes 7 and 8 are Blyth's; the rest are mine.

The myriad Laws are seen written in thin India ink.[1] But the beginner must do *zazen* earnestly. Then he will realize that there is nothing born into this world which will not eventually become "empty." Oneself and the original face of heaven and earth and all the world are equally empty. All things emerge from the "emptiness." Being formless it is called "Buddha." The Mind of Buddha, the Buddhahood, the Buddha in our minds, Buddhas, Patriarchs, and Gods are different names of this "emptiness," and should you not realize this you have fallen into the Hell of ignorance and false imagination. According to the teaching of an enlightened man, the way of no return[2] is the separation from Hell and rebirth, and the thought of so many people, whether related to me or not, passing through reincarnations one after another, made me so melancholy, I left my native place and wandered off at random.

I came to a small lonely temple. It was evening, when dew and tears wet one's sleeves, and I was looking here and there for a place to sleep, but there was none. It was far from the highway, at the foot of a mountain, what seemed a Samādhi Plain. Graves were many, and from behind the Buddha Hall there appeared a most miserable-looking skeleton, which uttered the following words:

> The autumn wind
> Has begun to blow in this world;
> Should the pampas grass invite me,
> I will go to the moor,
> I will go to the mountain.

> What to do
> With the mind of a man
> Who should purify himself
> Within the black garment,
> But simply passes life by.

All things must at some time become nought, that is, return to their original reality. When we sit facing the wall doing *zazen*, we realize that none of the thoughts that arise in our minds, as a result of karma, are real. The Buddha's fifty years of teaching are mean-ingless. The mistake comes from not knowing what the mind is. Musing that few indeed experience this agony, I entered the Buddha Hall and spent the night there, feeling more lonely than usual, and being unable to sleep. Towards dawn, I dozed off, and in my dream I went to the back of the temple, where many skeletons were assembled, each moving in his own special way just as they did in life. While I marveled at the sight, one of the skeletons approached me and said:

> Memories
> There are none:
> When they depart,
> All is a dream;
> My life—how sad!
>
> If Buddhism
> Is divided into Gods
> And Buddhas;
> How can one enter
> The Way of Truth?
>
> For as long as you breathe
> A mere breath of air,
> A dead body
> At the side of the road
> Seems something apart from you.

Well, we enjoyed ourselves together, the skeleton and I, and that illusive mind which generally separates us from others gradually left me. The skeleton that had accompanied me all this while possessed the mind that renounces the world and seeks for truth. Dwelling on the watershed of things, he passed from shallow to deep, and made me realize the origin of my own mind. What was in my ears was the sighing of the wind in the pine trees; what shone in my eyes was the moon that enlightened my pillow.

But when is it not a dream? Who is not a skeleton? It is just because human beings are covered with skins of varying colors that sexual passion between men and women comes to exist. When the breathing stops and the skin of the body is broken there is no more form, no higher and lower. You must realize that what we now have and touch as we stand here is the skin covering our skeleton. Think deeply about this fact. High and low, young and old—there is no difference whatever between them. When we are enlightened concerning the One Great Causality we understand the meaning of unborn, undying.

> If a stone
> Can be the memento
> Of the dead,
> Then the tombstone
> Would be better as a lavatory.

How dangerously foolish is the mind of man!

> We have
> One moon,
> Clear and unclouded,
> Yet are lost in the darkness
> Of this fleeting world.

Think now, when your breath stops and the skin of your body breaks, you will also become like me. How long do you think you will live in this fleeting world?

> To prove
> His reign
> Is eternal,
> The Emperor has planted
> The pine trees of Sumiyoshi.[3]

Give up the idea "I exist." Just let your body be blown along by the wind of the floating clouds; rely on this. To want to live forever is to wish for the impossible, the unreal, like the idea "I exist."

> This world
> Is a dream
> Seen while awake;
> How pitiful those
> Who see it and are shocked!

It is useless to pray to the gods about your destiny. Think only of the One Great Matter.[4] Human beings are mortal; there is nothing to be shocked about.

> If they can serve
> To bring us to loathe them,
> The troubles of this world
> Are most welcome.

> Why on earth
> Do people decorate
> This temporary manifestation,
> When from the first they know
> It will be like this?[5]

> The body of a thing
> Will return
> To the Original Place.
> Do not search,
> Unnecessarily, elsewhere.

> Not a single soul
> Knows why he is born,
> Or his real dwelling place;
> We go back to our origin,
> We become earth again.

> Many indeed
> The ways to climb
> From the mountain foot,
> But it is the same moon
> That we see o'er the peak.

> If I do not decide
> The dwelling place
> Of my future,
> How is it possible
> That I should lose my way?

> Our real mind
> Has no beginning,
> No end;
> Do not fancy
> That we are born, and die.

If you give rein to it,
The mind goes rampant!
It must be mastered
And the world itself rejected.

Rain, hail and snow,
Ice too, are set apart,
But when they fall,
The same water
Of the valley stream.

The ways of preaching
The Eternal Mind
May be different,
But all see the same
Heavenly truth.

Fill the path
With the fallen needles
Of the pine tree,
So that no one knows
If anyone lives there.

How vain
The funeral rites
At Mount Toribe![6]
Those who speed the parting ghost
Can they themselves remain here forever?
Melancholy indeed
The burning smoke
Of Mount Toribe!
How long shall I think of it
As another's pathos?

Vanity of vanities
The form of one
I saw this morning
Has become the smoky cloud
Of the evening sky.

Look, alas,
At the evening smoke
Of Mount Toribe!

Even it falls back and billows
With the rising of the wind.

It becomes ash when burned,
And earth when buried—
Could anything
Remain as evil?

With the sins
That I committed
Until I was three years old,[7]
At last I also
Disappeared.

This is the way of the world. Realizing how foolish they are who, not knowing that all things are and must be temporary and transient, are baffled, someone this very day asked how we should live in this fleeting world. A certain man[8] answered: "Quite different from past times, priests nowadays leave their temples. Formerly those who were religiously inclined entered the temples, but now they all shun them. The priests are devoid of wisdom; they find *zazen* boring. They don't concentrate on their *kōan* and are interested only in temple furniture. Their Zen meditation is a mere matter of appearance; they are smug and wear their robes proudly, but are only ordinary people in priestly garments. Indeed, their robes are merely ropes binding them, their surplices like rods torturing them."

When we think about recurrent life and death, we know that we fall into Hell by taking life; by being greedy we turn into hungry devils; ignorance causes us to be reborn as animals; anger makes us demons. By obeying the Five Commandments[9] we come back to earth as men, and by performing the Ten Good Deeds[10] we are resurrected in Heaven. Above these are the Four Wise Ones;[11] together, they are called the Ten Worlds.[12]

When we see this One Thought,[13] there is no form, no dwelling place, no loathing, no rejecting. Like the clouds of the great sky, the foam on the water. As no thoughts arise there is no mind to create the myriad phenomena. The mind and things are one and the same. They do not know men's doubts.

Parents may be compared to the flint and the steel used for making fire. The steel is the father, the stone is the mother, and the fire is the child. The fire is ignited with tinder material, and it will die out when the contributing causes of the fire, the wood and the oil, are exhausted. It is similar to this with the production of "fire" when father and mother make love together.

Since father and mother are beginningless too, they decline finally to a mind of burnt-out passion. In vain are all things of this world brought up from emptiness and manifested into all forms. Since it is freed of all forms, it is called the "Original Field." All the forms, of plants and grasses, states and lands, issue invariably from emptiness, so we use a metaphorical figure and speak of the Original Field.

> If you break open
> The cherry tree,
> There is not a single flower.
> But the skies of spring
> Bring forth the blossoms!
>
> Though it has no bridge,
> The cloud climbs up to heaven;
> It does not seek the aid
> Of Gautama's sutras.

When you listen to Gautama's preaching of more than fifty years, and practice exactly as Gautama preached, it is just as he taught at his last preaching when he said, "From beginning to end I have preached not a single word," and held out a flower, bringing a faint smile to Kāsyapa's lips. At that time he told Kāsyapa: "I have the exquisite mind of the right Dharma, and with it I acknowledge your understanding of the flower." When asked what he meant, Gautama said, "My preaching of the Dharma for more than fifty years may be likened to saying there is something in your hand in order to bring near a small child you want to take in your arms. My fifty years and more of Dharma-preaching have been like a beckoning to Kāsyapa. That is why the Dharma I transmit is like the taking up of a child to my breast."

Yet this flower is not to be known by bodily means. Nor is it in the mind. It cannot be known even though we speak of it. We must fully understand this present mind and body. Even though one may be called knowledgeable, he cannot therefore be called a man of the Buddhist Dharma. The Dharma Flower of the One Vehicle,[14] in which all Buddhas of past, present, and future have appeared in this world, is this flower. Since the time of the twenty-eight Indian and six Chinese Patriarchs there has never been anything in the world apart from the Original Field. As all things of the world are beginningless they are said to be Great.[15] All of the eight consciousnesses[16] appear from emptiness. Yet the flowers of spring and the plants and grasses of summer, autumn, and winter come from emptiness too. Again, there are Four Great Elements:[17] Earth, Water, Fire, and Wind (Air), though people are ignorant of this fact. Breath is wind; fire is what makes us hot; water a vital liquid that makes us wet; when we are buried or burned, we become earth. Because these too are beginningless, none of them ever abides.

> In this world
> Where everything, without exception,
> Is unreal,
> Death also
> Is devoid of reality.

To the eye of illusion it appears that though the body dies, the soul does not. This is a terrible mistake. The enlightened man declares that both perish together. Buddha also is an emptiness. Sky and earth all return to the Original Field. All the sutras and the eighty thousand dharmas are to be chucked away. Become enlightened by these words of mine and become a man of ease and leisure! But:

> To write something and leave it behind us,
> It is but a dream.
> When we awake we know
> There is not even anyone to read it.

The 8th day of the 4th month, the 3rd year of Kōshō (1457)
Ikkyū-shi Sōjun, formerly of Daitokuji, Tōkai.
Seventh generation from Kidō[18]

NOTES

1. The first sentence reads literally, "It is because they are written in thin India-ink letters that the myriad Laws [Dharmas] are seen." Ikkyū seems to be suggesting that the truth can be seen more readily in an informal, easily written work like this than in some elaborately conceived philosophical discourse. "Thin India ink" probably refers as well to the fact the work is written in Japanese instead of the Chinese usually employed by Buddhist writers.

2. "The way of no return" seems to refer to enlightenment; once gained one never again falls back into illusion.

3. The Sumiyoshi Shrine in Osaka.

4. The matter of birth and death.

5. That is, like a skeleton.

6. Mount Toribe is a hill east of Kyoto where corpses were cremated. The words "the smoke of Toribeyama" occur frequently in older Japanese literature.

7. Does this mean that one of the skeletons dies at the age of three? [Blyth]

8. Ikkyū himself, I suppose. [Blyth]

9. Not to take life, steal, commit adultery, tell lies, drink intoxicants.

10. This includes obeying the first four of the Five Commandments and in addition the bans on immoral language, slander, equivocation, covetousness, anger, and false views.

11. The four kinds of holy men: *srāvakas, pratyeka-buddhas, bodhisattvas,* and *buddhas.*

12. The Ten Worlds or states of existence: the states of the Four Wise Ones together with the Six Ways of sentient existence previously mentioned: of the Hell-dwellers, hungry ghosts, animals, demons, men, and heavenly beings (*Devas*).

13. Each thought-instant is said to encompass all the Ten Worlds in their totality.

14. I.e., the Mahāyāna teaching.

15. "Great" in the sense of absolute, eternal.

16. In Sanskrit, *vijñāna,* or the eight consciousnesses all sentient beings possess: sight, hearing, smell, taste, touch, and three different operations of the mind.

17. The Four Elements (*shidai*) said to constitute all matter.

18. Kidō is the Chinese Zen master Kidō Chigu (Hsü-t'ang Chih-yü, 1185-1269), the master of Daiō Kokushi (1235-1309), the founder of the main Japanese Rinzai line. Ikkyū's colophons often contain reference to him. *Tōkai* refers to Japan. The final page of the Ryukoku edition contains a head-and-shoulders image of Bodhidharma, with an accompanying *dōka*: Even doing nine years of *zazen*/Becomes hellish—/This body that becomes/The Earth of Emptiness.

II

The
Structure
of
Reality

7

SUZUKI TEITARŌ DAISETZ

The Buddhist Conception of Reality*

Suzuki Teitarō Daisetz (1870-1966), was born in Ishikawa Prefecture, the son of a doctor. He attended the Fourth High School in the area, where he was friendly with Nishida Kitarō. Nishida and Suzuki were to become symbolical for contemporary Japanese thinking on the basis of Zen realization in confrontation with Western philosophy. He started Zen meditation under Setsumon, a priest of Kokutai-ji, a temple in the area. In 1887 he left high school and became for a while a substitute schoolteacher. But in 1891 he entered Tokyo Senmon Gakkō, now known as Waseda University, while continuing the study of Zen under the Rinzai Zen master Imakita Kōsen at Engaku-ji, in Kamakura. The following year he entered Tokyo Imperial University. After the death of Imakita Kōsen, he continued Zen study under Shaku Sōen.

In 1893 he attended the First World Parliament of Religion in Chicago. On the recommendation of Shaku Sōen, he returned to America in 1897 to become the assistant to the philosopher-publisher Paul Carus in La Salle, Illinois, where he remained until 1908, translating Taoist works into English, and editing a scholarly journal. At the same time he published various works on Buddhism: an English translation of Ashvaghosha's *Discourse on the Awakening of the Faith in Mahāyāna Buddhism* (1901) and *Outline of Mahāyāna Buddhism* (1907). In 1908 he studied the thought of Swedenborg in London.

From 1910 to 1921 he taught at the Peers' School in Tokyo, then, in 1921 he was appointed to a professorship at Otani University in Kyoto. In 1927 his *Essays in Zen Buddhism* were published, followed by a collection of articles, and by a number of other works on Zen in English.

In the course of the years he became highly renowned as the scholar who drew attention to Zen Buddhism in Europe and America and gained general recognition as a man of both erudition and wisdom who did not treat Zen exclusively from an academic point of view, but wrote about it in the light of his own profound experience and thinking.

* "The Buddhist Conception of Reality," *The Eastern Buddhist* VII/2 (1974): 1-21.

Among Suzuki's achievements his work on the *Lankāvatāra Sutra* must be mentioned as well as the attention he drew to Bankei, the remarkable Zen master of the Edo Period, and to the often unlettered devotees of the *Nembutsu* practice, the *myōkōnin*.

The core of his thinking is the *sokuhi no ronri*, the "logic of identity through difference," which transcends formal logic and is the very basis of Zen thought. It may be summed up in the formula: "To say that A is A means A is not A; therefore A is A," in other words, that any statement of truth must include its opposite.

Suzuki's thinking influenced that of his friend K. Nishida profoundly.

While somewhat outside of strictly academic circles and vigorously claiming not to be a scholar, every one of his works bears the stamp of an exceptional erudition, vast knowledge, and deep spirituality.

Abbot Kobori Nanrei Sōhaku of Ryoko-in, Daitokuji, who was a student of D. T. Suzuki's, remarks in an article: "A distinguishing characteristic of Dr. Suzuki's thought is the spontaneous flow of his consciousness so deeply rooted in the Zen experience."

"He often said of himself, 'I am not a scholar,'" writes Kobori Rōshi, "by which he might have been suggesting where he differs from the ordinary scholar, who, so to say, lives in search of a certain reality through logical and objective thinking, setting himself apart from what he is pursuing," and he goes on suggesting that the Cosmic Unconscious, in which the consciousness of human beings is deeply rooted and to which Suzuki's mind broke through, goes beyond the limits of the intellectual realm and hence becomes capable of the awareness of the essence of nature and of man. It is this essence which seeks expression when, after going through its immersion in the Cosmic Unconscious, the field of consciousness is regained.

The essay which follows and which from a formal philosophical standpoint may at certain moments seem somewhat opaque, may refuse to yield its full meaning unless this is borne in mind.

If there is one question that every serious-minded individual will ask himself as soon as he grows up, or rather is old enough to reason about things, it is this: "Why are we here?" or "What is the significance of life here?" The question may not always take this form, but will vary according to the surroundings and circumstances in which the questioner happens to find himself. But once it has appeared on the horizon of consciousness, the question can be quite a stubborn one, constantly disrupting one's peace of mind. It will insist on getting a satisfactory answer, one way or another.

This inquiry into the significance or value of life is not an idle one readily gratified by mere words, but a matter for which the inquirer is prepared to give his life. We frequently hear in Japan of young people committing suicide, despairing of their inability to solve the question. This is a hasty and perhaps cowardly way out: they are too upset to know what they are doing; they are altogether beside themselves.

This questioning the meaning of life is tantamount to the search for ultimate reality. "Ultimate reality" may sound too philosophical to some people. They may dismiss it as being outside their sphere of interest, as being the professional business of a class of people known as philosophers. The question of reality, however, is as vital as the question of life itself. *What is reality?*

Reality is known by various names. To Christians, it is God; to Hindus, Brahma or *ātman*; to the Chinese, *jēn, tao,* or *t'ien* (Heaven); to Buddhists, Bodhi, *Dharma,* Buddha, *prajñā, tathatā,* etc. Buddhists seem to have a richer vocabulary than other religions or philosophies for speaking of ultimate reality.

How do we approach reality and take hold of it? A general approach to reality is the "objective" method. This is the attempt to grasp reality by means of logical reasoning, by appealing to the intellect, a very useful and frequently powerful instrument in dealing with practical, everyday affairs. The intellect is usually regarded as being something extremely useful and effective in countless ways, our most precious tool to use in our relation to the world, and it is therefore only natural that we resort to it in our attempt to grasp reality. And this is precisely what philosophers, those most intellectual of people, do.

But the question arises: Is the intellect really the key which will open the door of reality? It does raise all kinds of questions concerning the objective world and is probably able to solve most of them, but there is one question that defies the intellect, namely, the question of reality. Reality is that which lies beneath all things, mind as well as nature. (To say "beneath" is not exact, as will become clear as we proceed.)

It is due to the working of the intellect that the question of reality is raised. The intellect tries to establish a complete system of relations between the ideas we have formed in our contact with the world. In this attempt we come to postulate an ultimate reality which would make possible the harmonious unification of ideas. So far, however, we have not been successful at this, as the history of philosophy proves. A system of thought is formed by a great thinker who has put the best of his speculative powers to work on it, but his successors usually find it insufficient, defective in one way or another. They find flaws in his logic and, while not rejecting the system entirely, judge it to be incomplete. Then another great thinker appears and tries his best, with the same results.

In my view, the intellect is not an efficient weapon to deal with this question of ultimate reality. True, it raises the question, but this does not mean that it is qualified to answer it. The asking of the question in fact demonstrates the urge to find something ultimate on which we can earnestly stake our human destiny.

This urge for ultimate reality, while made conscious by the intellect, is really seated in far deeper recesses of the mind. If the intellect is unable to give it full satisfaction, where should we turn? But let us examine the nature of the intellect a little more closely.

The intellect looks outwardly, takes an "objective" view of things. It is unable to look inwardly so as to grasp the thing in its inwardness. It attempts to achieve a unitive view of the world by what is known as the objective method. This objective method may work well, but only when the inside view has first been taken hold of. For the unifying principle lies inside and not outside. It is not something we arrive at; it is where we start. It is not the outcome of postulation; it is what makes postulation possible.

According to the Vedas, in the beginning there was *ātman* or Brahma. It was all alone. Then it thought or willed: "I am one, I will be many." From this, a world of multiplicity arose.

According to Christianity in the beginning God was alone. He willed to create a world of the many and commanded light to appear: "Let there be light. . . ." A world of light and darkness thus came into existence.

When a thing is by itself and there is nothing else beside it, it is as being nothing. To be absolutely alone means to be a nothing. So it is not without reason that Christians speak of God creating the world out of nothing. If God created something out of something, we would naturally ask: What is it that made this something? We can go on asking the same question endlessly, until we finally arrive at nothingness, which is the beginning of the world.

Here is the most puzzling question we humans can encounter: Why did God or Brahma or *ātman* (or It) not stay all alone quietly in his absoluteness, enjoying himself? Why did he move to divide himself and create this world of woes, miseries, anxieties, and sufferings of all kinds?

To create something out of nothing, which is a contradiction in itself, and then to have this something not be a mass of joys but inextricably mixed with pain in all its possible forms, really takes us altogether beyond the realm of intelligibility. It is the most baffling question for the intellect. How can the intellect reconcile the idea of nothing, or nonbeing, with that of being, two conflicting ideas which defy the intellect—something coming out of nothing? As long as we resort to the objective method, there is no answer to be found, however ingeniously we manipulate the intellect.

Not only the intellect but the heart, too, refuses to be reconciled to the fact that God apparently commits himself to this act of inhumanity or ungodliness. Why did he put us in this world of iniquities and cruelties?

As long as we look at the world from the outside, as long as we try to effect a synthesis of the conflicting ideas by intellectualization, as long as we stand as mere observers and critics, this question of something coming out of nothing will never be solved, but must forever remain outside of logical comprehensibility.

It is not really the intellect that remains unsatisfied but the heart that is troubled to the utmost. The intellect and the heart are intimate, inseparable companions. When one is worried, the other shares in its worry.

The only solution to the problem, as far as I can see, is to become *ātman* itself and to will with it its creation of this world. Instead of staying in the world and looking back to its beginning, we must leap back at once to the spot where *ātman* stood when the world had not yet been created. That is, we must go back even to the point before the world came to exist, and plunge ourselves into the very midst of nothingness. For the Christian this means that one must become God himself and feel God's motive when he uttered that fatal cry: "Let there be light!"

This seems to be the only way to come to a definitive solution of the question. The intellect will naturally protest: How is this possible? We are not God, we are creatures, the created, and it is the height of sacrilege to think of our becoming God himself. We are forever separated from him by his act of creation; it is utterly beyond human power to cross the chasm. Besides, we are already created; the time of creation is past and gone forever. We can never go back to the time where there was yet no time. A timeless time is beyond our conception. To go out of time means annihilation. To use a Buddhist expression, we are what we are, swimming along the stream of *samsāra* (birth and death), and how can we stay in the stream and at the same time stand on the far shore in *nirvāna*?

This protest on the part of the intellect is rational indeed, since it is in the nature of the intellect to stay outside, not to enter inside. It is made to be an observer, not a mover. On the other hand, it knows how to raise all kinds of self-baffling questions, and as long as it can do this, there must be some way for it to quit its attitude of objectivity. It must somehow devise a means to kill itself and let something else take its place. This act of killing itself on the part of the intellect means a revolution in our life of relativity.

According to Buddhist thinking, we can not only *become* God or *ātman* or Brahma: we *are* God, *ātman*, Brahma. It is not *becoming* that is required, but becoming aware of the fact, recognizing it. Becoming is the movement, the transformation from one state to another—a dog turning into a cat, or a tree transforming itself into a man. Man being man and God being God, this transformation is impossible and Buddhist philosophy does not require it of us. It only asks us to realize the fact, to become conscious of the fact that man is God. By this transformation man can understand what moved God in the beginning to create the world out of nothing.

God made man in his own image. Man surely can go back to this fact—to the image that he possessed even before he came into this world. So it is not to become, but to be; not transformation, but simple recognition.

As long as we are outsiders, there is no way to get inside of things; and as long as we do not get inside, there is no end to our disharmony with life and the world at large. This is where we have to undertake a grand experiment with ourselves.

When a Buddhist devotee was asked whether or not Amida could save us, he replied to the inquirer: "You are not saved yet!" It is an experiment, one that you have to conduct yourself. You cannot leave it to others.

When Erō (Chin.: Hui-lang), of the late T'ang era, came to Baso (Chin.: Ma-tsu), Baso asked: "What do you seek here?"

"I wish to attain Buddha-knowledge."

"Buddha has no knowledge; knowledge belongs to the world of devils."

Erō later went to Sekitō (Chin.: Shih-t'ou) and asked him: "What is Buddha?"

Sekitō said: "You have no Buddha-nature."

"How is it that I have none?"

"Because you do not recognize yourself."

This brought the monk to awakening. Afterwards he shut himself up in his monastery and did not leave for thirty years. Whenever a monk came to him to ask for enlightenment, he said only this: "You have no Buddha-nature." Christ often addressed his disciples critically: "O ye of little faith!" Faith is generally considered as the opposite of intellection and often taken to be irrational; for this reason philosophy has nothing to do with faith. But life itself is a great affirmation, and philosophy or no philosophy, we cannot go on without taking this fact into account when we want to arrive at some solution to the question that is the subject of this essay. If so, philosophy, too, must have something of faith in it, must be standing on faith. Intellectual understanding of any sort must, after all, be an attempt to arrive at an integration of ideas, which is nothing but faith.

Underlying our intellection, there is faith. When the intellect gives shape to itself, it cherishes a doubt as to the presence of faith, and this makes the intellect wander further and further away from its roots. In fact, all intellectual efforts we make to solve the problem of reality are really directed towards the restoration of faith from which the problem started. The trouble with the intellect is that it does not realize what it is working for. Imagining that it has its own end, it goes on posing question after question. Or one might describe the process in another way: faith, negating itself, is turned into doubt, and doubt, which is at the bottom of curiosity and questioning, starts up intellection. When intellection comes to an impasse—to which it will surely come one day if it works honestly—it sees itself reflected in the mirror of faith, which is its homecoming. The intellect thus finally arrives at the great affirmation.

There is a good story, which I believe I quoted somewhere else but which I wish to quote here again, since it illustrates the character of the doubt we have just referred to. It also demonstrates how masters take up this question, giving it their own solution—a solution which in the end rests with the doubter himself.

A monk came to Yakusan (Chin.: Yeh-shan) to have his doubt settled. Yakusan said: "Wait until I come to the Dharma Hall, where I will have your doubt settled." In the evening the master appeared in the Dharma Hall as usual, and seeing the whole congregation assembled he announced: "Let the monk come out who wished to have his doubt settled today. Where is he?"

When the monk came forward and stood before the master, the latter came down from his chair and, taking hold of him, made this announcement: "Here is a monk who cherished a doubt!" Saying this, the master pushed the monk away and went back to his room.

Later another master, Gengaku (Chin.: Hsüan-chiao), remarked about this incident: "Let me see, did Yakusan solve the doubt for the monk? If so, what would be the solution? If there were still no solution, I would say this again: 'Wait until I come to the Dharma Hall, where the doubt will be solved!'"

Now, how do we come to a final settlement just by repeating the same words? Yakusan says somewhere else: "It is not difficult to say a word for you; but all that is needed is that you come to an immediate apprehension. If you begin thinking about it, the fault may turn out to be mine. It is after all better for each of us to see to the matter by ourselves, so that nobody will be blamed for it."

When the baby first separates itself from the body of its mother, it utters a cry that resounds throughout the universe, from the Akanishta heaven down to the deepest parts of the Naraka hell. But as it grows up, it becomes timid because of its so-called intellectual development, until it finally separates itself entirely from God. When it gets to this point, it loses its Buddha-nature and finds itself shyly asking if it ever had it in the first place. Is not the intellect here forgetting itself and plunging right into the abyss of utter darkness and confusion?

The intellect divides, dissects, and murders; faith unifies, puts the broken pieces together, and resuscitates. But division or analysis is possible only when it has something behind it that unifies. Without unification, division is not possible. To divide must after all mean to unite and consolidate. We cannot just go on dividing and analyzing. After all our dividing and analyzing, we must once more come back to the point where we started, for this is where we belong.

When a Zen Buddhist master of the T'ang dynasty was asked how to attain the ultimate goal of Buddhist life, he said, "Have an interview with who you were before you were even born."

This is getting back to the source of the universe, where even the intellect has not begun its dissecting business. This is the point where God has not yet spoken his *fiat* to light. This is where the Vedantic *ātman* has not yet stirred itself "to will." It is up to the intellect, if it can, to retrace its steps and put itself back to where it has not yet even started its work. But let us beware not to take this in terms of time!

If one says that God created the world out of nothing and looks at it "objectively," in the physical sense, "historically" or "chronologically," one is bound to be mystified. But the event of creation did not take place so many kalpas or aeons ago, astronomically or biologically speaking. Creation is taking place every moment of our lives. My writing this is a work of creation, and your reading it is a work of creation. We are creators, each one of us, and we are also created at the same time—created out of nothing and creating out of nothing.

The eye cannot see itself. The intellect cannot dissect itself. This is true as long as things are considered "objectively," as long as we are outside observers. But, after all, "the eye with which I see God is the same eye with which God sees me." To get the knack of this trick—if I may call it that—open your eyes and look at the flower in front of you or the starry heavens above. It is not the eye that sees the flower or the stars, nor is it the flower or the stars that are seen. The eye is flower and stars; flower and stars are the eye.

Or again, if I stretch out my arm, the intellect dissects this event or experience, and declares: "I move my arm, and my arm is moved." But the truth is that there is no agent called "I" that moves the arm, nor is there an arm that is moved. My arm is "I" and "I" is my arm; the actor is the acted, and the acted is the actor. There is only pure act, that is, pure experience. If one expresses this in words, though, one is bound to go far off the mark.

In this connection I wish to say a few words about the fact that Buddhism is often regarded as pantheistic. This is incorrect; Buddhism is neither pantheism or mysticism. It has a unique way of interpreting reality: it apprehends reality as it really is, or as it actually asserts itself. When Buddhist philosophers say that the green bamboos swaying in the breeze are the *Dharmakāya*, or that the yellow foliage luxuriantly growing in my front garden is *prajñā* or Buddha-nature (*buddhatā*), critics think this a pantheistic statement. But the Buddhist will reply: if the yellow foliage is *prajñā*, *prajñā* is a nonsentient being, and if the green bamboo is *Dharmakāya*, *Dharmakāya* is no more than a plant. When I eat a bamboo shoot, am I eating *Dharmakāya*, that is, the Buddha himself? No. *Dharmakāya* is *Dharmakāya* and bamboo is bamboo; they cannot be the same. What is meant is this: *Dharmakāya* or *prajñā*, being "emptiness" itself and having no tangible bodily existence, has to embody itself in a form and be *manifested* as a stalk of bamboo, as a mass of foliage, as a fish, as a man, as a Bodhisattva, as a mind, etc. But these manifestations themselves *are* not the *Dharmakāya* or *prajñā*, which is more than forms or ideas or modes of existence.

Most people are apt to become confused when they hear things like this. They fix on the bamboo and cannot think of it but as a real existence, as objective reality. Buddhists, too, do not deny the bamboo's objectivity, be it with a certain qualification, but would still insist that it is not the *Dharmakāya* itself.

The strangest thing is that the intellect raises questions and then separates itself from them without realizing that those questions are the intellect itself. When it understands this activity, that is, when the intellect apprehends its own way of moving out into questioning, the questioning will be the answering and the answer will be directly discovered in the question. As long as the intellect remains objective, it will never be free of the snare it has contrived for itself. But at the same time we must not forget that if not for the intellect devising all those innumerable questions out of itself, we should never be called back to look within ourselves and find the answer right there.

Animals and plants and inorganic objects are all endowed with Buddha-nature. They are acting it, they are living it, but they never come to a state of self-realization, because they have never awakened to an intellectual life. The intellect may also lead us astray in its attempts at interpretation. But once it is awakened to its true nature, man attains enlightenment. And it is for this reason that true enlightenment or illumination, corresponding to what in Sanskrit is called *bodhi*, has an intellectual connotation.

When a Buddhist teacher was asked, what it is that even transcends Buddhahood, he answered: "the dog, the cat."

Another teacher told his disciples: "If you wish to know what Buddhism is, go ask the peasants working in the fields; if you wish to know about worldly affairs, go ask those grand professors of religion."

These statements by Buddhist teachers are not meant to be ironical or sarcastic. They really point to the truth of Buddhism. The truth is where it is, and not where it is talked about or argued. Nevertheless, unless it is argued and discussed, it may never have the opportunity to be itself, to discover itself, to be back within itself. The main thing is to know how to make a judicious use of the intellect.

What the intellect aims at is a system of unification on the cosmic basis of all human experience. In the cry of a baby this unification is there; in the highest productions of art, it is there.

When Confucius said that at seventy he could follow his heart's desire without going beyond the natural order, he had reached his *citta-gocara*, that is, a state of spiritual unification.

To say that beneath intellection there is belief or faith or affirmation means that intellection conceals within itself a fundamental unification in which we all have our being, from which we work out our daily lives.

The main trouble with the intellect is that it gets away from itself, that is, it ignores the fact that it belongs to life, and undertakes to work out its own system independent of the original system in which it properly finds its meaning. However much it may try to achieve this, it can never work it out, even though it may sometimes imagine that it has.

Why this impossibility? Because its feet are firmly set on the great mother earth out of which it has grown up and without whose nourishment it cannot thrive. The intellect belongs where its roots are.

Intellectualization ought to be made the means of logically, or if necessary even "illogically," constructing a greater system of unification on the basis of self-realization.

Reality is all-inclusive, there is nothing that can be outside of it. Because it is all-inclusive, it is the fullness of things, not a content-free abstraction, as the intellect is too frequently apt to make it. It is not a mere aggregate of individual objects, nor is it something other than the objects. It is not something that is imposed upon things stringing them together and holding them together from the outside. It is the principle of integration residing inside things and identical with them.

To take hold of reality, therefore, we must find a means other than sheer intellection; which is always looking outward, running away from itself. If we can make the intellect turn within itself and achieve what Buddhists call *paravritti*, a kind of mental about-face, it may accomplish something. But this is to go counter to our ordinary intellectual habits. In other words, the intellect may in the end awaken to a more fundamental faculty lying dormant within it. Though it is going in the wrong direction, further and further away, one day it may well become aware of its having gone the way it ought not to have gone. Here a complete revolution will take place, which is called *paravritti*. The intellect must once and for all experience an impasse in the course of reasoning, and if it is honest with itself, this moment is sure to come. Then, faced with a blind alley, up against a wall that absolutely refuses to yield, it will for the first time realize its own nature. This means the surrender of intellect to something greater and stronger than itself. This surrender means salvation when suddenly, as if by a miracle, the wall opens up from the other side. The Bodhisattva Maitreya snaps his fingers and the heaviest door yields, and Sudhana sees at one glance all the treasures inside glowing in their glory (cf. the section of the *Gandavyūha Sutra* on Maitreya).

In speaking of the working of the intellect, I spoke of the need for "a more fundamental faculty," but I am afraid this is somewhat misleading. There is no special faculty rising from some special outside independent source and destined to take hold of reality. Actually it is reality itself which now comes in full view, shifting the stage, making the intellect see itself reflected in reality. Or put the other way around, the intellect seeing itself is nothing other than reality becoming conscious of itself. This self-consciousness on the part of reality, intellectually interpreted, is precisely where subject and object begin their differentiation.

This may be called "pure experience." The method leading to it is subjective experimentation in contrast to objective methodology. "Pure experience," if I remember correctly, is a term used by a noted American psychologist. I do not take it in a psychological sense but in a metaphysical one. Here there is no experiencing "I," nor is there any "experience" of reality. Here is experience in its purest form, in its most real aspect; here there is no abstraction, no "emptiness," no mere naming, no conceptualization, but an experience experiencing itself. Though there is neither subject nor object, and hence no combination, no synthesis of the two, there is a distinct experiencing possessed of a noetic quality. While it does *not* fall into what we ordinarily speak of as the individualized experiences of daily life, it is in the most eminent sense an experience.

When I see an object confronting me, this is generally taken to be a case of immediate apprehension. But "pure experience" is not this kind of immediate apprehension or intuition. Let it be clearly understood: in "pure experience" as I use it here, there is no subject seeing the object; that is, there is no apprehending or intuiting agent coming in contact with the apprehended or intuited, nor is there any event taking place which is called apprehension or intuition. Understanding "pure experience" in this fashion, as a combination or joint kind of "union" between subject and object, is the result of intellectualization. All these differentiated ideas come out of the experience itself, they lie deeply in it, they *are* it. First we must have the experience in its purest form, then the differentiation follows. The intellect, forgetting its own nature and limitations, persuades itself into thinking there is an "I" effecting union with a "not-I" and proclaims this "union" to be a mystic experience, the whole thing turns topsy-turvy and an "I" with all its egocentric impulses comes to assert itself. As long as mysticism is understood as the union of "subject" and "object," I cannot approve of the use of the term for the Buddhist experience. Though we can not avoid resorting to words even where they are not at all adequate, we must try for the expression that most closely approximates the facts.

Masters of Buddhist philosophy therefore exhaust their stock of terminology trying to impart this knowledge to those who have not yet been initiated. (It is after all a kind of knowledge, although we have to insist that it is knowledge of a different order.) In fact, not only do the masters exhaust the terminology but they also use a multitude of "skillful means" (*upāyakauśalya*).

A monk approached a master and asked: "What was Bodhidharma's idea in visiting this country (China)?" Bodhidharma, of course, came to China from India some fifteen hundred years ago, and is generally accepted as the founder of the Zen School of Buddhism in China. In Zen dialogues this question always means: "What necessity was there for him to come to China from the West to teach Buddhism, or rather, about the Buddha-nature which is said to be everybody's? There was no need at all for him to undertake such a hazardous trip from a faraway land to teach the Chinese—as if they were not already endowed with the

Buddha-nature." The real purport of the question, however, is about being informed about the Buddha-nature itself, that is "What is reality?"

The master, however, taking the question literally, tells the monk: "Why not ask about your own idea (or mind)? There is no use asking about another man's mind when the Buddha-nature concerns yourself. You ought to know your own Buddha-nature, your self, the ultimate reality."

Obediently, the disciple then asked: "What, then, is my own mind (or nature)? What is my inner self? What is ultimate reality?" For this is the question that had really been troubling the disciple.

The master said: "You must see into the secret working."

"What is the secret working?" asked the disciple.

The master opened and closed his eyes. And this, we are told, opened the inquisitive monk's mental eye to the secret working of "pure experience."

To add a superfluous comment: the secret working of reality is not confined to this master's opening and closing his eyes. Here is my hand, I make a fist by clasping the fingers together, I open it, and now I show you the palm. Here is no secret, it is all open, no evidence of whatever nature is needed, those who have eyes are the witnesses. But if you say there is still a secret, an obscurity, something "mystical," you cannot blame me; it is all on your end.

Dipankara Buddha is the first Buddha, according to Buddhist legend, under whom Sakyamuni took his first introduction in Buddhism. Dipankara therefore may be considered the first form God assumed in order to teach human beings ultimate reality. Now a monk in the Five Dynasties Era, about one thousand years ago, is said to have asked: "What was the world like before the appearance of Dipankara, the first Buddha?" The question may be understood in the sense of what the world was like even before the appearance of Adam and Eve in the garden of Eden, or, what kind of a world it was before God created this world of multiplicities.

The master said: "The same as after the appearance of Dipankara Buddha."

"What is the world like after the appearance of Dipankara?"
"The same as before the appearance of the Buddha."
"What is the world like at this very moment with Dipankara among us?"
"Have a cup of tea, O monk."

This *mondō*—the "questioning and answering" between monk and master—is, I suppose, clear and intelligible enough. If you do not find it so, I fear that making it intelligible and perhaps more rational would take much time and a great deal of intellectualization, and even after that, the matter might not be understood as it should. Indeed, unless there is a perfect and harmonious assimilation of all our ideas into the total body of thought in which all the opposites, such as subjective and objective, God and man, nature and mind, find their proper assignments, there cannot be a real understanding of the "absurdities" running through Buddhist philosophy.

Now the question remains, how one attains to a self-realization of "pure experience" whereby one takes hold of reality.

Realization means experimentation. Unless we experiment, we can never come to realization. Merely by talking about things, or looking at things, we never get anywhere. To get somewhere we have to use our own legs and tread every inch of the way. Nothing is more self-evident than this. Nobody will have any quarrel with it.

Philosophy is all very well. We are born to argue, to discuss, but if we do not move on, we are as on a treadmill, and never make progress. If one's purpose is only to work the treadmill, then means and end are in harmony. But if we aim to accomplish more than that, we must seek means suited to the purpose, that is, we must experiment in order to experience.

For this experimentation it is not at all necessary to sacrifice thousands of innocent human lives. If any sacrifice is needed, let it be the sacrifice of our own lives. By losing life, we find it—this is what we are told by wise men of all races. If it is so, is not the experiment worth trying?

Let me cite another *mondō*:

DISCIPLE: Because I do not yet see into the truth, I get involved in errors and falsehoods.
MASTER: As to the truth, do you see anything specifically to be so called, and pointed out as such to others?
DISCIPLE: No, it cannot be something to perceive as specifically definable.
MASTER: If so, where do you get what you call errors and falsehoods?
DISCIPLE: I am really puzzled here and am asking you about that.
MASTER: If that is the case, stand in a field ten thousand miles wide, where there is not an inch of grass growing.

97

DISCIPLE: Where there is not an inch of grass growing? But how can one possibly stand in such a place?
MASTER: Do not argue, just go ahead.

A field without an inch of growing grass in it, symbolizes *śūnyatā,* the ultimate reality of Buddhist philosophy. *Śūnyatā* is literally "emptiness." To say that reality is "empty" means that it goes beyond definability, and cannot be qualified as this or that. It is above the categories of universal and particular. But it must not therefore be regarded as free of all content, as a void in the relative sense would be. On the contrary, it is the fullness of things, containing all possibilities. Errors and falsehoods stand opposed to right views, and belong to the world of relativities. In *śūnyatā* no such contrasts exist; there are no such grasses growing in "the field." But you cannot say this by just walking around the field, or by just peeping through the fence; you have at least once to be in it, to "stand in it" as the original Chinese has it. This "going straight ahead" into things is a great experiment, a great experience.

The ultimate reality as conceived by Buddhist philosophy is "pure experience," *śūnyatā,* a grand integration which is prior to the intellectual differentiation of subject and object; it is the cosmic or divine unconscious becoming conscious.

The following may help the reader understand what is really meant by the Buddhist idea of *śūnyatā* ("emptiness"), "where there is not an inch of grass growing" and yet where we pass this bustling life of ours day after day, year after year.

Tōzan (Chin: Tung-shan) once spoke thus in a sermon: "O ye brethren, in early fall and late summer you go about east and west; only by going straight ahead in the direction of the field where not an inch of grass is growing can you get anywhere."

On another occasion he said: "As to the field where not an inch of grass is growing, how do you get there?"

When Sekisō (Chin.: Shih-shuang) heard of this he remarked: "Just out of the gate, and you see the grass growing."

Later Tōzen-sai (Chin.: Tung-ch'an chi) commented on this:

Let me ask whether Sekisō understood what Tōzan meant or not. If you say he did, O brethren, what about your running around here and there, attending to all kinds of things, day in day out? Is this not sowing grass all along the road? Or is it in harmony with the ancient usage? If you say Sekisō failed to understand Tōzan, how did he manage to make such a remark? O brethren, do you understand what I mean?

Let me ask, where do you want to go now? When you have a clear understanding you will be singing the "Homeward Ditty." Don't you see? Once, I made this response: "If so, I won't leave."

The Buddhist idea is always to start from the source, where the division of subject and object has not yet taken place—and this not by analysis, nor by postulation, nor by dialectics, but by the method which I call *prajñā* intuition. This is not an ordinary kind of intuition, for *prajñā* works where there is no differentiation yet. Let me introduce you to Tōsu (Chin.: T'ou-tzu), one of the great masters towards the end of the T'ang dynasty.

Someone asked Tōsu: "I am told that Prince Nata returns his bones to his father and his flesh to his mother. After this, where is his original body?"

In philosophical terms, it is a question about ultimate reality. The "original body" is reality. When Nata gives up everything that is regarded as constituting his body, his individuality, where is his self?

When an individual object is subjected to analysis, physically it is reduced to atoms and electrons; but what are atoms, what are electrons? Even when reduced to mathematical formulas, this does not add an iota to our knowledge of reality. The question is merely pushed further and further back into a mysterious recess where no illumination can take place.

When, on the other hand, speculative analysis is carried into the metaphysical field, the question grows more complicated; all kinds of hypotheses are proposed, great controversies take place. When a world of multitudes, of individual objects, of relative existences, of particular phenomena, is reduced to one reality which is called God, Brahma, Reason, the Absolute, *élan vital*, *śūnyatā*, emptiness, "undifferentiated aesthetic continuum," etc., what is it after all? We may give it all sorts of names, but mere naming does not give us much satisfaction. Philosophically, we may think that we have said the last word, but the heart does not seem to be quieted by it. The metaphysical questions we may raise one after another seem to issue from a deeper source than our rational nature. For this reason, what we speak of as the "heart" must be in more direct and concrete contact with what we call reality than the intellect is.

Prince Nata's "original body" must be found out not by some kind of analysis but by directly taking hold of reality itself, that is, by immediately apprehending reality, whatever it may mean.

But if it is directly and immediately apprehended, how do we express it? How do we communicate it to others? How do we transmit it to our fellow beings? Objects of direct apprehension as a rule cannot be realities themselves. Words are an efficient means of communication only when the one addressed has an experience that somehow corresponds to the contents of what is being communicated. Otherwise, words are empty, or cryptic, or "mystical."

Masters of Buddhist philosophy know that full well, so they have devised other means of communication, such as gestures, ejaculations, meaningless utterances, impossible statements, illogicalities, and irrelevant remarks.

"What then, is Nata's original body?"

Tōsu, the master, thus asked, threw down the staff he carried in his hand.

"Where do we now see Nata's original body?"

Tōsu was asked another time, "Who is Vairocana Buddha?" (Vairocana Buddha is ultimate reality.)

Tōsu said, "You have already named him."

The inquirer continued, "Who is the teacher of Vairocana Buddha?"

"Take hold of him before Vairocana Buddha was!"

When Tōsu was asked about his own "teacher," he answered in Lao-tzean style, "When you face him, you cannot see his head. When you follow him you cannot see his form."

This description of reality is more or less conventional. But how about the following?

Someone asked Tōsu: "I understand the Buddha exclaimed as soon as he came out of his mother's body: 'Above the heavens and below the heavens, I alone am the honored one!' Pray tell me what this 'I' is?"

Tōsu answered, "Why knock the old fellow down? What fault did he commit?"

To paraphrase this in more or less familiar terms: Why do you take the old Buddha to task by demanding he explain what "I" or reality is? He just cried, as all babies do when they come into this world of individualization. By doing this, he did not commit any fault. His cry comes out of the very depths of reality; there is in it no intellection, no dialectical analysis, no mediating postulation.

When I was once talking with a young philosopher about a baby's first cry, he said it was an "uninterpreted sensation." Yes, that is the way philosophers "explain" reality; they always resort to an "objective" method when dealing with the subject under consideration. But this means they can never come to an understanding of it. What they call the objective method will never penetrate into the realm of "pure experience," where the dichotomy of subject and object has yet to take place. Where there is no such happening, there is no room for objectivity of any sort.

The baby cries and the philosopher explains or interprets, but the baby goes on crying regardless of the intellectual subtleties. To "understand" it, we must become the baby and cry with it. It is on the side of "uninterpreted sensation." "Above the heavens and below the heavens, I alone am the honored one!" Let the baby not be "interpreted"!

Babies are one of the favorite subjects of Buddhist masters, as they were with Christ. Let us quote another case.

Sekishitsu Zendō (Chin.: Shih-shih Shan-tao) of the latter part of the T'ang dynasty, would lift up his staff whenever a monk approached him and say, "All the Buddhas of the past, future, and present come forth from this." When someone asked him about the difference between the Buddha and the truth (*tao*) the master said, "The truth is like opening the palm, and the Buddha is like closing it up into a fist." The questioner of course failed to understand what all this implied and wished a further elucidation. The master, waving his hand, said:

> No, no! If you go on like that you will never come to an understanding. All the teaching contained in the scriptures and canons is all very well, but if you endeavor to draw anything out of them [by means of the objective method], you will utterly fail. For you make the mind stand against its objects, and this leads to a bifurcation of the seer and the seen, which will draw you to further speculative complications and crazy casuistries. Don't have anything to do with the world of opposites; it comes to naught.

The ancient master says:

> From the beginning there is absolute nothing. [So do not fabricate a world of dualities out of that.]
> See the baby coming out of the mother's body? It does not say, "I

understand the sutras!" nor does it say, "I do not." It is never bothered with the existence or the nonexistence of the Buddha-nature, but as it grows it learns all sorts of things and will declare, "I know all that!" This, after all, is what was added to it later on, it is the working of the evil passions.

Here, however, we have to be on our guard and not be so hasty as to conclude that babyhood is the truth. For this is not quite to the point.

This last remark of Zendō's is significant. While the baby has its life to live ignorant of all scriptures of Buddhism and of the subtleties of *śūnyatā* philosophy, we grown-ups also have our lives to live, however sophisticated and involved in dialectical reasonings we may be. We are no more babies, and it would be the height of stupidity to aspire to their still-undeveloped mentality. What is important is to remain ourselves in every way possible with all our faults, moral as well as intellectual, and yet be "wise" as babies.

The Buddhist conception of *śūnyatā* is in one way the easiest and most direct to grasp—just as easy and direct as feeling hot water hot or as tasting sugar sweet. But when this approach is rejected and an appeal is made to intellection, *śūnyatā* can become a heated issue for a philosophers' conference. Masters of Buddhist philosophy, however, are fully aware of this interminable struggle for objective evidence and rationalistic treatment. They refuse to waste their time on this since they are not "philosophers" but men of fact, men of direct action, men of "experience."

Note how they respond to inquirers:

QUESTIONER: How about the golden chain which is not yet loosened?
MASTER: It is opened!

QUESTIONER: When the golden cock has not yet crowed, what about it?
MASTER: There is no sound whatever.
QUESTIONER: After it has crowed, what about it?
MASTER: Each of us knows time.

QUESTIONER: When the sun and the moon are not yet shining, where are the Buddha and we sentient beings?
MASTER: When you see me angry you say I am angry; when I am glad you say I am glad.

QUESTIONER: When not one thought is awakened, what comes out of
it?
MASTER: This is truly a nonsensical remark!

QUESTIONER: When not one thought is awakened what comes out of
it?
MASTER: What can you do with it? [or: You cannot do anything with it.]

The "chain not loosened," "the cock not crowing," "no thought
awakened"—all these refer to *śūnyatā*. And when the monk wants to
have some kind of information about it—that is, from an objective
point of view, for this is the only method so far known to him—the
master is disappointing. The master's standing is not that of the
monk; they are talking about different things. The master knows
this but the monk does not. When an object is approached from
outside, this means that we see it among other objects, that we put
it in relationship with them, therefore when we refer to it, the nets
of relationship are always woven around it; we can never single it
out from them. This means that it ceases to be itself. We may then
know many things about it, but as to its inner working we know
absolutely nothing.

If we are satisfied with this ignorance, all is well. But human
curiosity knows no end. It is better to say that the spirit is never sati-
ated until it finds the final abode where it belongs. Moved by this
spiritual anguish the intellect asks about "the golden cock that has
not yet crowed," about the "golden chain that is not yet loosened,"
or about "one thought unawakened." This is the intellectual
attempt to probe into the inwardness of things, wishing to take hold
of *śūnyatā* directly or absolutely, instead of surveying it in its inex-
tricable mesh of references, instead of pushing it into the labyrinth
of conceptual abstractions.

In other words, we need to apprehend the undifferentiated
immediately. When the golden cock crows it is differentiated; by
this, time is known. But what we are after is to hear the cock when
it has not yet uttered a sound—for it is by this experience alone that
the undifferentiated is immediately apprehended, and the only way
to get acquainted with the undifferentiated is to be personally introduced to it or rather to *be* it. The undifferentiated is never within
our apprehension as long as it remains undifferentiated; it becomes
apprehensible only as differentiation. To reverse what I have just
said: "We must hear the uncrowing cock when it crows!"

To repeat: hear the cock when it does not crow, or hear the cock remaining dumb all the while it crows.

The master stands where the intellect finds contradictions, and he goes on riding over them as if nothing stood in his way, whereas disciple and philosopher balk at every step because their intellect makes them too timid in the face of the threat of contradictions.

When the philosopher is told of "not one thought awakened," which is *śūnyatā*, he is puzzled and will ask, "What state of a thing could this be?" The doubt rises because he takes "no thought awakened" for some special state of consciousness to be distinguished from "all thoughts rising." When his thinking runs along these lines, he cannot comprehend that "no thought awakened" is none other than our everyday consciousness. For this reason, one master brands this philosophical way of thinking as truly nonsensical, while another retorts: "What do you want to do with it?" or "What can you do with it?"

When the master is ill-tempered his monks realize it; when he is pleased, that is always perceived by them. This is the way not only with the masters but with every one of us. Being human, we are all susceptible to joy, to irritation, to pleasure, to pain. As we all belong in a world of differentiation, we cannot be indifferent to conditions prevailing there. Buddha and all of us sentient beings have to submit to them. While thus conditioning ourselves to laws of differentiation we are all the time unconsciously conscious of that which is not differentiated, of that which is where sun and moon are not yet shining, of that which is when light was not separated from darkness.

The Buddhist conception of reality of *śūnyatā* is something concrete, but not in the sense of individualization. This can be seen again in the following *mondō*:

QUESTIONER: I am told that rain falls universally over all beings. What is this one rain?
MASTER: A pouring rainfall.
QUESTIONER: One particle of dust contains the universe. What is this one particle?
MASTER: Already differentiated into several particles!

QUESTIONER: The old year is gone and the new year is ushered in. Is there anything that does not belong to either of these two?

MASTER: Yes, there is.
QUESTIONER: What is that which transcends the two?
MASTER: An auspicious new era is ushered in and all things assume a fresh aspect.

These *mondō*, as we see, are after all more or less on the intellectual plane. While claiming to be above it, there is here a taint of ratiocination. Let the "philosopher" comment on the following:

QUESTIONER: When the moon is not full, what would you say?
TŌSU (THE MASTER): Swallow two or three of them.
QUESTIONER: What after the moon is full?
TŌSU: Vomit seven or eight of them.

8

NISHITANI KEIJI

Science and Zen*

From his earlier days as a philosopher it was "inconceivable" for Nishitani Keiji "that any thought that stresses outer events at the expense of existence itself could overshadow the problems of the inner life, of the soul, as being basic." His fundamental attitude therefore, as that of his teacher Nishida, was essentially a religious one.

About his lifelong fascination with, and search for, the "original countenance of reality"—a search which he resolved to pursue free from all religious and philosophical preconceptions—he explained that "having had frequent occasion to deal with the standpoint of Buddhism, particularly Zen Buddhism, this original countenance seems to me to appear there most frequently and unmistakenly."

Nishitani clearly locates the crucial problem of our time in its nihilism acting in symbiosis with science and technology. As such it has undermined the very foundations of our civilization, leaving the human in its humanness no refuge. He writes: "I am convinced that the problem of nihilism lies at the root of the mutual aversion between religion and science, and it is here that my philosophical engagement found its starting point, and from which my preoccupation with nihilism grew larger until it enveloped almost everything." The conquest of nihilism became for him not only his own duty but the imperative assignment for all contemporary thought, indeed for the world as such. His comprehension of Nishida's view on Oriental Nothingness, Absolute Nothingness (it has been suggested that the positive term *Suchness* or *Tathatā* might be preferable as less confusing) was at the basis of his struggle with the problem of contemporary nihilism, of which he spoke of as a "relative" nihilism, which could only be pierced and overcome by the radicalization of its relative nothingness, by the *metanoia* to Absolute Nothingness. He often referred to this Absolute Nothingness by its Buddhist appellation *śūnyatā*.

---

* "Science and Zen," trans. Richard de Martino, *The Eastern Buddhist* I/1 (1965): 79-108.

The concept of *śūnyatā*—insofar as it is concept instead of pure experience—was born from the realization of the abyss of nihility right under the feet of every human existence, quite independent of historical circumstances. In the current history of the world nihilism is encountered as the dominant historical direction taken by our entire culture, for it is no longer confined to Western culture, the nihilism of which has contaminated, colonized as it were, all other cultures.

It is not possible to turn around in an attempt to regain affirmative attitudes to existence. The negative direction has to run its course, to be pursued to its very limits, and then to pierce these limits, to nihilize this nihility in order to reach the point where the negative, so to speak, converges with the positive. This means that for Nishitani Western civilization will have to come to terms with Buddhist insights. It will, however, have to realize these from its own Western, hence to a great extent Christian, premises, for the predicament of our present culture must be seen as the end game of the Christian past. Christianity has to become aware of this and to admit it, if it is to overcome it. In its present form, however, Christianity seems unable to solve, or even face, these problems squarely, mired as it is in its Western provincialism and inhibited by the conventionality with which its values are generally interpreted. Christianity will have to reassess the ground of its own value system in confrontation with that of Buddhism (not that the reverse is excluded!) so as to attain a standpoint of true affirmation, whereby the negations which are the results of its past history may be overcome.

Nishitani's thinking, far from being negativistic, as it might appear at first sight, is radically positive, life- and future-oriented. The field of *śūnyatā*, while appearing as a radical negation, forms the basis for this life- and culture-affirming, regenerating attitude. The access to Nishitani's world of thought is not easy. It demands from the reader not only adaptation to oriental circumlocution, but especially intrepid reflection in which many traditional, more frequently conventional presuppositions must be relinquished.

The essay which follows here intends to present an aspect of Zen which seems capable of giving an answer to the question of the direction religion might take in our time. It presented particular difficulties in translation. The version presented is indebted to Richard de Martino's earlier one which appeared in *The Eastern Buddhist*, but has been reworked by Professor Jan Van Bragt and James W. Heisig.

I

When modern science excluded teleology from the natural world, it dealt a fatal blow to the whole of the teleological world view, which leads from the "life" of organic beings in the natural world, to the "soul" and "spirit" or "mind" of man, and, finally, to the "divine" or "God." The world was no longer seen as having its ground in what may be called a preestablished harmony of the "internal" and "external." Instead it came to be looked upon as an "external" world possessed of its own laws and existing by itself alone.

Max Planck once remarked, after touching on the universality of the invariables at work in the laws of heat radiation and gravitation, that if there were creatures endowed with intellect on other planets, sooner or later they, too, would inevitably come up against these same invariables. The laws of nature, as natural science has come to understand them in modern times, show this kind of cosmic universality. In that view, everything that exists in the universe under the rule of such natural laws is thought to consist of nothing but matter, devoid of life and devoid of spirit. Further, this view sees matter, in its usual state, as subject to conditions that could never serve as an environment for living beings (for example, in conditions of extremely high or extremely low temperatures). The range of the possibility of existence for living beings is like a single dot surrounded by a vast realm of impossibility: one step out of that range and life would immediately perish. Thus, to this way of thinking, the universe in its usual state constitutes a world of death for living beings.

At the beginning of *Thus Spake Zarathustra*, Nietzsche speaks of a camel going out into the middle of a desert. The progress of modern science has painted the true portrait of the world as a desert uninhabitable by living beings; and since, in this world, all things in their various modes of being are finally reduced to material elements—to the grains of sand in the desert of the physical world—modern science has deprived the universe of its character as a "home." Metaphorically speaking, the world has been reduced to a kind of greenhouse with all the windows smashed, to an egg with a broken shell—the boundary of its life-environment. Planck speaks of this as the utter detachment of modern scientific view of nature from anthropomorphism. But this also means that science has given the world a countenance entirely different from that presupposed by most traditional religions.

In other words, directly beneath the field of man's being-in-the-world, and the field of the very possibility of that being, the field of the impossibility of that being has opened up. The field where man has his being is his teleological dwelling place; it is the place where he has his life with a conscious purpose as a rational being. And yet it is disclosed as a field merely floating for a brief moment within a boundless, endless, and meaningless world governed by mechanical laws (in the broad sense of the term) and devoid of any *telos*. Our human life is established on the base of an abyss of death.

But the destruction of the system of teleology by science does not stop at the nullification and annihilation in their essence of the manifold forms of being and of the manifold functionings of "living" being. The various activities of human consciousness itself come to be regarded in the same way as the phenomena of the external world; they, too, now become processes governed by mechanical laws of nature (in the broader sense). In this progressive exteriorization, not even the thinking activities of man elude the grasp of the mechanistic view.

This means that all sorts of psychical and mental activities are reduced, together with the manifold modes of being, to a Nietzschean desert. In Buddhist terminology, the world of death comes to be seen through the veil, so to speak of the five *skandhas* of our existence (corporality, feeling, perception, volition, and consciousness). In a word, what is called "soul" and what is called "mind" or "spirit" become nullified in their essential mode of being. As a consequence, the concept of God is deprived of its foundation and its content becomes dubious, for the "soul" or "spirit" in man has provided the basis for this concept, as God himself has been conceived of as "spiritual," the "Holy Spirit" being a *persona* in the Trinity. Thus, the denial of the teleological view of the natural world by modern science necessarily results in the collapse of the whole system of teleology extending from the natural world through man to God. This result is what Nietzsche has called the advent of European nihilism. Modern science itself, however, has yet to "realize to the full" this grave consequence arising in the wake of its own activity.

When modern science took the natural world to be self-existing, regulated by its own laws, it did not, as we already noted, exteriorize the natural world alone. Its exteriorization was also directed to the field in which such "interior" things as life and mind are established. The necessary consequence was the annihilation of all sorts of *"eidos"* (or "substantial form"), not only the annihilation of the substantiality of visible things, but also the negation of the essence of life, soul, and the spirit.

Science is always outer-directed and facing the external world. Given that attitude, the field of what might be called the preestablished harmony between the external and the internal is relegated to the past by the scientific standpoint; it is hidden from its view. It is in the very essence of the scientific standpoint that this be so. Thus science, through its activity, takes effect on domains lying behind it without being aware of the fact.

The result is that, on the one hand, scientists destroy the teleological image of the world, and with it the characteristic feature of that image as an environment for life. In its stead they present material processes without life and spirit and devoid of *telos* and meaning as the true features of the world. On the other hand, as human beings engaged in scientific research these scientists live their own personal existence within a world that constitutes an environment for life. There is a contradiction here that is difficult to describe. It is a contradiction that, rather than being the fault of individual scientists, is natural to science itself and derives from the nature of the scientific standpoint as such. The same kind of contradiction appears in philosophy also, when it assumes the standpoint of "scientism." There, however, the contradiction is not natural as it is with science proper.

In its essential structure scientific knowledge harbors the certainty that its method of experimental analysis can prevail, at least in principle, throughout the whole realm of natural phenomena, and this certainty is expressed in the scientist as a personal conviction. This conviction in turn is supported by the actual accomplishments of science and by the efficacy of its methods as proved by those accomplishments—although, more fundamentally, it is thought in general to rest upon the certainty inherent in mathematical reasoning. This conviction of certainty contained in the scientific enterprise thus necessarily appears in two diverse forms. Objectively, it takes the form of the certainty of factual knowledge;

and subjectively, the form of a conviction as the immediate consciousness of self-evidence. But the nature of the scientific enterprise itself does not contain a basis on which to inquire into the ground of the possibility of the concurrence of these two forms. With this question we move into the dimension of philosophy, from which standpoint the scientific enterprise is seen as naive.

The scientific enterprise is based, to use Hegel's terms, on "certainty" and not on "truth." So-called scientific truth is in fact no more than certainty—which is all right as far as science is concerned. The philosophical standpoint of "scientism," however, takes scientific certainty in itself to be the same as philosophical truth. The philosophical naiveté of the scientific enterprise is thus raised to the level of philosophical sophistication, and scientific rationality is adopted as the standard for a system of value. In philosophy, this is a dogmatism altogether divorced from science itself. Because of this philosophical dogmatism, the various philosophical positions based on scientism were able to give rise to a common optimism biased to give glory to the enlightenment of mankind, i.e., to the progress of society brought about by science and its rationality. The grounding of this optimism, however, is all too shallow, as becomes apparent when we compare the atheism that inevitably accompanies it with the atheism of Nietzsche.

Nietzsche looked into the depths of the situation which gave rise to scientific optimism and saw that "God is dead," which he took as the highest form of pessimism, that is, as nihilism. By passing through this pessimistic nihilism and taking it upon himself, he was then able to transform it into what he called "active nihilism." In this way he was able to embrace the fact that "God is dead" with the feeling as if the shell in which mankind had hitherto been confined had cracked open, with the feeling of an adventurous sailor finding the horizon once again looming brightly ahead. He could feel a sense of emancipation and a sense of being unburdened. He could feel that joyful palpitation one comes upon when embarking on the exploration of an unknown continent. The depth of this affirmation of life wrenched from the very bottom of a pessimism where man was without hope is beyond the reach of all "scientific" philosophies and their atheistic attitudes—where the question of God is dissolved into the question of the "idea" of God, and this idea is then interpreted as originating from the fantasy of prescientific "primitives."

II

Religions have generally held science in abhorrence for dealing a fatal blow to the teleological world view and value system that constituted their foundations. They shunned it as if it were a work of the devil, a rebellion against God. It is a matter of fact that as a result of science and philosophies, both scientific and "scientistic," the religious sentiment of mankind has become more and more attenuated, and skepticism and indifference toward religious faith has become more widespread. As is well known, this tendency provoked any number of attempts at suppression or resistance from the side of religion. (These attempts run parallel to attempts by artists to resist the influence of science in defense of their aesthetic sentiments.)

But is the attitude of religions correct when they try to challenge science by holding on to their old teleological world view? Is it not first necessary for religions to reexamine the basis for their own world view in order to meet science on equal terms and to confront it competently?

As noted above, for the teleological view, the world is essentially like a hothouse. A theological viewpoint which locates the world under the rule of a divine order includes the fundamental assumption that this world must have been created as a "home" for man at work in this life, or at least as a harbor for *homo viator.* When, however, such a world view is contrasted with the callous indifference that science takes to be a normal feature of the universe, we can only say that such a teleological world view is "human, all too human." It is not yet free of the characterization of the world from the "inside," as an environment for *life.* In many religions, the deity has often been conceived as the bottomless fountainhead of life. The visage of bottomless *death* appearing in the universe seems scarcely ever to have cast its shadow on those religions.

Providing a way for the resolution of the conflict between science and religion is one of the fundamental tasks falling to philosophy in modern times. But the philosophical systems that have undertaken this task have not, on the whole, been free of teleological assumptions. Descartes, for example, in his investigations in physics, carried the point of view of scientific mechanism to the point of trying to use it to interpret the variety of forms that human passion takes.

113

But the metaphysic which functions as trunk of his whole system of philosophy, including his investigations into the physical sciences, is a teleological construction sustained by his proofs for the existence of God. As a result, he was unable to free himself from the dualism of *res extensa* and *res cogitans*. The same thing can be said with regard to the basic standpoint of Kant's philosophy, in whose concept of the "thing-in-itself" the whole issue appears in condensed form. For that very reason other modern philosophical systems which endeavored to be monistic by basing themselves on the absolute nature of God came to be, in general, teleological systems. In short, the various attempts on the part of modern philosophy to bring about a resolution to the conflict between science and religion have so far yielded unsatisfactory results.

It now becomes imperative for us to consider all the possible consequences that may be expected to arise necessarily, and in the form of a chain reaction, from the collapse of the teleological world view. In science as well as in philosophy, when it assumes the standpoint of "scientism," all phenomena in the universe are regarded as reducible to mechanical, material processes which are in themselves purposeless and meaningless. And yet the scientists and philosophers themselves who hold this view live as human beings, as if their lives had purpose and meaning and as if they were living outside of the mechanical, material universe they are observing. The problem with which we are now faced, however, does not permit us to rest complacent either with philosphical naiveté, as in the case of the scientist, or with the philosophical sophistication of that naiveté, as in the case of the philosophers of "scientism." Nor can we, as philosophers have heretofore done, stop at the stage of discriminating between the world to be ruled by mechanism and the world to be ruled by teleology, and then either regard the latter as transcending and comprehending the former or try to reorganize the whole system anew into a teleological hierarchy under the absolute nature of God. We must have the courage to admit that the "spiritual" basis of our existence, i.e., the ground from which all the teleological systems in religion and philosophy up to now have emerged and on which they have rested, has once and for all been completely destroyed. Science has descended upon the world of teleology like a sword-bearing angel, or rather a new demon.

For the spirit which has sustained most traditional religions and philosophies, the establishment of modern science, to use familiar

Zen terms, spells a sort of "destruction of the house and demolition of the hearth," that is, a fatal breakup of the "nest and cave of the spirit." This turn of events has to be accepted as it is. Like it or not, it is the historical "fate" of man, or rather, in Heidegger's term, his *Geschick*. It is a sort of fate assaulting man as a "fatal" question, so that man once more gets reduced fundamentally, in his own eyes, to a question mark. In this context, the essence of science itself constitutes a problem of a scope that goes beyond the scope of science itself. The essence of science is not "scientific." The essence of science is something to be brought into question in the same realm where the essence of man becomes a question to man himself. Of course, the scientist himself may not be aware of the meaning and the grave consequences which the establishment of modern science implies. It is probably the same with philosophers who adopt the standpoint of "scientism." The deadly sword of the new demon that science has called forth may have reached every last one of them. But somehow, for their part they do not dare to take it upon themselves to parry the sword. Hence the possibility of the simple optimism from whose perspective they speak only of "progress."

But let this "scientific" philosophy, which seeks to philosophize scientifically and objectively about science, proceed as it will, we may still take note of another philosophical attitude which shoulders the emergence of modern science as a "fatal" question of the possibility or impossibility of man's own "existence." It is an attitude emboldened to think *existentially* of the essence of science, and one that has made its appearance, contrary to our expectations, in the apparently most unscientific and fanciful of philosophers. Nietzsche, for example, discusses in his *Genealogy of Morals* the basic attitude of modern science, remarking of those who hold to scientism:

> These trumpeters of reality are bad musicians, their voices obviously do *not* come from the depths, the abyss of the scientific does *not* speak through them—for today the scientific conscience is an abyss—the word *science* in the mouths of such trumpeters is simply an indecency, an abuse, and a piece of impudence.[1]

What Nietzsche calls here the abyss of scientific conscience does not, of course, refer to the conscience of scientists in their scientific enterprises. He is not casting a skeptical eye on scientists regarding that point. The real issue at stake when he speaks of the abyss of the scientific conscience is whether or not one has pursued the consequences resulting from the establishment of modern science uncompromisingly to the end, whether or not one has dared to penetrate to the dimension where the question of the essence of science itself can be posed—the dimension where science is no longer scientific. The problem here is one of philosophical conscience inquiring existentially and essentially into what science is.

In other words, what we are talking about is submitting to science as to a fire with which to purge and temper traditional religions and philosophies, that is, as a new starting point for the inquiry into the essence of man. It was precisely in this way, as already noted, that Nietzsche actually accepted the historical situation which he characterized with the declaration "God is dead."

On this small planet of ours, nature has made an environment for "life" and provided a base for the "soul" and "spirit" to interweave the threads of historical events. But in the borderless universe that surrounds the earth, the usual state is one of a bottomless death which does not permit the subsistence of "life," or "soul," or "spirit." This same state also pervades the "underground" of the conditions for the life-environment on our own planet. It appears through living beings in their death. From the viewpoint of science, this constant feature of the universe may be regarded as nothing more than a material process, and the death of living beings merely one aspect of the same process. But from the viewpoint in which the essence of science is questioned on the same dimension as the essence of human existence, and in which the fundamental attitude of science itself is taken up as an existential problem, this constant feature of the universe and the death of living beings must be taken up in a totally different way. On that higher dimension our conscience, philosophical as well as religious, demands such a change of attitude.

It should be clear from what has been said so far that the fact that the teleological world view has been excluded by science can not simply stop there. It implies, as a further consequence, that the entire teleological system in traditional religions and philosophies has been robbed of its cornerstone. What we call life, soul, and spirit, including even God, who had been regarded as the ground of their being, have had their "home" destroyed. As has already been suggested, it is as if the very frame of the greenhouse had been dismantled. The human spirit has been deprived of its hearth. House and hearth have been torn apart.

III

For a thinker who faces science existentially, i.e., who accepts it as a problem for his own existence as such, that the usual state of the universe is explained by science in terms of lifeless materiality means that the universe is a field of existential death for himself and for all mankind. It is a field in which one is obliged, to adopt another Zen term, "to abandon oneself and throw away one's own life," a field of absolute negation. An example may help to illustrate the point. The ancient eschatological myth that the cosmos is doomed one day to burn up in a great cosmic fire found its way into Buddhism as well. In interpreting this myth, however, Buddhists have always taken it on the dimension of religious existence, transforming the idea of the end of the world into an existential problem. Seen from this standpoint, this world as it is—with the sun, the moon, and the numerous stars, with mountains, rivers, trees, and flowers—is, as such, the world ablaze in an all-consuming cosmic conflagration. The end of the world is an actuality here and now; it is a fact and a destiny at work directly underfoot.

Consider, for example, the famous Zen koan about Da-sui (Jap.: Dai-zui, 834-919) and the kalpa fire:

A monk asked Da-sui: "When the kalpa fire flares up and the great cosmos is destroyed, I wonder, will 'it' perish, or will it not perish?" Da-sui said: "It will perish."[2]

Undoubtedly, the monk meant by "it" the refreshing inner dimension of transcendence that he had realized in himself and in which he had extricated himself from "the burning house of the triple world" (i.e., this world). He stood apparently rooted in the firm realization of his "original self" that would not perish even in the face of the destruction of the thousand great worlds. And yet, even that original self is instantly burned up with the one remark of Da-sui: "It perishes!" "It," imperishable even in the destruction of the world, still contains in it a hint of "spiritual" realization and is not wholly free of the domain of teleology. Even if "it" should mean an infinite *âme ouverte* that exists in an identity with the All, it would still be a standpoint of "inwardness" and to that extent still contain the character of something closed, the character of "nest and cave." Such an "it" needs radically to be broken through.

The dialogue between the monk and the master continues:

> The monk said: "Then will it be gone with the other?"
> [The word *other* used by the monk here means the universe in the cosmic fire.]
> Da-sui said: "It will be gone with the other."

"It" must also follow "the other" and must perish together with the universe in the kalpa fire.

Here the myth of the kalpa fire receives an existential interpretation and is taken as an indisputable actuality by both questioner and questioned. A Buddhist demythologization is being carried out here. The same myth of the kalpa fire can, of course, also be interpreted in a scientific way. It is at least scientifically possible that the planet on which we live, the moon that today's scientists keep trying to get closer to, and the whole cosmos itself might be turned into a gigantic ball of fire. We might say that this possibility, as one mode of the usual cosmic state of bottomless death mentioned above, is already a scientific actuality hidden within the present condition of the cosmos. The state of Hiroshima immediately after the fall of the atomic bomb, for instance, gives us a glimpse of that hidden scientific actuality openly manifesting itself as an actuality in the human realm.

In the *mondō* just cited, not only was the myth of the cosmic fire dealt with as a scientific actuality, i.e., as a process of lifeless materiality and a state of bottomless death; but furthermore that scientific actuality itself was accepted as an existential actuality and made the subject of an interchange on the religious dimension. In the *Hekiganroku* ("Blue Cliff Records") in which this dialogue is recorded, the following verse is attached:

> Blocked by the double barrier,
> The monk asked from the heart of the kalpa fire.

The monk's question itself is then a question raised from amidst the kalpa fire at the end of the world, a question posed from a standpoint on the dimension where the universe has become a field for the "abandoning of oneself and the throwing away of one's own life." So, too, with the answer. Whereas, as we said before, modern science has become a deadly sword for teleology, traditional meta-physics, morality, and religion, here in the case of Da-sui it is trans-formed into a deadly sword in a religious sense. This means, as shall be explained later, that it is transformed into a sword of death that is at the same time a sword of life.

Another Zen master, T'ou-tzū (Jap.: Tōshi, 819-914), when asked a similar question: "How is it at the time of the all-consuming kalpa fire?" replied: "An unspeakably awesome cold!"[3]

One might argue that this answer points to the ordinary cosmic state of bottomless death. Terrible heat and terrible cold—either of which renders impossible the existence of any living being, includ-ing man himself (as *animal rationale*), who is exposed to it—are both equally ordinary phenomena of our universe. This being so, we may speak of an environment marked by conditions suitable for the sub-sistence of living beings as an altogether special place, somewhat like the greenhouse referred to earlier. In this sense, the unspeak-ably awesome cold, just like the all-consuming cosmic fire, may be interpreted as a demolition of the greenhouse of the teleological world view and an entry onto the field of the scientific world view. It would also be in keeping with common sense to interpret the answer as expressing the state of all things in the universe reduced to cold ash.

But the answer—"An unspeakably awesome cold!"—was intend-ed by the master to indicate a reality of religious existence on a dimension higher than that of science or common sense. It is an answer that destroys not only the teleological view of the natural world but also the whole world of soul, reason, and spirit based upon it, that is, the so-called intelligible world. That is, it represents a breakdown of the whole system of teleology. It spells a breakdown on all levels of everything "inner," of whatever constitutes green-houses or "nests and caves"; it means the spiritual "destruction of the house and demolition of the hearth." The very procedure of stepping out onto the field of the scientific world view is here trans-lated into the decision to accept the universe with its feature of bot-tomless death as the place for abandoning oneself and throwing away one's own life. The life-inhibiting universe of modern science is thereby exposed as a field where death in the religious sense, or the Great Death as it is called in Zen Buddhism, is to be realized existentially. In presenting the eschatological situation of the world in terms of an unspeakably awesome cold, the Zen master offered to the questioner—and through him to all things in the world—a place for the Great Death.

The myth of eschatology was thus demythologized and turned into the religiosity of the Great Death of the questioner and of the world itself. And this was made possible through a process in which the scientific actuality of the cosmos, or the cosmos in its aspect of abyssal death, was transmuted into the reality of the religious existence of the Great Death. When the scientific world view is returned to a deeper dimension in which the essence of science (which is in itself no longer scientific) is brought into question as inseparably bound up with the essence of man; and when that world view is taken on this dimension as a disintegration of one's spiritual household, i.e., as an essential transformation of man, and, therefore, as a mode of religious existentiality—then this whole process is also and at the same time a thorough demythologization of the eschatological myth. *In the religiosity of Zen Buddhism, demythologization of the mythical and existentialization of the scientific belong to one and the same process.* Religious existence in the Great Death makes possible at once the demythologizing of the myth of eschatology and the existentializing of the scientific actuality of the cosmos. The answer: "An unspeakably awesome cold!" was a presentation of the end of the world as the place for such a Great Death. To the questioning monk, it was like the thrust of a religious sword of death. The transposition of the cosmos beset by terrible cold to the level of religion was thus able to become like the brandishing of a religious sword of death and a demand to annihilate one's own self.

IV

The Zen masters, on their level of insight, answered the question in terms of a cosmic conflagration or an awesome cold of the spheres, each in his own way, thus making the universe under those conditions an expression of himself or, rather, a revelation of his own selfhood. The sword that kills is here at the same time a sword that gives life. In Da-sui's declaration that the "It" referred to by the monk must be demolished and that "it goes off following the other," we find what has been called "the solitary one laid bare amidst the myriad phenomena" exposing itself in the burning cosmos; or, again, we find what has been likened to "a piece of ice glistening in the midst of a fire,"[4] glistening in the midst of the kalpa fire that burns up all things. They stand where the universe is truly the universe as itself and the kalpa fire is truly the kalpa fire as itself, each of them in its own *alētheia* (truth), in the sense in which Heidegger would have us understand the term, i.e., as being unveiled and laid open. From there, too, the monk in the *mondō* is also taken in and brought to the dimension where he can find his salvation, the dimension where he truly exists as himself, where he is in his *alētheia*.

The very sword that kills is brandished here as a sword that gives life. At the very point where everything is negated radically and brought to ultimate extinction, the master points to a path of life. Something "immortal"—or rather, in Buddhist terminology, something that is "unborn and imperishable," something uncreated and undying, beyond the duality of life and death—stands self-exposed. Everything that subsists from the first has its subsistence only in virtue of having been delivered there, preserved there, and saved from dissolution into nothing. But, in order for man to realize the unborn for himself and to give testimony to it, he has to travel the path to it existentially, through the Great Death; he must unburden himself of himself, give up his tiny, egotistic self and deliver it over to his "unborn Self," setting himself free from all things including himself, and thus realizing in the unborn his own great Selfhood.

Da-sui indicated this existential path of self-deliverance in an existential way through his answer: "It perishes!" This is the aspect of Zen Buddhism we may call the Great Compassion. The light of the kalpa fire mentioned in the verse: "A question was raised within the glare of the kalpa fire; the monk tarries before a twofold barrier," may be called the shining rays emanating from the body of Da-sui.

To sum up, in Da-sui both the mystical kalpa fire consuming the whole world and the scientific actuality of the universe with its tremendous incandescence stand exposed as aspects of the reality of religious existence. This exposure, this "grand exposure," is none other than truth (*alētheia*) itself. But what precisely is the meaning and nature of "truth" here?

In terms of the scientific facticity of the universe, the conditions in which no living being can maintain its existence must be regarded as ordinary. The state of extraordinarily high or low temperatures is part of that ordinary cosmic condition. Further, these same conditions of scientific facticity lie hidden behind the life-environment of our world, which constitutes the stage on which the drama of history takes place and which has served as a base for the construction of teleological or anthropocentric world views.

All this should make it clear that the idea of the end of the world in the vast kalpa fire ceases to be merely mythical, but becomes an expression of scientific factuality. As stated above, however, there is something in this eschatological idea that goes beyond scientific fact. For example, the temperature of things, whether high or low, is always a quantity measurable in terms of number and therefore finite. Scientifically, even the kalpa fire must be of a finite temperature. But the idea of an end of the world spelling the termination of history and hence the downfall of every kind of teleological world implies something abyssal, something which might be called a bottomless death. The moment that this end of the world is accepted existentially as the reality at the ground both of our present existence and of our present world, that abyss or bottomless death becomes a present actuality for us. The temperature of cosmic matter can then be accepted as something abyssal in spite of the need for it to be finite, however extremely high or low. It can be accepted, so to speak, as a bottomless and infinite heat or a bottomless and infinite cold.

Infinite heat here does not, of course, mean heat of an infinitely high temperature. Infinity here is not infinity in terms of quantity, but infinity in terms of quality. Such a thing as an infinitely high temperature is an absurdity that cannot obtain in reality. Bottomless heat means that in spite of being quantitatively finite, heat of a certain temperature is bottomless, qualitatively infinite. In this sense, as will be subsequently explained, a heat that can be encountered in our environment—e.g., the comfortable warmth of hot tea—can be taken as warmth that is bottomless and infinite in the fact of its warmth, even though that fact be appreciated in a moderate temperature.

In this dimension of "bottomlessness" (*Ungrund*), any finite temperature, regardless of its degree of intensity, can be appreciated just as it is, in its respective being. All natural phenomena can be received, as they are, into the dimension of bottomlessness, even when they are scientifically reduced to quantitative or even mathematical relations. Natural phenomena of any form whatsoever do not, of course, cease to be facts. Whether they be taken in their concrete, natural forms or in the abstract forms they assume in such domains as physics, chemistry, and biology—that is, in the abstractions peculiar to each of these categories—they always retain the character of fact as understood in the particular discipline in question, and in this sense can also take on the characteristics of truth as limited by that discipline.

To talk of the dimension of bottomlessness does not mean that we overlook this. The aim is rather to point to this dimension as a field on which all natural phenomena take on even more "truth" and even more "fact," if one be permitted to express the transposition to the qualitative infinity of bottomlessness in this way.

Indeed, this dimension is nothing other than the place where all natural phenomena emerge manifesting themselves as they actually are. *We may call it the place where the concrete facts of nature emerge manifesting themselves as they actually are and possessed of greater "truth" than when they are ordinarily experienced as true facts; and the place where scientific truths emerge manifesting themselves as they actually are and possessed of greater "facticity" than when they are ordinarily thought of as truths concerning facts.* Here the *vérités des faits* and *vérités éternelles*, as distinguished by Leibniz, are together on the same level and enjoy equally the ultimate qualification of being fact and being truth. They all are ultimately *pragma* and ultimately *logos* at the same time. But, to repeat, such a dimension of bottomlessness can only open up in a religious existence that accepts the universe as a field for self-abandonment and for throwing away one's life; it can open only through the Great Death. Only in this way can the natural facts of the universe and the various forms of their truth be revealed as they really are. Only then can they stand as fact in the consummation of their facticity and as truth in the consummation of their truthfulness. *When anything, be it empirical or scientific, "is," its being always takes place as a manifestation on the dimension of bottomlessness.*

We have seen that all phenomena in the universe appear in a dimension of bottomlessness, manifesting themselves as they really are: things that exist individually, processes consisting of connections which can be further reduced scientifically to quantitative, abstract relations, and the universe itself as the whole wherein these things and processes subsist. Yet, the significance of the statement that the dimension of bottomlessness itself is truth (*alētheia*) itself is not yet clear. We just referred to that dimension as the field wherein all phenomena are possessed of greater truth and facticity, the field of the solitary one laid bare amidst the myriad phenomena. This "solitary one laid bare" represents the point on which every phenomenon is more itself than it is in itself. But what does all this mean? To answer that question more clearly, we need first to deal with a number of other points.

V

So far we have dealt with the effort of modern science to exclude teleology from both the natural and the spiritual worlds. But there is no denying the fact, as a moment's reflection will suffice to remind us, that terms like *life, consciousness, spirit,* and so forth point to actual phenomena of one sort or another. This fact is every bit as undeniable as the fact of the vast, unbounded "desert" of matter stretching all over the universe. Not even science can deny the existence of the world in which living beings are living, adapting themselves to their environment, or the fact that from the "inside" of certain living beings feeling, emotion, will, and thinking have come to evolve. It is one and the same world in which flowers bloom, birds fly, and men sing, and where even scientists may find themselves singing when spring comes. If, somewhere outside of our earth, there are beings of another sort endowed with intelligence and spirituality, developing their own art, philosophy, and religion, then they too should be taken into account here.

Now this perspective on the world, which has formed a basis for the erection of the teleological world view into a complete system, is born out of the womb of nature, whence it continues to emerge up to the present. Following Theodor Fechner, we may call this teleological perspective on the world the *Tagesansicht* (day-aspect) of the world in contrast to the mechanical perspective which is its *Nachtansicht* (night-aspect). The world seen from a teleological outlook, the world of concrete things like mountains and rivers, animals and trees, with their various "forms" (*eidoi*), can be reduced in a mechanistic world view to material processes which can, in turn, be described in terms of mathematical formulas. But it can never, in all its eidetic variety, be *deduced* from material processes. Even though we may think that whatever appears in its aspect of *eidos* (ontological form) can be assumed to be an idea or representation in our consciousness, and that all functions of consciousness can be further reduced to the activities of brain cells, the fact remains that the brain itself, along with its cells, belongs to the world of eidetic variety. Whatever appears in its aspect of *eidos* always presents itself as a whole. Man's intellect, too, takes its start from this whole as a given. Even though it can then go on endlessly analyzing this whole into component elements, our intellect is incapable of creating the original whole with its *eidos* by starting from the mass of analyzed elements as its given. Even in those instances where human technique may at first sight appear to have created new, artificial things never before present in the natural world (for example, nylon, plastics, etc.) it is nature herself that maintains the role of original creator. The technical procedures of manufacturing only serve to prepare the necessary conditions for her creative powers to function. The same may be said with regard to the effort of scientists today to "create" life, to produce some living being. Everything in its aspect of *eidos*, is a qualitative and therefore nonanalyzable unity; so, too, from the same point of view, any component element of any thing constitutes a similar qualitative unity. The world, when viewed eidetically, proves to be imbued with the character of *eidos* through and through.

As stated above, however, it is on the field of bottomlessness that phenomena in their eidetic variety can ultimately show themselves to be what they in fact truly are, and can manifest themselves in their original and consummate quality of truth and fact. In other words, *it is the field of emptiness (śūnyatā) or absolute nothingness—or what may perhaps be called the None in contrast to, and beyond the One—which enables the myriad phenomena to attain their true being and realize their real truth.*

Of course, this field of bottomlessness, or the None, is not something to be found right out in front of us, as we encounter things in everyday life. Rather, it is somehow always in back of us when we face "objects" in front of ourselves. It is therefore impossible for us to get into that background by pursuing the course of object-cognition common to everyday experience and scientific inquiry wherein the act of recognizing objects is essentially forward-looking. Ordinary self-consciousness, insofar as it is "consciousness," is not yet a true attainment of our background, because the self which we grasp in self-consciousness is only an idea or representation of our true self, which we grasp as if it were a sort of object. This representation is only a projection of our true self, a projection onto the screen of consciousness, where our true self does not manifest itself but is only represented by an idea of itself. From a posture of object-cognition, we always see and know the objects as they exist in the field of our own environment and, further, in the field of the so-called objective world, which our experiences and our science usually take as being the world (or the universe) itself. These two fields, our own environment and the objective world, are assumed to be in extension outside of us, whether "in front of" us or "around" us.

In order for us to get to our background, we have no alternative but to resort to an essential conversion of that posture and of the mode of being of everyday experience and scientific inquiry. That is, an essential conversion of our existence, of ourselves is required. This conversion is precisely what we previously referred to as the Great Death. We further noted there that it is only through this Great Death that the field of bottomlessness—which we have called here our background—can be opened up. When opened up, however, this background of ours is opened up also as our foreground, albeit now as a foreground more to the fore than the field of our environment or even that of the objective world, where "objects" are always encountered out in front of us. The field of bottomlessness lies beyond those fields. The field of "the beyond" constitutes the foreground where things and phenomena manifest themselves as they *appear*, i.e., emerge as they *are*, in their true facticity. To get to our background is at the same time to go beyond the universe as a world of objects. In the words of an ancient Zen saying: "Facing to the south I see the Great Dipper." It was in this sense that we spoke of the Great Death as meaning an acceptance of the universe as the field of self-abandonment and of throwing away one's life. It means receiving all phenomena of the universe on the field of bottomlessness. It means, to cite another Zen expression, "being held in a bottomless basket." Here the red flower "is" bottomlessly the red flower, and the green willow "is" bottomlessly the green willow.[5]

The world that manifests itself on such a field of bottomlessness lies beyond both the mechanistically viewed world and the teleologically viewed world. It is at once neither of them—and both of them. On the one hand, no living being whatsoever, with or without a soul or spirit, is there "reduced" to a material mechanism; on the other, no material thing whatsoever is there regarded as "living," endowed with a "soul." This world is neither the merely "scientific" world nor the merely "mythical" world, neither the world of mere "matter" nor the world of mere "life." In other words, it is neither the world merely in its aspect of death nor the world merely in its aspect of life. Although these conflicting viewpoints—the one of a positive orientation and the other of a negative one—partake respectively of one side of the truth, the truth itself demands a single vision that can grasp both sides simultaneously.

To describe this, Zen Buddhists often use expressions like "A wooden man sings and a stone woman dances," and "Iron trees come to bloom in the spring beyond the kalpas." The wooden man who sings and the stone woman who dances neither belong to the world merely in its aspect of "life" and teleology nor merely in its aspect of "matter" and mechanism. They belong to a world beyond these two world views, to a world where they directly interpenetrate each other and are canceled, elevated, and preserved (*aufgehoben* in the Hegelian sense). Yet that world is the actual world as we see it every day, the world in its truth and reality. The spring of this year with its flowers in full bloom, precisely because it is the spring of this year, manifests itself from beyond the universe, from beyond all kalpas and aeons. Here the cherry trees standing in full bloom in the garden are, as such, the "iron trees" in full bloom. Put another way, the actual world with its red flowers and its green willows is, as such, the world in its eschatological state, the world ablaze with the kalpa fire.

Such a bottomless field should not be thought of as something like mere space, for this "field" is nothing other than the essence of religious existence itself. This existence presents itself in its true essence only in emerging as a bottomless field. The world in which iron trees bloom in the spring beyond the kalpas, i.e., in which the cherry blossoms in the garden are blooming in the spring of this year—which is the same fact in its ultimate real truth—is the world on the field of bottomlessness, and this is the essence of religious existence. This field of bottomlessness is the solitary one showing itself in the midst of all things, mentioned above. This "solitary one laid bare" is truth (*alētheia*) itself. All things bear testimony to their ultimate facticity and truth through that solitary one.

For the sake of completeness our discussion of the essence of the religious existence should not fail to point out an entirely different aspect of this "self" which is at once original and ultimate as "the solitary one laid bare amidst the myriad phenomena." We have said that in this solitary and unveiled self all "things" (or phenomena) are attested to in their real, factual suchness and come to manifest themselves as they are in their own ultimate truth. This aspect of the essence of religious existence cannot be separated from its other aspect, which seems at first sight to be opposed to it by contradiction. According to this other aspect, the ultimate self constitutes the field on which all phenomena give perfect testimony to their character of *appearance*—appearance in the sense of unreal and untrue representation—in which they reveal themselves as a veil covering their own ultimate reality and hiding their own ultimate truth by substituting an "illusory" facsimile.

What, then, is this ultimate "reality" of theirs which they, as appearances, cover? What is their own ultimate "truth" which they themselves hide? What is being covered and hidden here? Or, what is it that *does appear* in and as those appearances, thereby *hiding* itself at the same time?

It can only be that solitary one laid bare, in which we have said that all things (or phenomena) attain their *ultimate* truth and *ultimate* facticity, where they possess a greater "truth" and are more "factual" than even when they are in themselves. The solitary one laid bare is precisely that which appears in and as all things (or phenomena), thereby hiding itself as itself and consequently making all things (or phenomena) its own "appearances" with their character of unreality and untruth. At the same time, it gives to these same appearances, in and as which it is appearing, the character of truth and reality that all things (or phenomena) possess as "facts." These two aspects are essentially inseparable; they constitute one and the same essence of religious existence.

The mechanistic world view of science, which reduces all things (or phenomena) to material processes, comes into existence in an orientation to the latter aspect, i.e., in the negative orientation. It nullifies not only the substantiality of visible things but also of life, soul, and spirit. It robs them all of their respective "substantial forms." All things (or phenomena) thus become appearances of "matter" or of physical processes—appearances that are unreal in themselves and irrelevant to scientific truth. This standpoint of science, however, is still confined to viewing the world from within the world; it is still "immanent" to the world. It needs to break through itself existentially, to attain self-transcendence and become "ecstatic" through the process of appropriating itself existentially. Only when the scientific standpoint steps out of the world, and thus also out of itself, can it attain to its own essence, which is no longer scientific. This means that the negative orientation witnessed in the aspect of untruth and unreal appearance is pursued to the end until it reaches consummation. At this ultimate point, the negative orientation converges, so to speak, with the positive orientation witnessed in the aspect of truth and real facticity. At this point, a field opens up in which these two aspects and orientations are revealed in their original identity, a field in which every "thing," every phenomenon, is at once a real fact and an unreal appearance, at once a truth and an untruth.

Once there came to China an Indian monk famous for his ability to discriminate various sounds and voices. A king invited Hsüan-sha (Jap.: Gensha, 831-908), a great Zen master of the ninth century, to subject the Indian monk to a test. The master struck an iron kettle with a copper tong and asked the monk, "What sound is this?"

The monk answered: "The sound of copper and iron."

Hearing this, the master said to the king, "Oh, my king, don't be deceived by strangers."[6]

Now, the monk's answer was entirely right: it was indeed the sound of copper and iron. Why then was it a deception? Would it not, on the contrary, be a deception to say that the sound of iron is *not* the sound of iron? Whence came the master's denial of the real facticity and truth of that true fact? It came from a place where that true fact is not *ultimately* true and not *ultimately* factual, a place where it becomes untrue and unreal. And yet this place is also the place where the same fact is also ultimately true and ultimately factual, that is, the place where the sound is as it is—where the sound sounds as it sounds—originally and ultimately. This was where Hsüan-sha stood when he spoke. Or rather, the place where he stood was simply Hsüan-sha himself as "the solitary one laid bare amidst the myriad phenomena." And it was there, too, that the sound came from.

This "place" is *Tathatā* (true Suchness), as it is called in Buddhism. It is there that the natural phenomena of a sprightly man singing and a lovely woman dancing are, as such, nothing more than the natural phenomena of a wooden man and a stone woman performing their wooden and stony functions. It is in such a world as this, amidst all such phenomena as these, that the solitary unveiled one, the Self at once original and ultimate, lays itself bare.

This Self lays itself bare, too, in the vast cosmic fire story of Da-sui mentioned earlier. The phenomenon there called "fire" *is* more truthful and more factual than what is called "fire" in the domains of science, myth, or the traditional religions. In the anecdote of Da-sui, the kalpa fire was the "other." Following this "other," the "immortal" spirituality of the questioning monk (his own "it") must go off and perish. This "other" is none other than Da-sui himself, in whom the fire *is* more truthful and more factual—indeed *is* more—than it is in itself. There, the fire *is* in its true Suchness. There, the solitary one is laying itself bare as the truth itself. It is the self of Da-sui that unveils itself as the ultimate truth-untruth of the kalpa fire, and as the "other" confronting the "immortal" spirituality of the monk. The same can be said of the self of the other Zen master who revealed himself as the unspeakably awesome cold amidst the vast kalpa fire. Such is the "scenery" belonging to the essence of religious existence.

VI

Generally speaking, religions so far have been too much oriented toward man. Even thought about "God" or "the gods" has been directed in such a way as to concern exclusively the affairs of a certain nation or of mankind at large. Conversely, man has understood his own relationship to "God" or "the gods" solely in terms of his own needs and goals. Even when man has tried to understand himself as man in a religious way, his viewpoint has been oriented toward himself. This means that the teleological orientation has narrowed the base on which traditional religions stand and narrowed their perspective. The resultant viewpoint has regarded the world as governed by a God who is oriented toward man—or as having been given by such a God to a mankind oriented toward itself—and as constituting the environment for man.

The *Weltanschauung* entertained by these traditional religions exhibits a similar orientation. Even in our own day when a religious faith pretends to be "theocentric" and rebukes the "anthropocentric" attitude of other faiths, that is, even when God is considered in terms of the "wholly other" and presumed to be utterly transcendent to man and the world, confronting man with his own claims and purpose, with his own providence and economy instead of complying with man's wishes and aims, the fact remains that faith is still essentially man-oriented so long as God in his demands is concerned exclusively with man and his history. Although it is generally in the "mythical" religions that the orientation to man in question appears in archetypal authenticity, other forms of religion which have outgrown the stage of myth nevertheless necessarily retain remnants of the mythical in their makeup insofar as they have not been emancipated in essence from that orientation.

Modern science, however, is of a stamp sharply contrasting with that of traditional religions. The horizon which lies open before modern science knows not the limitations of a teleological perspective. The image of the universe it sees is wholly exempt from the restriction of being an environment for man and is not in any sense man-oriented. As we said before, the universe of modern science is a universe in which the prevailing physical laws are of such universality that they would hold also for any other intelligent species, different from *homo sapiens*, that might inhabit other planets. No wonder that natural science has come to regard the old teleological world view as a product of the imagination, and has found the process of getting rid of that world view to represent a progression from fantasy to science, a movement of enlightenment from the realms of illusion to the realms of truth. Even the "metaphysics" which had constituted the theoretical foundation of the old world view, i.e., the philosophical principles of the "physical" sciences, received the same treatment as mythology and mystery. In general, there is no denying the fact that the teleological understanding of the world, including metaphysics, had produced profound clarity in matters concerning man and of concern to man. Yet as this teleological world view with its speculations on the natural world was broken apart by modern science and replaced by a mechanistic world view, the clarification it had achieved in matters related to man became open to question as a whole for having been too basically oriented to man, with the result that it is now under pressure to reestablish itself on the basis of the new image of the universe. The fact that man has once again become a question mark points finally to the fact that traditional religions have become radically problematical.

On the other hand, while it must be admitted that modern science has achieved brilliant results in its inquiry into the natural world, it has been unable to make a contact with the essence of man and so has exposed its own inadequacy as a way of investigating *man* himself. To be sure, parallel to the natural sciences other new branches of science such as the social sciences, sociology, psychology, anthropology, etc. have sprung up to undertake the study of the various mechanisms of society and its history, as well as the mechanisms of the various phenomena of consciousness. As such, however, these researches do not constitute an investigation of man himself. The latter is impossible without an existential quest of man by himself. Only such a quest can open the way for really coming in contact with the essence of man, a way which can then serve to channel all the results of the scientific research on man and the world into the investigation of man proper and lend them significance for that investigation.

The realization of such a possibility, however, has been impeded by the upheavals wrought by modern natural science, as well as by the later establishment of the social sciences. Consequentially, a confusion has arisen and still prevails today, in virtue of which those sciences all too often mistake man himself for a mechanism.[7] These sciences in turn have led man to make the same mistake about himself, and in this way have played a role in dissolving the substantial form of "man," in annihilating the essence of man.

The basic question, however, remains: What on earth is this man who is himself, among other abilities, endowed with the very capacity to inquire in so scientific a way into the mechanisms of nature, society, and human consciousness? To this question, the sciences are unable to provide an answer. Even if they try, there is no other course for them but to answer by way of inquiring again into the mechanisms of nature, the mechanisms of society, or the mechanisms of consciousness. What this means is that the very dimension on which that question emerges is closed to those sciences, and that they are even denied access to the possibility of posing such a question. Neither in natural science, which views man as a sort of mechanism of material processes, nor in any other of the available sorts of scientific research is there any way open that might lead to the investigation of man himself. Inherent in all of these sciences is only an orientation to reducing man finally into a material process of the world. In the last analysis, the mechanistic world view of modern science is totally incapable of making contact with the investigation of man himself.

From what has been said so far, it should be clear just how complicated and resistant to solution a problem we have here. What is needed is the unification of the two contradictory elements: the scientific view of the universe and the investigation of man himself. What is needed is, so to speak, some means by which the scientific view of the universe can directly become an element in the investigation of man himself and can then, by way of the investigation of man, be brought to the ultimate meaning of its own truth.

With regard to the former task, we have stated in this essay that the mechanically viewed universe, into which every sort of mechanism is finally reduced, including the mechanism of human consciousness, should be accepted existentially as the field of the Great Death of man, as a field in which "to abandon oneself and throw away one's own life." With regard to the latter, we have indicated that the universe as such should be seen on a field of "bottomlessness" (*Ungrund*), even while being "contained in the bottomless basket," and that it is there that every phenomenon in the universe emerges as a true fact, manifesting itself in its at once original and ultimate character of truth and facticity.

From another point of view, what is required here is a standpoint beyond the teleological and the mechanistic view of the world, a standpoint beyond the qualitative image of the world that consists of concrete eidetic variety, and the quantitative image of the world that yields to an indefinite analysis. Therefore, a new vision must needs open up in us, a vision in which these opposite (even contradictorily opposite) ways of viewing the world (the positive and the negative) interpenetrate each other and become one and the same way of looking at the world, a vision that can see "a wooden man sing and a stone woman dance." And this is precisely the vision that belongs to a religious existence embodying the Great Death and the Great Life. The "mental eye" of that vision belongs to "the solitary one laid bare amidst the myriad phenomena."

Like science, religion should not be relevant to man alone. The contents of its teaching should be such as to hold true even for any other species of intelligent beings that might be living somewhere else in the universe. That is, they ought to possess a cosmic universality. If other such species of living beings endowed with intelligence should actually exist, they would probably have environments entirely different in eidetic variety from "our" world, from the life environment of man. They might also have societies and histories vastly different from those of mankind, and perhaps also a totally different sort of consciousness. (As a matter of fact, even within "our" world, all species other than man—such as insects, reptiles, birds, and mammals—have their own special kinds of society and consciousness.) At any rate, the intellect of any imaginable beings on other stars would also demand a unity between the teleological view of the world which comprises their environment, society, history, consciousness, etc. and the scientific view of the universe—and this demand would not be fulfilled until a standpoint beyond both these views were opened up.

In short, the basic standpoint on which man's religion ought to be established must contain a universality analogous to that of science. Only when man's religion can cease to be something referring to man alone can it become something truly relevant to man. What this points to is the most essential task confronting all traditional religions. It seems to us, however, that such a religious standpoint with the requisite universal character discussed above has already been realized, at least in its basic outlines, in Buddhism, especially in Zen Buddhism, even though the traditions and actualities of Zen display various points to be amended, complemented, or perhaps radically reformed. We have tried in this essay to suggest tentatively an aspect of Zen which seems capable of giving an answer to the problem of "science and religion," and which thus seems to point to the future direction that religions ought to take in our time.

NOTES

1. Friedrich Nietzsche, *On the Genealogy of Morals*, trans. Walter Kaufmann and R. J. Hollingdale (New York: Random House, 1967), pp. 146-47 (III. 23).

2. Hekiganroku case 29. *Two Zen Classics*, trans. with commentaries by Sekida Katsuki (New York/Tokyo: Weatherhill, 1977), p. 223.

3. *Zenrinruijū* ("Zen hall miscellanea," a collection of sayings by Zen masters, published in 1307).

4. Both sayings are attributed to Chang-ching (854-932).

5. "The flower is red, the willow is green" is a popular Zen saying.

6. *Wu-teng-hui-yüan* (Jap.: *Gotō-egen*), Book 7 (a summarized rendering of the five chronicles of transmission of the Law, published in 1253).

7. Ruskin began his *Unto This Last* (1862) with the following words:

> Among the delusions which at different periods have possessed themselves of the minds of large masses of the human race, perhaps the most curious—certainly the least creditable—is the modern *soi-disant* science of political economy, based on the idea that an advantageous code of social action may be

determined irrespectively of the influence of social affection . . . "the social affections," says the economist, "are accidental and disturbing elements in human nature; but avarice and the desire of progress are constant elements. Let us eliminate the inconstants, and, considering the human being merely as a covetous machine, examine by what laws of labor, purchase and sale, the greatest accumulative result in wealth is obtainable."

9

KOBORI SŌHAKU NANREI

A Dialogue

*A Discussion Between One and Zero**

Kobori Sōhaku Nanrei (1918-1992) was born in Kyoto and graduated from Otani University, after which he began his Zen training in the Nanzen-ji branch of Rinzai Zen. He was the abbot of Ryōkōin, a sub-temple of Daitoku-ji and highly regarded as a Zen master. He counted numerous Americans among his students. In 1977 he was appointed Secretary General of the Daitoku-ji branch of Rinzai Zen. He was also well known as a calligrapher.

ONE: A few weeks ago I chanced to visit an exhibition of oriental arts in the K. Museum. Among the paintings, I noticed one which seemed to me quite simple and fresh—a few persimmons drawn in black ink. Though the arrangement of the fruit was monotonous, yet the whole produced a somewhat mystical effect and seemed to lead me into an unknown realm. Unfortunately, however, I could not understand the painter's intention. Therefore, the next day I dropped into the home of a Japanese friend to whom, since I have come to know him, I have been attracted by his rare personality and profound thought.

"Do you know the painting exhibit now being held at the K. Museum?" I asked him.

"Yes," he replied.

"Among the paintings on exhibition there I noticed a black and white drawing, of persimmons, I think. Thought it was quite simple, the painting attracted me, but its meaning was beyond my understanding. Since seeing it I have been wondering what it means, what its value is. And I am also eager to know something about the oriental spirit which could produce an art so alien to our styles and traditions. Won't you tell me something about this?"

---

* "A Dialogue: A Discussion Between One and Zero," *The Eastern Buddhist*, o.s. VIII/3 (1957): 43-49, and VIII/4 (1958): 35-40.

"Don't wonder about the painting," my friend replied. "It is use-less for you to try to discover the meaning of the persimmons through intellectual understanding. If you attempt to do so, you may be led up a blind alley. You had better cease seeking the mean-ing outside. But if you really wish to know something about it, you must first of all touch that which you yourself really are. You must begin with the reality within yourself."

At that time I could not quite grasp his meaning. I have been thinking about what he said to me and, having become confused, have come to you.

ZERO: Now I understand the reason for your visit this afternoon. Tell me what is in your mind.

ONE: I want to know what the persimmon painting means.

ZERO: It is just a simple expression of the painter's inner life. The painter is Mu Ch'i (Jap.: Mokkei), as I remember, a Zen monk who lived during the early part of the Southern Sung dynasty, and who was also a famous painter.

ONE: Oh, does the painting represent the simplicity of his monkish life, his wearing of black and white clothing? Or do the persim-mons, arranged so monotonously, symbolize Zen monks sitting in meditation?

ZERO: Absolutely not! You are quite an outsider. The door of the inner life is shut to you, for you are always unconscious of the true fact of life.

ONE: We generally consider that our daily life consists of material and spiritual elements. Does this differ from what you call the "inner life"?

ZERO: You cling to words. When you hear the term *material*, you grasp hold of it; when you hear the term *spiritual*, you grasp hold of that, too. You are continually deceived by the magic of terminology; you never touch the substance of the fact.

Every fact is alive; each has its own inner life respectively. But, in our daily life, the fact appears wearing clothing; that is, it seldom shows itself before us in its naked state. The clothing of facts is "ter-minology." Terms stand for concepts, and concepts are far from the inner life of facts. We speak of "spirit" or "matter," and by the mere use of these terms we think we have understood matter or spirit. It seems to me, however, that what we call our understanding is noth-ing but a mechanical handling of these conceptions according to traditional usage, unconscious though we may be of this. It is like gathering up and handing down clothing when the man who wore it is no longer there. The true man can never be known by making use of his former clothing. The inner life of a fact can never be caught by mere intellectual treatment.

ONE: Can we see the inner life too?

ZERO: Certainly. But first we must once throw off every kind of garment, must free ourselves from the influence of concepts and terminology.

Look! Here on my desk is a white rose in a vase. You see it as white, don't you? Now you must see the flower that is not white, and see the flower that is not a flower, too. It is from here that the inner life of the flower will begin to reveal itself to you.

ONE: Do tell me more, please!

ZERO: You are now observing the white rose. You and the flower are a certain distance apart. You observe the flower; the flower is observed by you. But reverse the point of view to that of the flower. The flower does not know that is is called a white rose. The flower knows no name, no color, no time, no space. The real life of the flower simply goes on within its own unknown mystery. Even the term *mystery* is not adequate to convey what its real inner life is. Listen, here is a story:

> The monk Chosei once questioned master Rei-un:
>
> CHOSEI: When there is chaos and undifferentiation, what then?
>
> REI-UN: A naked pillar has conceived.
>
> CHOSEI: When there is differentiation, what then?
>
> REI-UN: It is like a wisp of cloud appearing in the ultimate transparency.
>
> CHOSEI: I wonder if the ultimate transparency can yield a wisp of cloud or not?
>
> Rei-un did not answer.
>
> CHOSEI: If so, then anything that has life cannot be there. Again Rei-un did not answer.
>
> CHOSEI: The instant that the purest transparency is without a single speck in it, what then?
>
> REI-UN: The ultimate reality still ever renews its flowing.
>
> CHOSEI: What do you mean by "the ultimate reality ever renews its flowing"?
>
> REI-UN: It is just like the everlasting clarity of a mirror.
>
> CHOSEI: Then, on the path to enlightenment, is there anything to do?
>
> REI-UN: There is.
>
> CHOSEI: What is there to do on the path to enlightenment?
>
> REI-UN: Break the mirror, then you and I shall see.
>
> CHOSEI: When there is chaos and undifferentiation, what kind of beings appear?
>
> THE MASTER (REI-UN): It is as if a naked pillar has conceived.

ONE: You have spoken about the inner life of the flower and told me an interesting dialogue. But I do not understand the relationship between the two.

ZERO: Remember that *rose* is merely the name we give to an unfathomable substance according to our conceptual usage. From the beginning of the universe, however, the inner life of that which we name "rose" has not been conscious of its name. It is clear that any kind of name is nothing but a sign attached from outside by some accident to a material substance of fact. The name and the substance, therefore, are definitely unrelated to one another. The name is a differentiating insignia which assumes the role to bring willy-nilly into the spotlight of the intellect something anonymous that has been dwelling in chaos. But the actor's role always ends in failure; for, whenever that which is anonymous is brought into the light of intellection, its original nature or substance is metamorphized and takes on a quite different character.

ONE: Then what you call the real life or the inner life is something akin to "chaos" or "the undifferentiated"?

ZERO: That is what I would say.

ONE: How can I see the real life?

ZERO: The only way is to grasp it directly from the inside, without any medium.

ONE: How can I get inside it?

ZERO: Here, right now, you are, aren't you?

ONE: ———.

ZERO: You don't know where you are, even when you are in the midst of the fact. This is because unfortunately you yourself are always repudiating the fact.

ONE: What can I do about it?

ZERO: To put yourself into it, you must first of all see your own real self, which is no other than the true dweller in the chaos. I urge upon you the necessity of discovering your own real self. This is enlightenment. You, however, are not truly aware of your real self, so you cannot see that there is no question but that you are in the midst of reality now.

ONE: May I ask you about the real self?

ZERO: Oh yes, you may ask about it as much as you like. And you may know a great deal about it, too. But though your parent may tell you how you have been brought up since your birth, or a philosopher explain to you endlessly about the existence of the self by means of abstract reasoning—epistemologically, ontologically, ethically, physically, sexually, socially—yet you will grasp nothing of your real self.

ONE: Acccording to what you say, it would seem that the self is, so to speak, twofold. Is that so?

ZERO: In a certain sense that is true. Buddhist philosophy tells us that man must return to his own real self, namely, to non-ego. He must awaken to the fact that the self he normally considers to be his self or ego is a false self, full of ignorance and subject to suffering. He must get rid of this false self and see his real self. This real self is the Buddha-nature within every man.

From my own point of view I might state this as follows. We have our daily life in this visible world in which all things exist in a necessary relativity. This mutual relativity is, after all, ego-centered. The visible world in which we live might be called an ego-centered system. In the network of this ego-centered system everything is named and each name designates an individual ego. You were named "One" by your parent. Under this name you were a student; your school teacher distinguished you from the others as a clever boy. Under your name you got a job in an office; you worked day after day and attained a certain position in society, where you wake up, eat, sleep, talk, love, hate, compete, suffer, desire, dream, become old, and die. When that time comes your name will be put on a tombstone, though you yourself will already not be there.

There is, however, another system which might refer to the real self, that is, the non-ego-centered system. Within this non-ego-centered system you are not you, the flower is not a flower, the persimmon is not a persimmon, time is not time, space is not space, life is not life, death is not death, love is not love, hate is not hate, competition is not competition, suffering, desire, good, bad, all different kinds of existences, all forms and non-forms, are not themselves. There is only chaos, the undifferentiated fact that "ever renews its flowing."

You noticed that you seem to be a "twofold" you, as you spoke of it. The "you" who has a name may be taken as the *rūpa* self. *Rūpa* means "form" in Buddhist philosophy. And the "you" who dwells in the undifferentiated may be taken as the *śūnyatā* self. *Śūnyatā* generally means "emptiness," but in my view the word *emptiness* is apt to be thought of as "endless void." Therefore one must see emptiness as Suchness, as "As-it-is-ness." As long as you never step into the midst of undifferentiation, the *śūnyatā* self and the *rūpa* self continue to remain at a distance from one another, separate and unrelated. When, however, by your own effort you break the mirror, you will realize your twofold self to be one actual body. This is the real self. Do you understand?

ONE: Oh please, let me show it directly! I am really eager to see my real self.

ZERO: Hey, One!

ONE: Yes, sir.

ZERO: Hey, One!

ONE: Yes, sir.

ZERO: Hey, One!

ONE: Yes, sir.

ZERO: You blockhead! Where are you?

* * *

ONE: Good evening, sir, when I met you last, you were kind enough to instruct me about Mu Ch'i's picture of the persimmons. Since then I reflected on your words but arrived at no clear understanding. May I repeat some of my questions?

ZERO: Oh yes, certainly.

ONE: I hear that most of the Buddhist Paintings in China and Japan are generally displayed as a diptych or triptych. If this is so, could you tell me if there is any particular reason for this.

ZERO: Well, paintings or sculptures of Buddha are, in actuality, made as a triptych. This seems closely related to Buddhist Philosophy. If you visit Nara, the oldest city in Japan, you will find many beautiful old sculptures and paintings in the temples. You will see among them an image of Amitābha Buddha, with Avalokiteśvara Bodhisattva at his right and Mahāsthāmaprāpta Bodhisattva at his left. If the image is of Sakyamuni Buddha, he is accompanied by Samantabhadra to his right and Manjuśri to his left. The Bodhisattva to the left represents the wisdom of Buddha's enlightenment while his compassion is represented by the Bodhisattva who stands to his right. They always stand as a trinity. The Buddha after long years of meditation attained the final awakening. Then he started on his endless pilgrimage to save all the people in the world, however numberless they might be. The two Bodhisattvas accompanied him to support his work. The awakening of Buddha is not only the penetrating insight into the basis of all existence but is backed by the deepest feeling of compassion for others. If awakening lacks this deep emotion, the awakening is incomplete or may be a selfish one. And if this compassion is not based upon the fundamental insight into truth, it may be nothing but a sentiment of sympathy. Therefore truth, awakening (wisdom) and compassion are indispensable principles in Buddhist philosophy. But you must remember that these three principles are not to be understood as separated from each other, but they are originally one and the same. There is no fundamental truth without awakening. There is no true awakening without compassion and no compassion without awakening. But Buddhist philosophers and artists came to represent them in the form of a trinity.

ONE: Oh, I see.

ZERO: As I see it, Buddhist painting in China, in the course of history, underwent a striking change in the form and meaning of the triptych, having been influenced by the philosophy of Zen. Instead of the traditional arrangement of the the three venerated ones, pictures of a tiger and dragon, monkey and crane, mountain and river, flowers or fruits appeared and came to be placed to the right and left of a central Buddha image. For instance, among Mu Ch'i's works, many representative triptychs are kept now in Daitoku-ji, a famous Zen temple in Kyoto. One of them has an image of Avalokiteśvara in the center. The picture on the right shows a monkey, stretching his long hand out to catch the moon in the water; the picture to the left shows a bamboo grove with an elegant white crane about to move.

Again the famous landscape painter, Li T'ang (1100-1130) has painted two wonderful landscape pictures which are placed to the left and right of a painting of Avalokiteśvara. Later, it seems to me these side pictures came to be treated independently and a diptych form of painting developed: Mu Ch'i's persimmon and chestnut are kept as two pictures and accompany no central painting.

ONE: I don't quite understand why such a change was introduced into the form of painting in China, particularly by means of Zen influence. Is Zen a kind of nature worship?

ZERO: In Buddhist philosophy, as you know, to understand what Buddha is has been the prime matter of concern. In this respect Zen was a unique departure which contributed greatly to the philosophy of Buddhism. I won't spend much time talking about this important subject here but let me just tell you the following story:

> A monk asked Tōzan: "What is Buddha?"
> He replied, "Three pounds of flax!"

I suppose you may not understand what this reply means. Your mind may be perplexed by it. This is the utterance of a famous Zen master. Zen is a religion designed to awaken oneself to the last state of one's existence, which is no other than the awakening of Sakyamuni, the Buddha. In other words, to open our spiritual eyes to the world of the absolute reality which is the realm of the true Buddha. This is "the undifferentiated world" which you may remember from the story of Chosei I told you last time. To enter this world, to realize this "undifferentiated world" and to live in it while we are living our workaday life (at the moment you are listening there I am speaking here), this is the *sine qua non* for the Zen student.

At the moment "the undifferentiated" is awakened, it cannot stay as such but changes itself into this real world, the world of differentiation, where a flower is a flower, a willow is a willow, a mountain is a mountain, you are you and I am I. Here is a new world where the undifferentiated Buddha appears as a willow, a flower, a mountain, even as a man who has a name, a man who is six feet tall, with two eyes opened, a straight nose, flat mouth, with no physical features lacking. While the world of phenomena is the world of phenomena it is that of noumena at the same time.

If you try to trace this connection with a logical reasoning, your mind is sure to be confused and suffer, but if you examine it with your full body,[1] you will be sure to come to a real understanding of it. From then on we need not necessarily refer to Buddha or Bodhisattva, but instead, in our everyday life, we see a flower as a flower and that is enough, a persimmon as a persimmon and that is enough too. Do you see?

ONE: Well, well, I don't think I do, but. . . . Could I say that the persimmon or the chestnut drawn by Mu Ch'i are nothing but his depiction of a Buddha image?

ZERO: You are apt to understand things with a knowledge which is given by others. Then the understanding you have is not your own. You have first of all to understand things without reference to what others have said. The immediate understanding is the only way through which you will be able to live a creative life. Just look at a flower, just listen to a bird singing, just place your foot upon the floor. Out of the midst of a total undifferentiation let your single step move, let a flower bloom, let a bird sing, let your lips touch a cup of hot tea. Even though this total absolute undifferentiation cannot be expressed in words, yet we are men who have an inner impulse to express it some way. A painter may symbolize it by a pure white space of paper on which no ink nor color is spotted. If it is a Nō player, he must use a definite period of silence without a word and without the sound of a drum. If it is a genius of a garden designer, he might symbolize it with a vast space of white sand without a single plant, or a single stone. But just as the total undifferentiation will have nothing to do with our actual life, so a mere whiteness of paper, a silence from the beginning to the end, or a vacant expanse of white sand without a single plant or a single stone does not make any sense to man. Look! In the midst of the pure white paper, an instant touch of black ink is flashed and with the minimum possible number of strokes a persimmon is composed. There are no unnecessary strokes at all. The brush has caught a purest moment of change in which beginningless, endless undifferentiation has cut into differentiation—persimmon! Do you understand?

ONE: Ah, I feel better!

ZERO: If it is a Nō player on the polished wooden stage, for a long period he will be silent and make no sound. Suddenly he stamps powerfully on the boards; the sound of one step breaks the entire silence and may be followed by words, the beating of a drum . . .

The silence and the sound make a delicate interpenetration where the eternal soundlessness penetrates into a sound and a sound inspires the eternal soundlessness. Again in the case of a garden like Ryōanji Temple, on the vast white sand, one central stone is placed accompanied by a few small ones in harmony with it. Here "undifferentiated form" has changed itself into a visible form, that of a stone. The stone inspires a formless undifferentiation—form and formlessness accomplish a creative interpenetration with each other. In Mu Ch'i's picture, "undifferentiated" color has changed into simple black ink—the colorlessness and color here make a delicate interpenetration.

There is an old Zen verse:

> The landscape with flowers and birds is
> As beautiful as gold brocade;
> Let us change them to become
> A black and white painting by Genki.

As you know, art in the Ear East is called "an expression out of nothingness." Black is a color to transform the colorless, infinite undifferentiation into the simplest color where a spot of black ink is a creation out of the infinite possibility, nothingness. Here the infinite just cuts into the finite. Now you see what the painting of the persimmons means, don't you?

ONE: Oh, thanks a lot. I feel most relieved.

NOTES

1. Examination with one's full body. This term seems first to have been used by Rinzai in his record *Rinzairoku* and later is referred to by Hakuin, the reorganizer and the revivifier of the Japanese Rinzai Zen. It means that the study of Zen is not to be concerned only with our intellectual investigation. Intellect is the function of man's brain, which is nothing but a partial function of man's body. Instead, with all one's total functions, one has to wrestle with the problem which is fundamental to one's life. The whole personality, without a single bit lacking, should be in operation. Even the nail on a finger, a strand of hair, each one of the cells which compose our body should partake in the awakening. This is not only the attitude of a Buddhist in the pursuit of awakening but should also be that of those who lead the Buddhist life, dedicated to helping others.

10

ABE MASAO

Man and Nature in Christianity and Buddhism*

Professor Abe has written various studies on Dōgen (1200-1253) and has translated some of his works. Dōgen is no doubt the most original thinker in Japanese Buddhist history. In his essay "Dōgen on Buddha-Nature" Abe shows how Dōgen rejected traditional interpretations of Buddhism as inauthentic and expounded the Dharma according to his own realization attained while studying in China under the Zen master Ju-ching (1163-1228), convinced that this was the Buddha Dharma as directly transmitted from Gautama to the Patriarchs. Although he was the founder of the Sōtō Zen sect, he categorically refused to have Zen described as a sect. He is unique in the history of Buddhism in Japan as a lifelong meditator who combined profoundest religious insight with an extraordinary philosophical ability and literary gifts. As Abe puts it, he is comparable to his contemporary, Thomas Aquinas.

The most poignant reformulation of Dōgen is perhaps that of this passage in the *Nirvāna Sutra*: "All sentient beings without exception have the Buddha-nature; Tathāgata (Buddha) is permanent with no change at all." This passage Dōgen understands as: "All is sentient being, all beings are, all being is the Buddha-nature; Tathāgata is permanent, being, nonbeing, and change."

This, according to Dōgen's understanding, expresses the fully authentic Mahāyāna position. In other words, not only humans, not only all living beings, but all beings have the Buddha-nature in common. Their common denominator is generation-extinction. The birth-and-death predicament is no longer anthropocentrically seen; instead it is perceived as being integrated in the generation-extinction contingency all beings share and hence of the salvation from it. Moreover, this generation-extinction process takes place at every moment. Dōgen radicalizes the traditional Buddhist view that does away with any special or superior position of man

* "Buddhism and Christianity as a Problem of Today," *Japanese Religions* III/2, pp. 11-22; and III/3, pp. 8-31.

as compared with other living beings, and on this point Buddhism contrasts sharply with Christianity, where man according to Genesis is created in God's image and assigned mastery over all creatures. Death here is "the wages of sin," the result of man's free acts in rebellion against the word of God. In Buddhism it is only his capacity for self-awareness that is the distinguishing characteristic of man which gives him the capacity to realize his own life and death as integrated in a reality that transcends his own condition, namely, the generation-extinction of all beings. Man's special position therefore is simply that he exists as man, the "thinking reed" who can realize and fulfill the Dharma, and this is the full extent of the anthropocentrism Buddhism allows us. The salvation of human existence, which in Christianity is personalistic in the personal relationship of man with God's word and is hence anthropocentric, in Buddhism becomes radically cosmocentric.

Professor Abe's essay referred to sees the Buddha-nature of Dōgen's insight as neither transcendent nor immanent and hence is in contrast with Spinoza's idea of the immanence of God, *Deus sive natura*, however much closer this may be to the Buddhist concept of reality than to the orthodox Christian one. In Buddhism, however, "all beings" and Buddha-nature are totally nondualistic, a view that is as "unpantheistic as it is non-theistic." The Buddha-nature, ultimate reality for Dōgen, is realized precisely in the infinite and ontological dimension in which all beings "exist respectively as they are." And this Buddha-nature is not *something* unnameable, it is *the* unnameable, and, conversely, this unnameable is Buddha-nature. Going to the extreme limit of his position, Dōgen says, "*Mu-jō* ('impermanence') is the Buddha-nature." Hence *nirvāna* is the realization of impermanence as impermanence, it is not the world seen *sub specie aeternitatis* but under the aspect of impermanence. This is not arrived at as a philosophical construct but through the pain and suffering of all beings and the universe itself by the religious sensitivity of a human mind.

I

"Has man as man, and the finitude of man in its positive aspect, ever been seriously taken into consideration by Buddhist scholars? The extension of *shujō* (sentient beings) to man, animals, and even, as we find it in Dōgen, to all things, makes this doubtful."[1] This question raised by Hans Waldenfels, S.J., leads us to an examination of the problem of "man and nature" in Buddhism and of the Buddhist idea of "naturalness" or *jinen*.

In the Buddhist way of salvation, it is true that man is not simply or exclusively taken as "man." Man is rather taken as a member of the class of "sentient beings" or "living beings," and further, as clearly seen in Dōgen, even as belonging among "beings," living and nonliving. This presents a striking contrast to Christianity, in which salvation is almost exclusively focused on man as "man." In Christianity it is taught that man *alone*, unlike other creatures, was created in the *imago Dei*, and that thereby he *alone* can respond to the Word of God. The fall and redemption of nature takes place through and with the fall and redemption of man. This man-centered nature of Christian salvation is inseparably connected with Christian personalism, according to which God is believed to reveal himself as a person, and the encounter of man with God as an I-Thou relationship is taken as essential.

In Buddhism, however, there is no exact equivalent to the sort of man-centeredness and personalism found in Christianity. The problem of birth and death is regarded in Buddhism as the most fundamental problem for human existence and its solution is the primary concern in Buddhist salvation. But birth-death (*shōji*) is not necessarily taken up as a problem merely within the "human" dimension. It is rather dealt with as a problem of generation and extinction (*shōmetsu*) that belongs to the total "living" dimension. This points to the Buddhist conviction that the human problem of birth and death cannot be solved basically unless one transcends the generation-extinction nature common to all living beings. Thus it is in a non-man-centered dimension, the dimension common to all living beings, that the Buddhist idea of birth and death, i.e., *samsāra*, as well as that of emancipation from birth and death, i.e., *nirvāna*, are to be grasped.

Further, by going beyond the "living" dimension to the "being" dimension, Buddhism develops its non-man-centered nature to its outermost limits. This dimension of "beings," including both living and nonliving beings, is no longer only that of generation-extinction but is that of appearance-disappearance (*kimetsu*) or being-nonbeing (*umu*). The "living" dimension, though trans-man-centered, is of a "life-centered" nature that excludes nonliving beings. The "being" dimension, however, embraces everything in the universe, transcending even the wider-than-human "life-centered" horizon. Thus the "being" dimension is limitless, beyond *any* sort of "centrism," and is most radical precisely in terms of its non-man-centered nature. It is this most radical non-man-centered and cosmological dimension that provides the genuine basis for the salvation of man in Buddhism.[2]

Accordingly, in Buddhism man's *samsāra,* i.e., succession of births and deaths, is understood to be inescapable and irremediable unless one transcends man-centeredness and bases one's existence on a cosmological foundation. In other words, not by doing away with the birth-death nature common to all living beings, but only by doing away with the appearance-disappearance nature—i.e., the being-nonbeing nature common to everything—can man's birth-and-death problem be properly and completely solved. Herein one can see a profound realization of that *transitoriness* common to man and to all other beings, living or nonliving. This realization, when grasped in its depth, entails a strong sense of solidarity between man and nature. The story of a monk who, looking at the fall of a withered leaf from a tree, awakened to the transiency of the total universe, including himself, bespeaks the compelling power of such a realization.

When transiency as such is fully realized and is thereby transcended in the depths of one's own existence, then the boundless dimension of *jinen* or "naturalness," where both man and nature are equally enlightened and disclose themselves each in its own original *nature,* is opened up. It is for this reason that, referring to such familiar Buddhist phrases as "All the trees and herbs and lands attain Buddhahood" and "Mountains and rivers and the earth all disclose their *Dharmakāya* [their essential Buddhahood]," I once wrote: "Indeed, unless all the trees and herbs and lands attain Buddhahood together with me, I shall not have attained Buddhahood in the true sense of the word." Here the non-man-centered, cosmological emphasis of Buddhism is very conspicuous.

The non-man-centered nature of Buddhism and its idea of *jinen,* however, do not imply, as is often mistakenly suggested, any denial of the significance of individualized human existence. In fact, it is precisely the other way around: the very act of transcending man-centeredness is possible only to a human being who is fully self-conscious. In other words, without self-consciousness on the part of human existence, it is impossible to go beyond "human" and "living" dimensions and to base one's existence on the "being" dimension. Man alone can be aware of universal transitoriness as such. Accordingly, the fact of transitoriness, common to all beings, is a problem to be solved by him as man. Now this self-consciousness is actualized only in an individual self, in one's *own* self. Further, the problem of birth and death is in its very nature the subjective problem *par excellence* with which everyone must cope alone and by himself. In this sense Buddhism is concerned in the deepest sense with the individual self, with the person, i.e., with man as man.

In Mahāyāna Buddhism, as a preamble to the *Gāthā* "The Threefold Refuge," the following verse is usually recited:

> Hard is it to be born into human life.
> We now live it.
> Difficult is it to hear the teaching of the Buddha,
> We now hear it.
> If we do not deliver ourselves in this present life,
> No hope is there ever to cross the sea of birth and death.
> Let us all together, with the truest heart,
> Take refuge in the Three Treasures!

The first and second lines express the joy of being born in human form during the infinite series of varied transmigrations. The third and fourth lines reveal gratitude for being blessed with the opportunity of meeting with the teaching of the Buddha— something which very rarely happens even among men. Finally the fifth and sixth lines confess to a realization that so long as one exists as a man one can and must awaken to one's own Buddha-nature by practicing the teachings of the Buddha; otherwise one may transmigrate on through *samsāra* endlessly. Herein it can be seen that Buddhism takes human existence in its positive and unique aspect most seriously into consideration. Thus in this sense one may say that Buddhism is also man-centered.

However, for man to transcend his man-centeredness within his own individuality means for him to "die" in the death of his own ego. For only through the death of his own ego is the cosmological dimension, the dimension of *jinen*, opened up to him. And only in that moment does he awaken to his true self—by being enlightened to the reality that nothing in the universe is permanent.

As regards the above discussion, someone may raise this question: Does the doing away with the distinction of birth and death, for instance, in the liberated consciousness actually "do away" with these "realities" themselves? By realizing impermanence as the essence of everything whatsoever, is one thereby freed from its bondage not only psychologically but also ontologically? To answer this question is to be led to the crux of the problem. The "doing away" with the distinction of birth and death means to overcome the dualistic view in which birth and death are understood as two different realities. From what position does one understand birth and death as two different realities? From the standpoint of life or death? Since it is impossible for one really to distinguish life and death as two realities by taking one of the two as one's own standpoint, it must be done from a third position that in some sense transcends both life and death. But such a third position is unreal because it is a conceptualization resulting from looking at life and death from a position external to them. Rather, one comes to reality only by overcoming such a third position and its outcome, i.e., the relative realities of life and death. In this overcoming, realizer and realized are not two but one. Only in this way is Ultimate Reality realized.

Strictly speaking, however, to attain reality one should transcend not only the duality of life and death but also the wider dualities, i.e., the dualities of generation-extinction and appearance-disappearance. Only by transcending the duality of appearance-disappearance, i.e., the duality of being-nonbeing, does one attain reality, because there is no wider duality than that of being-nonbeing. Herein there is no "centrism" of any sort at all and the limitless dimension of transitoriness common to all beings is clearly realized as such. The oneness of realizer and realized is attained only through the realization of this universal transitoriness. Situating one's existence in the boundless dimension of being-nonbeing, one realizes universal transitoriness as the only reality—including oneself in this realization. Reality is realized by the person who has that awareness of reality which is not a psychological, but an ontological awareness: the ontological awareness *par excellence*.

In Buddhism the non-man-centered and cosmological aspect is absolutely inseparable from its existential and personalistic aspect. Indeed, in Buddhism one can be genuinely existential and personal only when one's existence is based on the boundless cosmological dimension that transcends the human dimension. But this cosmological dimension is opened up, not objectively, but subjectively through one's existential realization of absolutely universal transitoriness. And the mediating point, or place of confrontation, of the cosmological and the personal aspects is the death of one's ego.

Buddhist salvation is thus nothing other than an awakening to reality through the death of ego, i.e., the existential realization of the transiency common to all things in the universe, seeing the universe really *as it is*. In this realization one is liberated from undue attachment to things and ego-self, to humanity and world, and is then able to live and work creatively in the world. "Awakening" in Buddhism is never for a single instant ever in the slightest something other than, or separated from, the realization of universal transitoriness. *What is referred to as Buddha-nature in Buddhism and is said to be inherent in everyone and everything, is simply another term for the realization of universal transitoriness, or* jinen, *in which everyone and everything discloses itself as it truly is in itself. And it is from this realization of* jinen *that the Buddhist life of wisdom and compassion begins.*[3]

II

The opening question raised by Father Waldenfels concerning the Buddhist understanding of man and his finitude has, I hope, been answered in the preceding section. "The extension of *shujō* ('sentient beings') to man, animals, and even to all things" should not imply a mere one-dimensional expansion of standpoint beyond the human sphere, but, as stated above, a transcendence of man-centeredness in the direction of the cosmological dimension through the realization of absolutely universal transiency. Moreover, this kind of transcendence can be achieved only by man, who alone of all beings is self-conscious. The transiency common to everything in the universe is clearly apprehended as what it is by man alone through his uniquely subjective realization. In this sense "The extension of *shujō* to man, animals, and even to all things" does not obscure the finitude of man but, on the contrary, makes it clear and unambiguous.

However, Father Waldenfels's question concerning the Buddhist understanding of man's finitude seems to me to be intrinsically related to another important aspect of our subject, viz., the issue of the direction of transcendence in Buddhism and Christianity.

In Christianity man's finitude is realized over against divine justice and divine love. "No human being will be justified in his [God's] sight by works of the law. . . . They are justified by his grace as a gift, through the redemption which is in Christ Jesus, whom God put forward as an expiation by his blood, to be received by faith" (Rom. 3:20, 24-25). Man's finitude is realized in the light of God's righteousness as death, which is "the wages of sin" (Rom. 6:23). Accordingly, faith implies the death of the "old man" as well as the birth of the "new man" in Christ.

Insofar as the death of the human ego is essential to salvation, no distinction can be made between Christian conversion and Buddhist awakening. In Christianity, however, because death is "the wages of sin" it is grasped within the context of man's personalistic and responsible relationship to God; due to his own injustice and sin, man can never be saved by his own efforts but only through faith in Christ as the redeemer, i.e., the incarnation of God.[4] The divine-human relationship in Christianity is thus essentially vertical, with Christ, the mediator, originating in God as the transcendent or supernatural reality. Thus, in the last analysis it is an irreversibly vertical relationship with God as the superior. Even the *unio mystica*, in which the soul of man joins to God in an indescribable experience, is not altogether an exception. And this irreversible relationship between man and God is inseparably bound to man's deep realization of his own finitude.

Viewed from this Christian standpoint, the Buddhist understanding of man's finitude may not appear to be clear enough. For in Buddhism man's death is not seen as the result of "sin" in relation to something transcendent or supernatural, such as divine justice, but only as one instance of that transiency common to all things whatsoever in the universe. Again, because Buddhism emphasizes that everyone can attain Buddha-nature without a mediator, man's finitude seems not to be properly realized.

Does this Buddhist position, however, indicate a failure in its understanding of man's finitude? It is clear that Buddhism, especially its original form, did not admit the supernatural in the form of God as creator, judge, or ruler, of the universe. This is so precisely because Buddhism is convinced that man's finitude is so deep that it cannot be overcome even by the supernatural. Now, this conviction is a pivotal point for Buddhism. And in this connection Buddhists would put this question to Christianity: Is man's finitude a kind of finitude which can be overcome by faith in God? What is the ground for such a faith?

Dependent origination, a basic idea in Buddhism, indicates that there is no irreversible relationship even between man and "God," nature and the supernatural, the secular and the holy. This is especially clear in Mahāyāna Buddhism, which stresses the relationship of *soku* as seen in its familiar formula *"samsāra-soku-nirvāna"* (*samsāra* as it is, is *nirvāna*). Accordingly, "naturalness" or *jinen* is not something merely immanent, nor a counterconcept of the supernatural, but implies the total negation of the supernatural or transcendent. Thus, as I have written before:

> It [naturalness) does not simply mean naturalism as opposed to personalism. . . . The naturalness intended by *jinen* is thought to underlie both the natural and the supernatural, creature and creator, man and God, sentient beings and so-called Buddhas, as their original common basis. In the *jinen* all things, including man, nature, and even the supernatural, are themselves, and as they are.

Only in the realization of this kind of *jinen* can one become a real person, i.e., an awakened one who has compassion and wisdom for all things in the universe.

Christianity transcends man and nature in "God," who, being the God of love and justice, is understood to be supernatural. The Christian loves his neighbor as himself in harmony with the first commandment to love God, who is his savior from sin, with his whole heart. Buddhism, on the other hand, transcends man and nature in the direction of "naturalness" or *jinen*, which is identical with Buddha-nature or suchness. Thus, the "direction" or "location" of transcendence is not the same in Christianity and Buddhism, although the death of the human ego and the realization of the new man are in each case essential to transcendence.

NOTES

1. Hans Waldenfels, "A Critical Appreciation," *Japanese Religions* IV/2 (1966): 23.

2. See also A. Masao, "Dōgen on Buddha-nature," *The Eastern Buddhist* IV/1 (1971): 28-71.

3. Italics added [Ed.].

4. It is interesting to compare this statement with Soga Ryōjin's later remarks. See, below, "Dharmākara Bodhisattva," section VI [Ed.].

11

UEDA SHIZUTERU

"Nothingness" in Meister Eckhart and Zen Buddhism

With Particular Reference to the Borderlands of Philosophy and Theology*

Ueda Shizuteru, born in 1926, has been a disciple of Nishitani Keiji for over fifty years and his successor in the Department of Religion at Kyoto University, thereby assuring the continuation of the Kyoto tradition which began with Nishida Kitarō. After receiving doctorates from Kyoto University and the University of Marburg, he contributed numerous studies in the fields of German mysticism and modern German thought, on Zen Buddhism, and on the philosophy of Nishida, to both Japanese and German journals. He was also a regular speaker at the Eranos Conferences in Ascona, Switzerland. His major work on the mysticism of Meister Eckhart, *Die Gottesgeburt in der Seele und der Durchbruch zur Gottheit*, has been received with particular interest.

I

According to Meister Eckhart, God gives birth to his Son in the solitary soul. "The Father begets me as his Son, as his very same Son. Whatever God works is one. Thus he begets me as his Son without any distinction."[1] The "birth of God in the soul,"[2] spoken of here in the language of the Christian doctrine of the Trinity, is the leap to realization of his own authentic life that man experiences in "solitariness" with the surrender of the ego. "The Father begets me as his Son without any distinction." This means that the absolute event of salvation touches each and every individual in its full originality, without first passing through a mediator. This being the case,

---

* "Nothingness in Meister Eckhart and Zen Buddhism with Particular Reference to the Borderlands of Philosophy and Theology," in *Transzendenz und Immanenz: Philosophie und Theologie in der veränderten Welt*, ed. D. Papenfuss and J. Söring (Berlin, 1977), trans. James W. Heisig.

Eckhart stands very close to Mahāyāna Buddhism, the philosophical-religious base of Zen Buddhism. According to Mahāyāna teaching, the very same awakening to the very same truth transforms each and every individual into the very same Buddha—that is, it makes of each individual the same "Awakened One" that it made of the historical Buddha, Gautama.

So far the similarity is only of a general nature. A more deep-reaching spiritual kinship appears when Eckhart speaks of a "breakthrough to the nothingness of the godhead."[3] "The soul is not content with being a Son of God." "The soul wants to penetrate to the simple ground of God, to the silent desert where not a trace of distinction is to be seen, neither Father nor Son nor Holy Spirit."[4] By carrying out in radical fashion his Neoplatonically laden understanding of "being one," Eckhart transfers the essence or ground of God back beyond the divine God to the simply modeless, formless, unthinkable, and unspeakable purity that he calls, in distinction to God, "godhead" and that he describes as a nothingness. This means that the essence of God is withdrawn from every objectification on the part of man, from every representation. God is divine in turning towards his creatures: for in his essence, beyond the opposition of God and creatures, he is a nothingness pure and simple.

Eckhart's thought exhibits a gradual ascent to this nothingness of the godhead. He begins with statements like "God is good" and "God loves me," which still represent statements of faith. But he goes on to say that "God must be good, God must love me." These represent statements of knowledge, for it is in knowledge that the reason for God's being good is disclosed. Lastly, however, he arrives at the position that "God is not good" (i.e., in his essence). This statement belongs to negative theology, which Eckhart not only pursues in a very radical way but also accords a strongly existential tone.[5]

For Eckhart, the nothingness of the godhead is, in a non-objective manner, the soul's very own ground. Hence the soul, in order to return to its original ground, must break through God and out into the nothingness of the godhead. In so doing the soul must "take leave of God" and "become void of God." This is accomplished only if the soul lets go of itself as what has been united with God. This is what Eckhart understands by extreme "solitariness," the "fundamental death." At the same time, the original source of genuine life that lives of itself and from itself, "without why or wherefore," is thereby disclosed in the ground of the soul, so that the soul now lives from its own ground. Eckhart has the soul speak at this point: "I am neither God nor creature."[6] Here is true freedom, freedom without God, a "godlessness" wherein the nothingness of the godhead, and thus the essence of God, is present. Eckhart's thought draws him here beyond the opposition of theism and atheism, beyond the opposition of personalism and impersonalism.

Eckhart links this "beyond" in the "godless" life directly to the *vita activa* of the everyday reality of the world. In unison with the movement "away from God to the nothingness of the godhead" goes a movement "away from God to the reality of the world." In his exposition of the gospel passage on Mary and Martha (Luke 10:38ff.), Eckhart sees a completeness in Martha at work in the kitchen to take care of the guests that is lacking in Mary who sits at the feet of Jesus and listens to what he has to say,[7] thus inverting the usual interpretation of the story. Martha toils away in the kitchen. In her, the return to the everyday reality of the world is at the same time the real achievement of a breakthrough beyond God to the nothingness of the godhead. For Eckhart, God is present as the nothingness he is in his essence in and as Martha at work in the kitchen. He points the way to overcoming the so-called *unio mystica* and to arriving at a non-religious religiosity.

We may also note the structured dynamic at work in Eckhart's thought here. He proceeds through radical negation back to the ground of essence at its first beginnings, and from there back again to the *vita activa* and to the reality of the world. It is a dynamic that we might describe as a coincidence of negation and affirmation, of nothingness and here-and-now actuality. Here, too, we have Eckhart's solution to the crisis of faith of his time, torn between a radical Aristotelianism on the one hand, and a popular religious movement for the witness of poverty in the apostolic life on the other.

In Zen Buddhism this same coincidence is at stake—except that there negation and affirmation are effected more radically than they are in Eckhart. The radicalness of Zen is evident from the fact that it speaks of nothingness pure and simple, while Eckhart speaks of the nothingness of the godhead. For Eckhart, to say that God is in his essence a nothingness is to treat nothingness merely as the epitome of all negative expressions for the purity of the essence of

God, after the manner of negative theology. Conversely, when Eckhart arrives at affirmation, he does so in the first instance mediately, through God who is the first affirmation. Thus we find him choosing an example like the following: "To one who looks at a stick in the divine light, the stick looks like an angel." Eckhart's affirmation of the stick is not an affirmation of the stick as stick, but of the stick as an angel in the divine light. Zen Buddhism speaks more straightforwardly: "Mountain as mountain, water as water; long, long and short, short."[8]

In Eckhart's thought it is the category of "substance" that is, in the last analysis, definitive. But concomitant with his arrival at, and insistence on, the imageless and formless nature of substance pure and simple, Eckhart advances a radical de-imaging of the soul which is consummated in and as a ceaseless "letting go." This "letting go" accords his teaching its extremely dynamic quality, corresponding to the dynamic of the Zen coincidence of negation and affirmation—except that in Zen, where we see a radical execution of the Mahāyāna Buddhist thinking on relatedness, the scope of this coincidence is wider than it is in Eckhart. This brings us, then, to a discussion of nothingness in Zen Buddhism.

II

Absolute nothingness is concerned with the coincidence of ceaseless negation and straightforward affirmation, such that the coincidence as such is neither negation nor affirmation. In the history of Buddhism, it has been Zen that has given this coincidence a fresh, existential concreteness to cut through the layers of speculation surrounding it. This Zen has achieved by having the concepts of absolute nothingness and the self interpenetrate one another. In a word, we are presented with a nothingness-self—or, one might say, a nothingness viewed as *someone* rather than as *something*. This nothingness-self is presented graphically in a classic Zen text through three pictures dynamically connected to one another.[9] Together they are intended to show the perfection of the Zen way of self-becoming, reached after various stages of the religious life have been left behind, one after the other.

The first picture is in fact not a picture at all, but the mere drawing of an empty circle with nothing inside of it. It points to absolute nothingness functioning "in the first place" as radical negation. The text accompanying this empty circle says of it: "holy, worldly, both vanished without a trace." It gives us a radical neither/nor: neither religious nor worldly, neither immanence nor transcendence, neither subject nor object, neither being nor nothingness. It indicates a fundamental and total negation of every sort of duality, albeit not for the sake of a unity. It is "neither two nor one." It is absolute nothingness.

This is not to say that there is simply nothing at all, but that man needs to be set free of substantializing thought. For Buddhism, everything that is, is in relationship to others, indeed in a reciprocally conditioned relationship. For anything to "be related," therefore, means that in itself it is a nothingness, and that in this nothingness the totality of all relationships is concentrated in a once-and-for-all, unique manner. Corresponding to this coincidence of nothingness and the dynamic of relatedness, Buddhist thought makes frequent use of the typical formula: "It is and likewise it is not. It is not and likewise it is." In the double perspective that this "and likewise" opens up on *a* and *not-a*, Buddhism sees the truth of both being and nothingness. Insight into this "and likewise" of *a* and *not-a* inhibits substantializing thought. For Buddhism, at the core of substantializing thought lies the substantializing of man, which in turn has its roots sunk deep in the ego as such. Ego here means ego-consciousness, the elementary mode of which is expressed as "I am I," or better, "I am I because I am I." This "I am I" that has its ground again in "I am I," and in that way is closed off and sealed up in itself, represents the fundamental perversity of man. In contrast, the true man is able to say of himself, "I am I *and likewise* I am not I." The man of ego, whose egoity reaches even into the realms of religion, must in a basic sense die. As a radical neither/nor, absolute nothingness signifies this "fundamental death" of man.

Now absolute nothingness, the nothingness that dissolves substance-thinking, must not be clung to as nothingness. It must not be taken as a kind of substance, or even as the nihilum of a kind of "minus substance." The important thing is the de-substantializing dynamic of nothingness, the nothingness of nothingness. Put in philosophical terms, it refers to the negation of negation, which entails a pure movement in two directions at the same time: (1) the negation of negation in the sense of a further denial of negation that does not come back around to affirmation but opens up into an endlessly open nothingness; and (2) the negation of negation in the sense of a return to affirmation without any trace of mediation. Absolute nothingness, which first of all functions as radical negation, is maintained as this dynamic coincidence of infinite negation and straightforward affirmation. In this coincidence, and because of it, a fundamental transformation and a complete return—a sort of "death and resurrection"—are achieved in *ex-sistence*.

This brings us to the second picture, where we see merely a tree in flower alongside a river, and nothing else. In the accompanying text we read the words: "Boundlessly flows the river, just as it flows. Red blooms the flower, just as it blooms." It is not a picture of an external, objective landscape; nor even of a metaphorical landscape meant to express an inner condition of man or to project an interior spiritual landscape. It is a picture of reality seen as an actual appearance of the selfless self. Since in absolute nothingness subject and object, which have been split from one another, are returned to their state "prior to the split," so too in our example here, the tree blooming alongside a river is none other than the selfless self. This should not be taken as a statement of the substantial identity of man and nature, but rather as a statement that things like trees in flower—just as they bloom—incarnate the selflessness of man in a nonobjective manner. The blooming of the tree and the flowing of the water are at the same time the self at play in its selfless freedom. Nature "naturing," as in the way trees bloom, represents here the first resurrected body of the selfless self.

The Chinese-Japanese equivalent for the word "nature" properly connotes something like "being so from out of itself." Here nature is not seen in the sense of one realm of beings within the whole of being, but as the truth of the being of beings. If man, in his nothingness and hence not from out of his ego, experiences flowers just as they bloom from out of themselves—or more appropriately put, if flowers actually bloom in the nothingness of man just as they bloom from out of themselves—then at the same time and in the truth of his own being, man makes himself present just as he is from out of himself. Here, grounded in selflessness, we have a particular joining together of the subjective/existential and the objective-factual. Nature, as the "just-as-it-is-from-out-of-itself," is synonymous in Buddhism with truth, whose Sanskrit word is *Tathatā*—literally, "thusness." This "thus" means an unveiling of what is present, and thereby also an elementary confirmation, an original concept of truth prior to the differentiation of the truth of being and the truth of knowledge or propositions.

Next, on the basis of this incarnational reality that confirms selflessness and sustains it, there appears the selfless self which, by its very selflessness, takes the hyphenated "between" of the I-Thou, as its own existential inner realm of activity. The third picture shows us an old man and a youth meeting on a road, but it is not the chance encounter of two different people that is being depicted there. "An old man and a youth" means the selfless self-unfolding of the old man. For the self in its selflessness, whatever happens to the other happens to itself. This communion of common life is the second resurrected body of the selfless self. The self, cut open and disclosed through absolute nothingness, unfolds itself as the "between." I am "I and Thou," and "I and Thou" are I. What we have here is the self seen as a double self grounded on selflessness in nothingness. It is a coincidence—a reciprocal coincidence—of absolute self-sufficiency and absolute dependency, which takes us further than the I-Thou relationship that Buber speaks of.

To review what we have been saying, these three pictures portray a threefold manifestation of the self, at any given moment of which the same reality is fully present in a special way. This same reality, the selfless self, is for its part only fully real insofar as, in a threefold process of transformation, it is able to realize itself on each occasion in a totally different way. Hence the self is never "there," but is at each moment in the process of transformation, now losing every trace of itself in nothingness, now blooming selflessly with the flowers and like one of them, now meeting another and making the encounter into its own self. The nonsubstantiality of the selfless self is evident in the freedom of one aspect to be interchanged with another. It does not portray a permanent identity with itself in itself, but an *ex-static* process of drawing with *ex-sistence* an invisible circle of nothingness-nature-communication. This movement of *ex-sistence* constitutes for the first time the truly selfless self. In so doing, the various aspects of the selfless self are still able to be objectified and depicted in images like those represented in the three pictures referred to, but the process as such, which is the main thing, is never able to be fixed as an object or image. This is also the case with absolute nothingness. When absolute nothingness is spoken of in Zen Buddhism, it is this entire dynamic complex that is meant.[10] Still, we are left with the question: Why speak of merely nothingness then, if it is this entire complex that one has in mind? The answer lies in the nonobjectivity of the process, in its nonsubstantiality, and in the fact that Buddhism locates the decisive moving force of this process in dynamic negation, in the nothingness of nothingness. Man grounds the positive only by means of and as his *ex-sistential* dynamic, at any given moment fully concrete and individual.[11]

III

What is represented in the three pictures just referred to and their accompanying text shifts back and forth, as we have seen, between two different dimensions. We may distinguish *Dimension A*, where what is depicted is actually taking place; and *Dimension B*, where that event is presented, or presents itself, as such. In a word, we must distinguish between the dimension of the event and the dimension of its self-presentation or self-articulation.

Presence (for instance, the presence of flowers in the nothingness of man) occurs on Dimension A, while the phrase, "the presence of flowers in the nothingness of man" (or in its earlier formulation, "flowers bloom just as they bloom from out of themselves") lies on Dimension B where it originates as a self-unfolding of the event to self-clarity in the form of an elemental proposition. Did it not so unfold itself, the event would needs remain a *small* nothingness. Only in that unfolding is the original event signified as a *great* nothingness. Thus nothingness points directly back to the original event where it retracts what had been unfolded. In so doing, however, nothingness does not leave the event to rest in itself but returns it again to its unfolding. Thus nothingness makes an open field for the inter-dimensional process: unfolding *and likewise* the retraction of unfolding, the retraction of unfolding *and likewise* unfolding. Therein lies the supreme paradox *and likewise* no paradox at all, for in the retraction to nothingness the paradox is also retracted.

In this way of looking at how an event unfolds into an elemental proposition, Zen Buddhism, as is its wont, avoids faith propositions. Dimension A deals originally with nothingness. Dimension B unfolds into a treatment of the knowledge of reality as it is. There is no faith proposition involved here, but an elemental proposition in which reality articulates itself, as in the formula, "Flowers bloom just as they bloom from out of themselves" or "Self and other are not two." This state of affairs gives Zen its special significance for philosophy. Already on Dimension B, where in most cases theology is concerned with specific dogmas, Zen is able to "neutralize" itself, so that the elemental propositions it speaks there—despite the difference of dimensions—might be taken as an elemental form of philosophical principle. Of course, it is altogether a matter of individual philosophical initiative whether this is taken into consideration in the quest for principles or not. To clarify this further, however, we must bring into the picture a third dimension, the dimension on which philosophy operates. In so doing, I should like to adopt as my model a work from the early philosophy of Nishida Kitarō (1870-1945), *A Study of Good* (1911).

In his Foreword, Nishida writes: "I would like to try to clarify everything in the light of the claim that pure experience is the only real reality." What unfolds here is a threefold process that in turn represents a manifold of different levels: (1) pure experience, (2) pure experience as the only real reality, and (3) clarifying everything in the light of the claim that pure experience is the only real reality. In connection with this threefold process, we see at work the characteristic relationship found in Nishida between East Asian Zen and Western philosophy. In this relationship there is effected a "transformation of Zen into a philosophical principle." It may also serve as an example of the multidimensional process that belongs to the open field of nothingness.[12] We are not concerned here directly with the content of his statement, but rather with the structure of the process of thought to which it gives expression.

A. Pure experience as event: "In the moment of seeing or hearing prior to reflection—e.g., 'I see a flower'—and prior also to judgment 'This flower is red'—in this moment of actual seeing or hearing, there is neither subject nor object, but only the simple presence that obtains before their split." In this sense, "neither subject nor object" is a nothingness that is nothing other than genuine fullness. This experience immediately experiencing, which for Nishida guarantees the original unity of the empirical, the metaphysical, and the existential, is what he designates as "pure experience" because it has not yet been elaborated by reflection and judgment. For Zen, this pure and simple experience obtains on Dimension A.

B. The context then points to an unfolding on another dimension: "The only real reality is pure experience." Pure experience as an event next arrives at an epistemic realization of what it itself is, and that in the form of an elemental proposition. What we have here is the self-articulation, or the primary articulation, of an event wherein that event *de-cides* itself in an elemental proposition and presents itself at any given moment in its entirety. By itself, this elemental proposition would count as a Zen saying, a saying in which a Zen insight is assigned its initial verbal expression—for instance, "Endless expanse, nothing hidden."

C. Finally, the full context: "I would like to try to clarify everything in the light of the claim that pure experience is the only real reality." Here Nishida directs his method onto a philosophical dimension, to clarify everything (philosophy as the science of the totality) through a single principle (philosophy as the science of principles). Once incarnated into this philosophical context, both pure experience as well as the elemental propositions of knowledge no longer have a distinctive Zen character. In this full context of Dimension C, the phrase "pure experience" is already a philosophical term. Here, "the only real reality is pure experience" is no longer an elemental proposition of knowledge but a philosophical principle, the first principle through which everything is to be clarified. That is why Nishida states his aim as "to clarify everything." In one respect, "everything" has already been grasped on Dimension B. But there, within the self-unfolding of the event A, the unity is the elemental givenness, so that "everything" is grasped concomitantly in its unity in that elementally given unity. The connection of unity, as an elemental givenness, with everything contained therein can also be explicitly unfolded on Dimension B. As the Zen saying has it, "Oneness is everything, everything is oneness." Another Zen saying goes, "In the spring wind, steady and invisible, the long branches with their blossoms are long, and the short branches short, each from out of itself."

Far from being philosophical thought, however, this is more analogous to theology, for which first principles are given in advance as an original source, and for which this original givenness functions as an axiom. But when philosophy seeks to clarify everything, the given is everything in its particularity of manifoldness, distinction, and opposition—for example, nature and spirit, or reflection and intuition—not in an original unity given from the start. To produce for the first time a unified (that is, here, a systematic) clarification of "everything" in its distinction and opposition, and thereby at the same time to seek a first principle, is the task of philosophy. And any possible philosophical principle must be submitted to criticism (the ineluctable self-criticism of philosophy) as to whether or not it clarifies everything in a factually adequate and systematically consequential fashion. As such, this critique can come to no definitive end for the simple reason that everything is inexhaustible in its distinction. In this regard, a philosophical principle that is supposed to have the certainty of self-evidence remains hypothetical within the totality of philosophical thought. Philosophy must be ever prepared for methodical rethinking, for thinking all over again from the start.

Nishida himself faced this point full consciously: "I would like to *try* to clarify everything. . . ." This does not mean, however that for Nishida the realization and upholding of the first principle of knowledge on Dimension B loses its footing. But Nishida knew that an elemental principle does not admit of being taken over directly onto the dimension of philosophy as a first principle, or more precisely put, that the content of a proposition may indeed remain the same while it may change from something unconditionally valid on Dimension B to something hypothetically valid on Dimension C. Zen is aware that it finds itself in a certain foreign element here. If in Nishida Zen succeeds in mediating a principle to the philosophical dimension, it is only hypothetical. In other words, in Nishida, the self-sufficiency of philosophical thought is not encroached upon by Zen. Seen from the standpoint of Zen, Nishida's philosophy *qua* philosophy is a second, indirect articulation of Zen through which Zen transforms itself into a non-Zen so as to make its way into a world that was previously foreign to it.

This threefold complex that unfolds in Nishida's philosophical position contains two different processes moving in opposing directions. *Starting from the standpoint of Zen*, A-B-C represents a movement of unfolding, in the process of which B and C are separated by a gap that Nishida, as a philosopher, was the first in the history of Zen to bridge. *Starting from the standpoint of philosophy*, C-B-A represents a movement of retreat back to the original. In this movement a certain affinity obtains between philosophical principles and the elemental principles of knowledge, and this smoothes the way for philosophical thought into Dimension B, since both are already expressed in propositional form and can therefore be thought out in conceptual terms. In contrast, there is a gap between B and A in this reverse movement of philosophy back to the original, since A is unthinkable and unpreconceivable as an event. In the history of philosophy, Nishida was the first to bridge this gap, that is, to think the unthinkable by means of non-thinking and so to go all the way back to Dimension A in the quest for an original principle. This he did as one engaged in the practice of Zen.

As philosopher, Nishida was at the same time a practicer of Zen; and as practicer of Zen, at the same time a philosopher. In general, philosophy and Zen—crudely put, thinking and non-thinking— stand opposed to one another. This tension, however, became something creative in Nishida through Zen and philosophy bringing one another into question. In the light of Zen, philosophy was made into a question about the origination of principles. In the light of philosophy, Zen was made into a question about the possibility of the project of building a world and the possibility of cultivating a logic. The result of this encounter of East Asian Zen and Western philosophy was the complex, A-B-C, discussed above, with its double mobility in opposing directions. In the last analysis, it is absolute nothingness that for Zen Buddhism throws open a field for A-B-C and its interdimensional mobility. Because of the character of nothingness that belongs to the original event, it can be neutralized on Dimension B, relativized on Dimension C, and likewise be returned once again to Dimension A. And the relationship at work in this encounter is thus different from that which obtains between theology, grounded on its faith propositions, and philosophy.

NOTES

1. *Meister Eckhart: Deutsche Predigten und Traktate*, ed. and trans. by Josef Quint (Munich, 1955), p. 185 (hereafter abbreviated as Q).
2. For an extended treatment of this notion, see S. Ueda, *Die Gottesgeburt in der Seele und der Durchbruch zur Gottheit* (Gütersloh, 1965), pp. 27-97.
3. See Ueda, *Die Gottesgeburt*, pp. 99-139.
4. Q, p. 316.
5. On the relationship of these various statements to one another, see S. Ueda,

"Uber den Sprachgebrauch Meister Eckharts: 'Gott muss . . .'—Ein Beispiel für die Gedankengänge der spekulativen Mystik," in *Glaube, Geist, Geschichte,* Festschrift for Ernst Benz (Leiden, 1967), pp. 266-77.

6. Q, p. 308.

7. Q, Predigt 28, pp. 280ff.; and *Meister Eckhart: Die deutsche Werke,* ed. by Josef Quint and commissioned by the German Research Society (Stuttgart), Vol. III, Predigt 86, pp. 472ff (hereafter abbreviated as DW).

8. See S. Ueda, "Der Zen-Buddhismus als 'Nicht-Mystik'—unter besonderer Berück-sichtigung des Vergleichs zur Mystik Meister Eckharts," in *Transparente Welt,* Festschrift for Jean Gebser (Bern and Stuttgart, 1965), pp. 291-313.

9. Published in English translation by M. H. Trevor as *The Ox and His Herdsman* (Tokyo, 1969). The work comprises a graphic presentation of the progress of man's self-becoming according to the way of Zen through ten stages. Here we are concerned only with the last three.

10. On the theme "nothingness = self," see S. Ueda, "Das Nichts und das Selbst im buddhistischen Denken—Zum west-östlichen Vergleich des Selbstverständnisses des Menschen," *Studia Philosophica,* Annual of the Swiss Philosophical Society, Vol. 34 (1974): 144-61.

11. Concerning this existential dynamic in the light of the three oxherding pictures treated here, see S. Ueda, "Das wahre Selbst—Zum west-östlichen Vergleich des Personbegriffs," in *Fernöstliche Kultur,* Festschrift for Wolf Haenisch (Marburg an der Lahn, 1975), pp. 1-10.

12. See here S. Ueda, "Das denkende Nicht-Denken—'Zen und Philosophie' bei Nishida unter besonderer Berücksichtigung seiner Frühphilosophie der reinen Erfahrung," in *Denkender Glaube,* Festschrift for Carl Heinz Ratschow (Berlin, 1976), pp. 331-41.

12

HISAMATSU SHIN'ICHI

Zen as the Negation of Holiness*

Hisamatsu Shin'ichi (1889-1980) was born in the city of Gifu. He was brought up in the Buddhist atmosphere of the Shin Sect.

He received a doctorate in philosophy from Kyoto Imperial University in 1918. However, his primary concern was a religious rather than a philosophical one. On the advice of his professor, Nishida Kitarō, he started Zen study at Myōshinji Temple under Ikegami Rōshi, and combined this with an intense concentration on Zen classics and Buddhism in general, deeply influenced by his teacher Nishida Kitarō's philosophy.

He became acquainted with Western mysticism—Plotinus, Dionysius the Areopagite, Meister Eckhart, and Jakob Böhme—and studied its relationship to Zen. He also became thoroughly familiar with the works of Kant, Fichte, Schleiermacher, Feuerbach, Windelband, William James, Bergson, Rudolf Otto, Max Scheler, Barth, Heidegger, and Jaspers, and pursued a critical comparative study of these philosophies with Zen. In 1939 he published his book *Oriental Nothingness*, which included an early work *Beyond the Separation of Subject and Object*. This was followed by *The Human Problem Regarding the Awakening of Faith* (1947), *The Spirit of the Tea Ceremony* (1948), *The Way of the Absolute Subject* (collection of theses, 1949), *Man's Authentic Existence* (1951), and *Zen and the Fine Arts* (1958). Among his published lectures and papers are *A Discourse on the Nature of Profound Subtlety* (1949), *On Atheism beyond Atheism* (1949), *The Christian Image of Man and the Buddhist Image of Man* (1949), *Buddhism and the Spiritual Formation of the Japanese People* (1955), *The Religion of Self-Awakening* (1955), and *Zen's Task in the World* (1959).

In 1915 he was appointed professor in the Hanazono University, Kyoto; from 1929 he lectured on religion as a professor at Ryukoku University, Kyoto. He was appointed assistant professor at Kyoto Imperial University in 1937, and taught Buddhism there until his retirement in 1949. In 1944 he started a new religious movement with his students, stressing the oneness

---

* "Zen as the Negation of Holiness," trans. Sally Merrill, *The Eastern Buddhist* X/1 (1977): 1-12.

of religious practice and scholarship in the service of a renewed world order. In 1949 he was appointed lecturer at Otani University, Kyoto, and starting in 1952 he also taught philosophy and religion at the Kyoto College of Fine Arts as well as at Kyūshū University and Bukkyō University, Kyoto. In 1958 he was invited as a visiting professor at Harvard Divinity School to lecture on "Zen and Zen Culture."

Shortly before his death at age ninety-one he returned to Gifu City.

> *All worldly desires have fallen away*
> *and at the same time the meaning of holiness*
> *has become completely empty. Do not linger*
> *where the Buddha dwells. Go quickly past*
> *the place where no Buddha dwells.*
>
> The Ox and His Herdsman, VIII[1]

I

For Kant the term *holiness* had an exclusively ethical connotation. It was the ultimate goal of morality, yet it belonged as a matter of course to some dimension, some ideal perfection of morality not realizable in the actual world. Holiness here assumed a meaning quite distinct from the good that can be actualized. Kant, however, did not pursue the question of holiness to the point where the particularly religious element could be discerned as distinct from the ethical.

Holiness, as a term properly rooted in philosophy and expressive of the religious realm as such, may probably be traced back to the neo-Kantian German philosopher Wilhelm Windelband (1848-1915). For Windelband, however, although holiness had a transcendental constituent, it remained bound up with truth, good, and beauty and had no specific identity or characteristic beyond the realm of moral values.

For Rudolf Otto (1869-1937), author of the *Idea of the Holy*, holiness assumes a meaning which differs in principle from that of Windelband. According to Otto, holiness has its basic form in the *numinous*,[2] a category completely different from that of truth, good, and beauty. The numinous cannot be conceived of in a moral frame of reference. It is not rational *per se*, and cannot be cogitated: it is a nonrational, "absolute other" which has an independent existence.

172

One might say that for Otto holiness is not simply synonymous with the numinous as such, but is a compound category that synthesizes the numinous with rational and especially moral elements. The holy, therefore, is not bereft of moral reference, but neither is it, as it was for Kant, based on morality, or as it was for Windelband, on truth, good, and beauty. In this sense, Otto's holiness, based on the numinous, is of a totally different order from that of Kant and Windelband.

The Swedish theologian and historian of religion Nathan Söderblom (1866-1931) considered holiness not as something purely moral but as something beyond morality, specifically "religious." However, insofar as for Söderblom it still requires a moral perfection unattainable by man, this "religious" finality is still conceived in a moral frame of reference. As such, holiness never comes into its own as a nonrational or superrational category, however much Söderblom sees it as a religious concept and excludes those for whom the holy has no meaning as irreligious.

Although at first glance Söderblom's view of holiness seems akin to that of Otto, on closer examination it differs fundamentally from it. For Otto holiness is a state of human consciousness which is *sui generis* and autonomous, and which cannot be derived from any other form of consciousness. Hence imperfect morality as such does not necessarily conflict with the possibility of holiness.

But even Otto's concept of holiness invites the criticism of being all too humanistic. For it falls short of the concept which dialectical theology has of holiness. Dialectical theology speaks of it as "the divine" or the sacred in the Christian sense of the Holy One, of God. That is to say, in dialectical theology, the holy is never a state of human consciousness. It is something entirely outside of man and has the characteristic of "absolute otherness." For Otto "creature-feeling"[3] is our response to the numinous; and although this numinous seems to be beyond and outside of us, it proves on closer examination to be only a particular state of consciousness within us at the base of our "creature-feeling," awaiting its chance to be evoked. Obviously it is not located beyond and outside of us.

From the point of view of dialectical theology, therefore, Otto's view of holiness is bound to be criticized for its similarity to the immanent sacredness of mysticism. The "divine" of dialectical theology has nothing in common with levels of human consciousness or creaturely feeling. It sees holiness as an objective reality absolutely transcending man: divine holiness. In this respect, the holiness of dialectical theology may be said to grasp religious reality even deeper than Otto's idea of the holy. Although Otto's concept of holiness is nonrational and "absolutely other," it does not transcend man but dwells within him. It may be an immanent nonrationality or Otherness, but it is not a transcendent one.

The nonrational core of the religious, however, has to be grasped in the very quality of transcendence. That Otto was unable to penetrate to this level is due to his psychologism, which is close to that of Schleiermacher and similar to the humanistic approach of Feuerbach and others. The radically transcendent character of the divine cannot be grasped from such a standpoint. For this a perspective similar to that of dialectical theology is needed.

And yet, even though the term *holiness* is interpreted there on a most "religious" level, we believe there exists a point of view which, instead of accepting this, strives for an even higher level of the religious in the very negation of holiness. This is precisely the point of view of Zen. The words in the *Lin-chi lu* ("The Record of Lin-chi"): "When meeting a Buddha, slay the Buddha. When meeting a Patriarch, slay the Patriarch," alludes to the attainment of this highest reach, this ultimate depth.

II

The term *holiness* originally refers to the transcendent. Between holiness and the everyday world of man, there persists an unbridgeable gap, a radical separation. The *divine* of dialectical theology represents the most consistent expression of this separation. Reflecting on the concepts of holiness in Otto, Söderblom, and Windelband, this transcendent, unbridgeable gap would appear to be intrinsic, for without it holiness does not exist. Terms such as Otto's *creature-feeling*, or *absolute otherness* or *mysterium tremendum*, as well as Emil Brunner's *sich verlieren* (self-extinguishing), while not all possessing exactly the same meaning, convey the same notion of a transcendent gap implied by holiness or sacredness.

This gap, however, does not exclude interaction between the holy and man. On the contrary, the gap itself is the link that unites man to this holiness. This is what Otto recognizes in speaking of the quality of *fascinans*[4] in the numinous, and why dialectical theologians paradoxically emphasize that this gap and all this absolute disparity in itself is an approach to, a conjunction with God. This conjunction, however, does not obliterate the distance, the separation from the holy, for the gap itself is the conjunction and the conjunction is the gap. Since gap and conjunction coexist, one might speak here of a *disparate conjunction.*

A religion of holiness is a religion of disparate conjunction. Brunner says that faith is discovering the self in the annihilation of self. Brunner's "extinguishing of self," denotes entering into a disparate conjunction with God. This *sich verlieren* is not, however, the same as the extinguishing of self in the *unio mystica* with the divine. The self that is not extinguished is a self wanting in faith and unable to enter into conjunction with the divine. Only the self-extinguished self—in Zen terms we would speak of a self that becomes *mu* ("no-thing")—may be seen as the true self of faith which enters into conjunction with the divine. This is why Zen concurs that one cannot embrace religious faith unless one becomes *mu.*

The no-thing of mysticism should be strictly distinguished from the no-thing of religious faith. In speaking of extinguishing the self, Brunner states that this extinguished self still exists and remains absolutely separate from the divine. It is not dissolved into the sacred, as is the case in mysticism. Instead, he stresses that only by the extinguishing of self can one come to the realization of this absolute gap, and that it is this realization through which one establishes "unity" with the divine. At this point a deeper religious content becomes apparent in such concepts as holiness, dependence, extinguished self, and faith.

Schleiermacher's *absolute dependence* also indicates the union between the sacred and man, and as such is suggestive of a disparate conjunction. Without a gap, a dependent relation cannot be established. For Schleiermacher the *feeling of freedom* is absolutely negated.

In Buddhism, the Jōdo-Shinshū sect has points of similarity with dialectical theology. It, too, is a religion of disparate conjunction. It absolutely negates the self by extinguishing it and by uniting it with Amida Buddha. This union, however, does not dissolve one into Amida Buddha. Rather by "entrusting oneself" to Amida Buddha, one enters into a relation of absolute dependence, a relation in which there is an absolute gap between the base and evil self on the one hand and Amida Buddha on the other; and nevertheless there is union of the two. This union, as an element essential to holiness, has the gap as its prerequisite. No order of holiness is possible without this separation. Precisely because it is transcendent and separate from us, holiness can be revered, worshiped, trusted, and believed in.

Zen, however, negates this transcendent and objective holiness which is so radically separated from us just as it denies a Buddha existing apart from human beings. As such it is radically nonholy. Retrieving the holy Buddha, so far removed and separate from human beings, it realizes the Buddha within these human beings, a "nonholy," a human Buddha. Searching neither for Buddhas or Gods outside of man, nor for paradise or Pure Lands in other dimensions, Zen advances man as Buddha and actual existence as the Pure Land.

In the *Hsüeh-mai lun* ("On the lineage of Dharma"), a work traditionally attributed to Bodhidharma, we read:

> Being in tremendous turmoil, the unoriented do not know that their own mind is Buddha. They search about, outside of themselves, spending the whole day contemplating the Buddha and paying homage. But where is the Buddha? Do not entertain any such false views. Awaken to your own mind: outside the mind there can be no Buddha.

In the *Platform Sutra of the Sixth Patriarch*:

> The unenlightened person does not understand his own true nature, does not realize the Pure Land in his own body, and thus petitions all over. The enlightened man never differs no matter where he is. For this reason the Buddha says, "Wherever I may be I am always in comfort and bliss. . . . If only your mind is pure, your own nature is itself the Pure Land of the West."

From the very outset, Zen lays the emphasis on man by using words like *self, self-mind, self-nature, original nature, original face, true man, mind-nature, self-Buddha*, and *original-nature-Buddha*. The reason for this lies in a sort of Copernican effort to bring the transcendent objective holiness down to the ground of the human self and to grasp it as the subject of the self. In this regard Lin-chi says:

> The pure light in your single thought—this is the *Dharmakāya* Buddha within your own house. The nondiscriminating light in your single thought—this is the *Sambhogakāya* Buddha within your own

house. The nondifferentiating light in your single thought—this is the *Nirmānakāya* Buddha within your own house. This Threefold Body is you—listening to my discourse right now before my very eyes.

We see from this passage that Zen does not regard the Threefold Body of *Dharmakāya, Sambhogakāya,* and *Nirmānakāya* as something mythological or transcendent, but tries to verify it existentially here and now within one's own body.

In Zen, the traditional thirty-two (or eighty) distinguishing features of the Buddha are regarded as symbolic features of the self, not to be taken literally. In Zen, no Buddha exists outside of the self. There is no Buddha to be worshiped or revered as something separate from one's self. Huang-po says, "If you seek the Buddha outside of yourself and practice Buddhism by attaching yourself to the form of the Buddha, you are on the wrong way and sully the way of awakening." And in the *Hsüeh-mai lun* ("On the Lineage of Dharma") we find the words:

> One's own mind is Buddha, so you should not worship Buddha with Buddha. Even if the distinguishing features of Buddha and the Bodhisattva should suddenly manifest themselves before your eyes, you need not pay homage to them.

Since in Zen objectifying or giving form to Buddha is always cautioned against, there is little interest in making Buddha images. This is one reason Buddhist sculptors are not found among the Zen Patriarchs as they are among the Patriarchs of the Tendai, Shingon, and other Buddhist sects.

Human Buddhas, as in the portraits of *Arhats* and Zen Patriarchs, are more natural to the Zen mentality than transcendent Buddhas like Amida or Mahāvairocana, or the *Devas*. Depictions of the Buddha's body in a mountain scene or as preaching the *Dharma* in a valley stream are preferable to portraits of transcendent paradisical realms such as the Pure Land or to mandalas. For Zen, all is wondrous just as it is: the head big, eyes small, nose vertical, mouth horizontal, mountains towering, valleys plunging deep, birds crying, monkeys gamboling are, as such, mandalas. Ch'an-yueh's *Arhats* and Mu-ch'i's landscapes are Zen paintings. In periods when Zen flourished, in the Sung dynasty, in the latter Kamakura, Muromachi, Momoyama, and up to the beginning of the Tokugawa period, it was not only in painting but also in literature, social etiquette, performing arts, architectural design, crafts, and landscape gardening that expressions of Zen as negating holiness were to be seen. The special characteristics of the culture of these periods, distilled in such words as *wabi, sabi, yūgen*, simplicity or nonconstraint, are qualities rooted in Zen.

Okakura Tenshin[5] regarded *sadō*, the Way of Tea, as an expression of Zen. In his *Book of Tea* he wrote: "The secret of Tea lies in its appreciation of something that is incomplete." The exquisite beauty of Tea, however, lies in the negation of completeness: it is not that, in Okakura's words, "by deliberately not finishing something, one completes it by virtue of one's own imagination." The philosophy of Zen does not consist in that one, as Okakura would have it, "attaches importance to the procedure by which one searches for completeness rather than completeness itself." On the contrary: importance is attached to the *negating of completeness* rather than to completeness itself. Asymmetry and incompleteness in the Way of Tea do not point in the direction of symmetry and completeness. They indicate the self-negation of symmetry and completeness. In the Way of Tea, *sabi* should not be taken in the sense of the rust over something yet to sparkle, but as the extinguished gloss of that which once sparkled.

III

I mentioned Zen as being a religion of "man simply being Buddha," which negates the "holy" and transcendent and does not search for the Buddha separated from or external to man's self. This does not mean, of course, that man in his "usual state" is a Buddha, as is the view of the anthropocentric idealism prevalent in the modern age, or that the Buddha is some idealized form of man. Zen's affirmation of man is not so simplistic. It is precisely the position of Zen to negate absolutely that "usual state" of man. Po-chang Huai-hai emphasizes the need for a great "abandoning" when he says:

> You should first abandon all ties with the world and cease everything. Do not imagine all manner of things as being good or bad, worldy or unworldly. Be not involved in thoughts, and so doing, abandon body and mind.

We see here the radical negation of the "usual state" of man. In this respect Zen and dialectical theology are in agreement that the elements of separation and transcendence are of crucial importance. For Zen, however, the absolute negation of the "usual state" of man does not occur in the stellar distance between God and man, but rather man dissolves in the divine, literally becoming the *unio mystica* himself.

Unlike in dialectical theology, in Zen it is not a union that takes place across the gap of the great separation. It is a union of nondifferentiation, which, being nondualistic, leaves no trace of contradiction. The Buddha and the unenlightened one are thus of one form. Buddha and sentient being are not two. But this does not imply a uniformity in the sense of a Buddha who has form. Lin-chi says that the true Buddha is formless, has neither spatial nor spiritual form. Hence the Sixth Patriarch says:

> The capacity of Mind is vast and great:
> It is like the emptiness of space;
> It has neither breadth nor bounds;
> It is neither square nor round; neither large nor small;
> It is neither blue nor yellow nor red nor white;
> It has neither upper nor lower, long nor short;
> It knows of neither anger nor pleasure; neither right nor wrong; neither good nor evil;
> It is without beginning and without end.

What the Sixth Patriarch calls "mind" in this passage is not different from what Lin-chi calls the "true Buddha." They are merely different names for the same thing. Lin-chi also speaks of a true Buddha as mind-dharma, saying, "the mind-dharma, being formless, penetrates the ten directions." This true Buddha in Zen is referred to by different names and explained in various ways, but it is "the self which eliminates distinctions internally and goes beyond opposition externally." Only then can the self of Zen be characterized as being "formless, penetrating the ten directions," "like empty space," "completely clear: not a single thing to be seen," "the nothing (*mu*) outside the mind, unattainable even inside of it," or "one mind only," "neither born nor extinguished, neither increasing nor decreasing," or "mind in itself is Buddha."

The union of nondifferentiation in Zen is a union of Buddha and man such that the true man as such is not outside the true Buddha even as the true Buddha as such is not outside the true man. The term *union* here points simply to one and the same thing and does not indicate a combined union of two different entities. If there were two entities, they could not possibly be made to combine. But since the true Buddha and the true man are one and the same, it is not a matter of either combination or unification. This is what the Sixth Patriarch spoke of as the "one form *samādhi.*" In Zen, unlike dialectical theology, there is neither a "Thou" to be found in the sense of "all is Thine," nor an "I" that is completely nothing. The "I" of Zen is rather the "all" and stands in contrast to dialectical theology's "I-as-completely-nothing." Although "I" is "all," this "all" is itself "one," as in "all is one." In the "I" of Zen there is no opposition externally, and no discrimination internally, which is why it is called "no-thing." It is what the Sixth Patriarch speaks of as "not a single thing" and Huang-po "like empty space." In the *Pi-yen-lu* ("Blue Cliff Records") it is referred to as "vastness." These are all different expressions for "no-thing" in Zen.

The "no-thing" in Zen could be seen as the "no-thing of mysticism." However, as mere self-negation, the "no-thing" is not really mystical. For if it were to be called mystical, then mysticism would merely be the self-negating element that all religions have in common. Zen, however, much as Western mysticism, is not based on this "no-thing" of mere self-negation. It is based on the "no-thing" of the true Buddha, and as such is not to be considered sheer self-negation.

Neither does Zen present some kind of "deification" of man—a naive figment of the modern imagination—nor does it posit a transcendent God, as does dialectical theology. The critical focus of Zen is the affirmation of the "sacred in man" by retrieving the sacred from the realm of the transcendent and returning it to that of human subjectivity. Zen is not simply a rational position. It is a rational position paradoxically identical with the nonrational. It is not simply an immanent position, but one of transcendental immanence. Zen and Mahāyāna Buddhism must be seen in this light.

NOTES

1. *The Ox and His Herdsman: A Chinese Zen Text,* trans. H. M. Trevor (Tokyo: Hokuseido, 1969), p. 19.

2. Otto coined the term *numinous* from the Latin *numen*, meaning "god," "spirit," "divine," on the analogy of *ominous* from *omen*. In his exploration of the nonrational aspects of religion, Otto used the term *numinous* to refer to the awe-inspiring element of religious experience which "evades precise formulation in words. Like the beauty of a musical composition, it is nonrational and eludes complete conceptual analysis; hence it must be discussed in symbolic terms."

3. In place of Schleiermacher's *absolute dependence*, Otto substituted the term *creature-feeling*, which, in his words, "is itself a first subjective concomitant and effect of another feeling element, which casts it like a shadow, but which in itself indubitably has immediate and primary reference to an object outside of the self."

4. The dual qualities of *mysterium tremendum* and *fascinans* are characteristic of Otto's way of expressing man's encounter with the holy.

5. Okakura Kakuzō (1862-1913), known by his pseudonym Ten-shin, was a reformer of Japanese art in the Meiji era. As curator of the Oriental Department of Boston Museum he was also instrumental in introducing oriental art to the West.

13

TAKEUCHI YOSHINORI

The Philosophy of Nishida[*]

Takeuchi Yoshinori (1913-2002) was born in the industrial city of Yokkai-chi. His father was the priest of the local Jōdo-shinshū temple, but also a famous Sinologist and professor at Tōhoku University in Sendai. The young Takeuchi Yoshinori succeeded his father as priest at the temple in Yokkaichi. After graduating from Kyoto University and studying with Tanabe Hajime, and later with Nishitani Keiji, he became in time a full professor in the Department of Religion of Kyoto University. At the invitation of Friedrich Heiler, he accepted a visiting professorship at the University of Marburg in Germany and also held visiting professorships at Williams College and at Columbia University, where he lectured on Japanese philosophy and on Shinran. His books in Japanese and important articles established his rcputation as a philosopher. His *The Heart of Buddhism*, edited and translated by James W. Heisig, appeared as volume 4 in the Nanzan Studies on Religion and Culture.

I

At the present juncture of history, our world, hitherto divided into East and West, is in a rapid process of integration. Our great prob-lcm in this connection is the failure of spiritual progress to keep up with progress in science and technology. There is still not a little misunderstanding between cultures and ideologies. But I suspect that where there is misunderstanding there is also the possibility of understanding.

Fortunately there is today, both in the West and in the East, a growing interest in the problem of the East-West synthesis. And per-haps it is not unwarranted to seek in the spiritual traditions of the East for something that will contribute to the development of

---

[*] "The Philosophy of Nishida," *Japanese Religions* III/4, pp. 1-32.

183

thought in our contemporary world, a world menaced with dehumanization as a result of technological progress.

Having assimilated various cultural traditions of the East, Japan has developed her own culture. And in our philosophy, attempts have been made to interpret the spirit of the East in terms of modern Western thought. Up to the present, philosophical thinking in Japan has shown more creativity in the field of religious philosophy than in other fields. But it is likely that it will extend the scope of its thinking into all the domains of human culture and try to meet the challenge of cultural problems arising from our contemporary situation. In the West too, there are persons who are seriously concerned with the meaning of Oriental culture. American pioneers in Chinese studies, such as Ezra Pound and Irving Babbit, are men of broad vision who have approached Chinese literature and philosophy not merely with a historical interest, but also with the expectation of finding there something that appeals to the mind of contemporary man, something which can be revivified and reconstructed for the new, wider horizon of the coming age. Here in Japan I have met many a scholarly visitor whose loftiness of spirit has likewise impressed me. On my recent visits to universities in Germany and the United States I could sense that there prevailed everywhere an open-mindedness, which is indeed absolutely necessary for the study of philosophy and culture. I have therefore ventured to attempt here an interpretation of Nishida's philosophy, mainly for the sake of Western readers. It is my hope that it may provide them with an aid to penetrate into the spirit of Oriental-Japanese culture.

Preliminary Remarks

1. The history of Japanese philosophy during the last half century or so may be divided into three periods, each of which is represented by a group of thinkers. First, we have those philosophers who had accomplished their work by the middle of the century. Dr. Suzuki Daisetz belongs to this group though he was still active after that. However, his case is an exception. Generally speaking, the works of the philosophers of this group already belong to history so that a fairly clear-cut outline of their thought may be drawn for appraisal from our present situation. By well-nigh unanimous consensus, the first place of distinction among these philosophers has been assigned to Nishida Kitarō (1870-1945).

Then, there came those who built their structures on the foundations laid by the first group. It is noteworthy that many of them were inspired by the thought of Nishida. They studied it carefully, commented on it—a task difficult even for a Japanese[1]—and applied his philosophical principles to many special problems untouched by Nishida himself. "As Nishida restricted himself rather to the pursuit of basic principles, so the development of the special areas became their work. They developed logic, ethics, aesthetics, and philosophies of religion, history, and science based on his thought," as Professor Shimomura Toratarō says.[2]

It is rather difficult to form a judgment as to the value and merit of their work, because they stand too near to us; proper distance will be required for an objective estimation.

In the third place, there are philosophers of a still younger generation. Some of them came under the influence of Tanabe Hajime (1885-1962), while others are much inspired by Hatano Seiichi (1877-1950). Other philosophical influences, including those of more recent philosophies in Europe and America, are also felt by them. And their thought is still in the process of formation.

2. In the historical context mentioned above, the role and significance of Nishida Kitarō are especially great. It is no exaggeration to say that in him Japan has had the first philosophical genius who knew how to build a system permeated with the spirit of Buddhist meditation, by fully employing the Western method of thinking.

Nishida began his philosophical activity around the turn of the century and was for decades a leading figure in his field. It is hardly possible to talk about Japanese philosophy apart from Nishida's influence. Tanabe was also at first a disciple of Nishida, though he later criticized Nishida's philosophy and through this criticism established his own philosophy. After the death of Nishida, Tanabe became the most notable philosopher not only among those who had learned from Nishida but in the entire philosophical circle in Japan. It may indeed be said that the path of philosophical thinking in Japan was beaten mainly by these two men, who criticized each other through lectures and seminars and through writing. Thus they stimulated each other so that each developed his own philosophy further and more profoundly. Not only did they learn from each other, but they constantly kept abreast with the philosophical trends of the West, thus receiving much incentive to delve further down.

Nishida's Philosophical Pilgrimage

1. Nishida derived his basic insights from his long, concentrated practice of Zen. But he was also much inspired by the philosophy of William James and tried to interpret his own basic insights philosophically with the use of psychological concepts borrowed from James. The opening page of Nishida's *Zen no Kenkyū*[3] ("A Study of Good"), 1911, indicates the general direction of his thought:

> To experience is to know events as they are. It means to cast away completely one's own inner workings, and to know in accordance with the events. Since people usually include some thought when speaking of experience, the word "pure" is here used to signify a condition of true experience itself without the addition of the least thought or reflection. For example, it refers to that moment of seeing a color or hearing a sound which occurs not only before one has added the judgment that this seeing or hearing is related to something external or that one is feeling this sensation, but even before one has judged what color or what sound it is. Thus, pure experience is synonymous with direct experience. When one experiences directly one's conscious state there is as yet neither subject nor object, and knowledge and its object are completely united. This is the purest form of experience.[4]

The concept of pure experience, here expounded, is the Western philosophical mold into which Nishida poured his own religious experience cultivated by his Zen training. As it is beyond the dichotomy of subject and object, so it is far removed from the difference of whole and part. The whole universe is, as it were, crystallized into one's own being. In the *total activity* of one's own pure and alert *life* one's entire being becomes transparent, so that it reflects, as in a mirror, all things as they become and also participates in them. This is "to know in accordance with the events." The profoundness of reality, the directness of one's experience of reality, a dynamic system developing itself in the creative stream of consciousness—these are indeed motifs characteristic of Nishida's philosophy, all suggesting where his thinking was ultimately rooted.

But James was not the only philosopher who influenced Nishida in his initial stage. The impact of Hegel's philosophy was likewise conspicuous, as pointed out by Professor Noda Matao:

> Thus, pure experience comes to cover actually the whole range of knowledge, physical, mathematical, and metaphysical. The "pure-

ness" of it, in part, means ultimately to be free from egocentricity.

Here Nishida's thought is akin to the dialectic of Hegel. Nishida's pure experience proves to be a spontaneously developing totality which includes even reflective thinking as its negative phase, and in the end pure experience is identified with ultimate reality. The title of one of the chapters in his "Study of the Good" characterizes Nishida's position somewhat crudely as "Consciousness Is the Unique Reality."[5]

According to Nishida, judgment is formed by analysis of the intuitive whole. For instance, the judgment that a horse runs is derived from the direct experience of a running horse. The truth of a judgment is grounded on the truth of the original intuitive whole from which the judgment is formed through the dichotomy of subject and predicate or that of subject and object. For the establishment of its truth a judgment is, through its dichotomy itself, referred back to intuition as its source, because intuition is here considered a self-developing whole, similar to Hegel's Notion (*Begriff*). As Hegel says, "All is Notion," or "All is judgment," so could Nishida say, "All (reality) is intuition," or "All reality is immediate consciousness." For this is practically the import of his dictum, "Consciousness Is the Unique Reality."

2. Next came to Nishida the influence of Bergson's philosophy. But he tried to synthesize it with Neo-Kantian philosophy, which was at that time quite prevalent in philosophical circles in Japan. He thus entered the second stage of his thinking, the result of which was incorporated into a book entitled *Jikaku ni okeru chokkan to hansei* ("Intuition and Reflection in Self-Consciousness"), 1917. His basic notion did not undergo any change, but he tried to express what he once called pure experience in a different way.[6] Neo-Kantian influence led him to eliminate from his thought all psychological terms and to follow strictly the path of logical thinking to the end. Actually, however, he found himself standing at the end of a blind alley, where he was met by something impenetrable to his logic. "After a long struggle with the Unknowable my logic itself bade me surrender to the camp of mysticism," so he himself says in effect. Thus the self as the unity of thought and intuition now requires a mystical background. According to Nishida, the self as the unity of thought and intuition is pure activity, similar to Fichte's "pure ego." But the self ultimately finds itself in the abyss of dark-

ness (corresponding to the *Ungrund* or *Urgrund* of Jakob Böhme) enveloping within itself every light of self-consciousness. This darkness, however, is "dazzling obscurity" (cf. Dionysius the Areopagite) giving the self an unfathomable depth of meaning and being. The self is thus haloed with a luminous darkness.

3. The third stage of Nishida's philosophy was marked by a reversal of his whole procedure, as is shown in his *Hataraku mono kara miru mono e* ("From the Acting to the Seeing Self"), 1927. Whereas he had always made the self the starting point for his philosophical thinking, he now parted definitely with transcendental idealism, or rather, broke through it, to find behind it a realm of reality corresponding to his own mystical experience. This may be called the realm of non-self, which should not be confused with Fichte's non-ego as the realm of the objective over against that of the subjective. The "non-self" of Nishida is the ultimate reality where all subject-object cleavage is overcome. In accordance with Buddhist tradition he called it "nothingness" (*mu*),[7] and sought to derive the individual reality of everything in the world, whether it be a thing or a self, from the supreme identity of Nothingness.

The "pure ego" of Fichte, as the universal consciousness or consciousness in general, is still abstract, while the "non-self" of Nishida establishes itself as individuality in the Absolute Nothingness, which includes, not excludes, the individual reality of the thing-in-itself. Indeed, the problem of the individual now became Nishida's chief concern. In his quest for a solution, he made an intensive study of Greek philosophy, especially Plato and Aristotle. He found the thinking of these philosophers to be relatively free from the cleavage of subject and object, in comparison with modern Western philosophy which always presupposes, consciously or unconsciously, the *cogito* as the starting point of thinking. The ontology of Plato and Aristotle rather makes a *logic of reality* reveal itself, a logic which explains the world of reality as seen from within. Whether one calls it "explaining" or "seeing," it is to be understood here as an act taking place in the world of reality itself.

In the judgment *S is P*, the subject denoting an individual or singular substance and the predicate representing a universal concept are joined in unity. But here there is a paradox in that the individual and the universal are, on the one hand, independent of each other, and yet, on the other hand, include each other.[8] How is it possible to reconcile Plato and Aristotle with their different views of the universal and the individual? As a matter of fact, this is precisely the problem taken up by Hegel with regard to dialectics and developed in his *Science of Logic*. According to Hegel, "being" is the truth which makes a judgment possible by joining within itself both the subject and the predicate. "Being," however, is the Notion, which is the universal concept represented by the predicate. In spite of his emphasis on the subject as individual, the whole truth of the judgment is, in the last analysis, absorbed into the act of the universal concept subsuming the individual to itself. In contradistinction to this universalism of the Notion, Nishida seeks to clarify the meaning of the individual from a different viewpoint, viz., from that of Absolute Nothingness. Thus he propounds that Nothingness or *mu* is the universal which is to be sought behind the predicate as a universal concept. He then developed the idea of the "locus of Nothingness" (*mu no basho*), adopting the concept of *topos* from Plato (cf. *Timaeus*) and that of *hypokeimenon* from Aristotle (cf. *Metaphysica*). From this time on Nothingness is explained as the uniqueness of the *locus*.

4. In the fourth stage of the development of his thought, Nishida applied the idea of the locus of Nothingness to the explanation of the historical world. The following account is an attempt to interpret the thought of Nishida as it matured in his later stages.

II

It is clear that the idea of Nothingness is derived from the "intuition" of Zen Buddhism, called "pure experience" by Nishida. In his third stage he suggested a different attitude to be taken toward the real nature of things in contradistinction to that taken by Westerners. It is the attitude of seeing the form of the formless and hearing the voice of the voiceless. This is, according to Nishida, what has been cultivated in the tradition of the East. The following words may be quoted in this connection: "By intuition (or seeing) I mean our way of seeing the being of things in the world, through which we see a being and also our own act of seeing, as a shadow of the Self-reflection of Nothingness—I mean the shadow of the Self-reflection of Nothingness which performs its function by projecting itself on one point within its *locus.*" This may be a thought rather difficult for the Western mind to follow, so I give here some illustrations.

(1) Let us consider the *haiku* of Matsuo Bashō, because the relationship between his *haiku* and Zen Buddhism is particularly noteworthy.

Furu-ike ya	The old pond—
kawazu tobikomu	a frog jumps in;
mizu no oto.	the water sounds.

For the appreciation of this *haiku*, if you imagined yourself to be a frog jumping into the old pond, and making a splashing sound, you would have missed the point. The purport of this short poem is rather to describe the silence that prevails. Bashō always pictures his theme with a touch of vivid action, but only in order to emphasize stillness by contrast—to form a synthesis of both, so to speak. Although the sound made by the frog suddenly, and only for an instant, breaks the tranquility of the place, the latter is all the more heightened thereby.

Of similar import is an old Chinese poem, which may be translated as follows:

A bird gives a cry—the mountains quiet all the more.

A psychological analysis of this experience will show that for the one who has, through the voice of a bird, realized the stillness in the mountains, the voice is felt first as disturbing; then by contrast the first stillness is recollected, and this deepened feeling of stillness prevails in his mind by integrating all the three moments of stillness, voice, and Stillness into one single impression. The voice of the bird here becomes the voice of the stillness itself.

In the light of Nishida's *pure experience* as the truth of experience, from the outset the voice of the bird expresses the feeling of stillness. For the voice of the bird is as a voice, a "shadow of stillness," or rather, a mirror which reflects the quiet mountains. Here the audible thing acquires its existential, i.e., *ex-sistential,* background, from which it appears in a transparent and transfigured form.

Shizukesa-ya	Oh! the stillness—
iwa ni shimi-iru	the voices of the cicadas
semi no koe.	penetrating the rocks.

Here the cicadas, noisy in one sense, are with their voices revealing the voicelessness of the silent whole of the landscape. As the cicadas' chorus, like showers, penetrate the rocks, so the stillness of the place where he stands sinks deep into the heart of Bashō. There he stands still and does not move an inch. Even the slightest movement on his part would be enough to make the cicadas stop at once.

Thus the hearer himself participates in the stillness. One's hearing a bird or a cicada, and one's *existing* there as a bird or a cicada, are one and the same thing, since in the pure experience the reality of a thing includes one's realization of it.

One might think the bird remains the same, both before and after the hearer's presence at the place, thus reducing the feeling of stillness to his private emotion. But this is no way of meeting the bird as an individuum communicating to you the mountain-stillness, nor of meeting anyone whom you may address, "thou." For the compassionate relationship of "I and thou" always implies mutual participation in being. The bird participates in the stillness of the mountains; and the hearer participates in the meeting between the bird's cry and the mountains' silence. This relation of the three, the bird, the hearer, and the mountains, may find an analogy in a national flag which communicates the dignity of the nation represented by it to the person who shares the life and being of it—unless one thinks of a flag merely in terms of its material.

The "objective" way of seeing and hearing does not reveal the true nature of a thing seen or heard. It is rather by self-negation on both the side of the subject and the object that true communication between them is established. On the one hand, the hearing of a voice as an isolated sound is to be negated and, on the other hand, the apparent objective being of a bird is also to be negated. Only in this way, the voice of stillness will be realized on both the side of the subject and the object. Thus a poet opens his eyes in the "place" where the bird he hears is transfigured, and the bird on its part gets its living environment wherein to fly and sing as a true individuum. The poet and the bird, as "I and thou," are joined on the same spot, to exchange words of silence, whereby the stillness of the whole atmosphere is enhanced the more. And now the stillness widens its expanse more and more—into the locus of Nothingness.

Therefore, the appreciation of the above-quoted poems may be made easier by repeating the first lines after the last. Thus:

> Oh! the stillness—
> the voices of the cicadas
> penetrating the rock;
> Oh! the stillness!

> The old pond—
> a frog jumps in;
> the water sounds—
> The old pond!

In this case the description of the scene is itself part of the reality; furthermore, the poet himself belongs to the activity of the locus of Nothingness. The truly dynamic character of Bashō's poems is thus clear. We have already spoken of his synthesis of action and stillness. Its ground may be shown in the following way: (a) On the one hand, the poet who sees and describes the scene belongs to the scene in its entirety: the whole act of description is done from within the scene itself. He himself is the point of self-reflection of the world from within itself, in the Stillness in which he whole-heartedly participates. This Stillness of *sabi*, as Bashō calls it, is the spirit of his *haiku*. (b) On the other hand, stillness is there in contrast with an action in which the poet himself participates. Thus the stillness of the old pond is contrasted with the motion of the frog jumping in. But, at the same time, the stillness and the action work on each other and out of their interaction and interrelation in the deepest dimensions comes the "sound of stillness," the sound of the still water prevailing ripple by ripple over the whole length and breadth of the pond as a wave of voiceless voice. Therefore in the result, the description of a motion may thus be considered as a part of the Stillness itself, and this suggests the idea of *shiori*, another favorite idea of Bashō.[9]

(2) Another example may be taken from Japanese archery. A German philosopher, Herrigel, has written a very telling book on the subject, entitled *Zen in the Art of Archery*. From olden times the

discipline of archery has cultivated an attitude of mind which approaches the serene mind of a sage. If one's arrow doesn't hit the mark, the first thing one should do is to reflect on oneself and to reform one's own attitude instead of looking for the cause of the failure in externals.

In Japan, the beginner in archery learns the use of bow and arrow in front of a simple bundle of straw as target, set three or four feet from him. He must be trained to get his posture right and to keep his mind in good order. After a long preliminary training of this sort, he is then permitted to confront a real target, not yet to aim at it, but simply to acquire the knack of meeting the bull's-eye by intuition. If an archer simply aims at the bull's-eye, there is a chance of his hitting it, but he may also miss it. But if the bull's-eye and the bowman become one so that the arrow by itself arrives at the bull's-eye, he will never miss it. Psychologically this implies a kind of incubation in the subconscious. At any rate, the bowman must forget the fact that he is standing in front of the bull's-eye, to let the arrow leave the bowstring by itself without any effort on his part. This absorption in archery is similar to the self-concentration practiced in Zen. Having mastered the art of archery, Herrigel himself could very well appreciate the quintessence of Zen meditation. As a matter of fact he was the first man who introduced Zen philosophy to the German-speaking world.

Now, according to Rinzai (Chin.: Lin-chi, died 867), the famous Chinese Zen master, a fourfold consideration is needed for enlightenment:

    (a) to let the subject (man) go and the object (environment) remain;
    (b) to let the object go and the subject remain;
    (c) to let both subject and object go;
    (d) to let both subject and object remain.

The meaning of this "fourfold consideration" may be clarified by means of the poems already quoted: (a) In order to hear a bird or cicada as a voiceless voice of the mountain, the ordinary way of hearing and seeing is first to be negated, so that one may participate in the Stillness of the mountain by returning to the depth of one's own being. (b) But, even if one could apprehend the voiceless voice of the bird, thus to be overwhelmed by it—even so, if one could not make a poem to describe it, one's understanding of the Stillness would not be complete. (c) Therefore, the distinction of subject and object should be negated to enable one to return to the common ground of absolute negativity (the locus of Nothingness). And then (d) from there, from the profundity of negation, one will be able to let the thing reappear in absolute Stillness, in which both subject and object stand as they really and truly are.

Or, to take again the example of archery, the man who practices it must (a) reform his own self, (b) then face the target; but (c) in the consummate skill of his art one will have learned to forget both himself and the target. Between the shooter and the bull's-eye something like a magnetic field will thus be prepared, (d) so that the arrow now flies to the bull's-eye as a piece of iron is attracted by a magnet.

This fourfold consideration of Rinzai suggests stages of spiritual development similar to the Hegelian dialectic of *An-sich-sein, Für-sich-sein*, and *An-und für-sich-sein*. In Hegel too, the absolute negativity, which performs its function of negation with respect to both subject and object, has the two aspects of a simple negation (*Vernichtung*) and preservation (*Aufbewahrung*). So it might seem to correspond exactly to the third and fourth stages of Rinzai's dialectic. But the latter should rather be considered a dialectic in locus. It is to be noted here that Hegel also, in his "dialectic in process," presupposes the whole process in its perfection, as it has recently been discussed by Heidegger.[10]

Therefore, the dialectic in locus includes within itself the dialectic in process. But the former surpasses the gradual process, and can reach any stage at any time according as the occasion demands. The difference between them may be compared to that between a teacher and his disciple.

The teacher is he who has already attained his goal and retraces his steps for the benefit of his disciples who are on their way to the goal. For them it is obligatory stage by stage to follow the dialectical process, while the teacher himself is able to attain any point at any time regardless of dialectical sequence. Rinzai's four categories are the master's way of meeting his disciples. "Sometimes I let the subject go and the object remain, sometimes I let the object go . . . , sometimes I let both subject and object go, and sometimes I let both subject and object remain." These words may well indicate that Rinzai had in mind, in contrast to Hegel, a dialectic taking place within the locus of Nothingness, comprehending everything in the world as the topological self-determination of Absolute Nothingness.

With regard to the awakening of the religious consciousness, Kierkegaard, in contrast to Hegel's idea of the continual development of the spirit from immediate sense perception to absolute knowledge, advocated "stages" of life maintaining that from stage to stage a leap intersects the gradual development. It seems, however, that Kierkegaard was all too eager to criticize the immanental dialectic of Hegel, to stop to think what difficulties his own so-called qualitative dialectic might have.

The same problem also emerged in Chinese and Japanese Buddhism in the form of the relation of *ton* (sudden awakening) and *zen* (gradual awakening). Thus, Nishida's dialectic in the locus of Nothingness is to be understood in relation to the essential problem of dialectic in religious awakening.

III

In the fourth stage of his development, the idea of the locus of Nothingness is applied to the explanation of the historical world. Although the basic character of the locus does not undergo any change in this development, yet his method of treatment shows much progress in precision and refinement of expression. About this time, senior philosophers in Japan were being attacked by their younger contemporaries who advocated leftist philosophy. Facing this abrupt change of philosophical climate, Nishida as well as Tanabe found it necessary to restudy Hegel in order to think through the problem of dialectic and to meet the challenge of Marx squarely. Another current of thought, which obliged them to re-examine Hegel, was the dialectical theology of Karl Barth.

Dilthey's philosophy of history, with its hermeneutic method, also influenced them. Thus their philosophical interest now shifted from epistemological and metaphysical problems to those of history and society. How was Nishida to proceed in this new field with his "topology" of Nothingness?

For an explanation of Nishida's mature thought, it is necessary to direct attention to the three key ideas developed in succession during this stage of his thought (1930-1945): (a) the Eternal Now, (b) action-intuition, (c) the historical world as an identity of contradictories.

(A) *The Eternal Now*

The "topos" character of Nothingness becomes clear, when we consider the concept of the Eternal Now. The being of every thing in the world has its presence in time. Presence in time means being in the present, in contrast to the past and the future. In the present, one is aware of one's self as an *individuum*. This way of being present in time, where one's entire being, both self-consciousness and freedom included, and the being of other things in the world are involved, is a fact of immediacy, from which one starts one's search for truth. (a) But this kind of presence is momentary and therefore transitory: "It appears to be, only to disappear, and disappears, only to let a new present appear." Being and non-being are mixed in their very structure. The present, therefore, is a unity of contradictory moments. Further, (b) although it is momentary, the present envelops the whole succession of the temporal order, because past, present, and future, all belong to the present. As St. Augustine said in his *Confessions*, "The past is the present of the past, the present is the present of the present, and the future is the present of the future." All of them are measured from the standard of the present, without which we could never understand their meaning. So the infinite series of moments in the temporal order from the incalculable past to the incalculable future, depends on the momentary present of "here and now." The present is the monad of time which represents in itself the infinite span of past-present-future, although itself belongs to this series as an infinitesimal part of the whole. (c) It follows that the present determines itself. It is the present of the present. From this center of "self-determination of the present," time flows—it flows, as it were, from the present to the present. This is an evidence of the immediate self-consciousness. It is a fact of man's being and sense of freedom. But man's consciousness of being and freedom is closely bound up with the sense of his transiency—we are those "whose names are written in the water." (d) On the other hand, the infinite time series, though not to be identified with Eternity itself, must nevertheless be regarded as representing one of its essential qualities. How is it then possible that the transient moment, the infinitesimal atom of time, should include in itself a property of Eternity?

According to Nishida, it is because the present is rooted in the Eternal, insofar as the Eternal is another name for the locus of

Nothingness. It reflects itself, and the focus of its self-reflection is the present of the present. The rectilineal reckoning of time may be compared to the rutted road as the wheel of the "topological" world-whole turns around, i.e., as the locus determines itself. Thus into the present itself, as well as into the past-present-future series, the Eternal projects itself. The clarification in this way of the character of the present, as the center of the "topological" self-determination, is a most important contribution made by Nishida to our understanding of time. That the present is Eternity is not to be understood in the mystical sense, in which time is, as it were, a running horse, while the present is its saddle, so that only by sitting in the saddle of *nunc stans*, can one realize the eternity of the present. Nishida's conception of time is more dialectical. To him, the present and Eternity are in contradictory opposition to each other, on the one hand; while, on the other hand, the one may be regarded as the same as the other, seeing that they are related to each other through their ultimate self-identity. These two points need further explanation:

(a) The relation of the present and Eternity is not simple identity; from the present there is no road leading to the Absolute (Eternity). On the contrary, the whole series of time, to say nothing of the transient present instant, is a mere nothing in the face of Eternity. (b) But Eternity, as the locus of Nothingness, envelops within itself every individual instant, giving life to it. Eternity establishes the instant as a true (independent and self-determining) *individuum*, i.e., as the present. Therefore, Eternity and the present are related to each other in a relation of disjunctional conjunction (or conjunctional disjunction).

This means that Eternity is reflected in the present, while at the same time, the present itself is reflected in the mirror of Eternity. If the meaning of Eternity is sought objectively, not a trace of it will be found. There will be nothing but a stream of time. For time and Eternity are as far apart from each other as the sky in the clearest moonlight is from the stream below. But to the one who rows along the stream, every ripple reflects the moon, every moment reflecting the light of Eternity. But Eternity, in its turn, reflects in its mirror every instant of time. All the monads are included in the world (Leibniz); as Nishida interprets it, this means that the world reflects in itself all the monads within it. All things in the world do not pass into the past (non-existence) in vain. They are all recollected by

Eternity. Thus the being "whose name is written in the water" is at the same time the one "who is registered in the presence of Eternity."

Bergson and more recently an American philosopher, Professor Charles Harthshorne, also think that all the events of the past are restored in a metaphysical remembrance.[11] It seems that Nishida thought through the problem more radically: not only the events of the past, but also those which will happen in the future, are all reflected in the mirror of Eternity. They are all present in the Eternal Now.

As the independent, self-determining *individua* relate to each other in the self-determination of the locus of Nothingness, so one self-determining present relates to another in the self-determination of Eternity, which is the locus. Every present moment is an independent monad of time. But all the moments of time put together form the continual time series of past-present-future. The linear time is made up of the instants in their "disjunctional conjunction." Time is thus a "continuity in discontinuity." Each instant leaping into the next is thereby interwoven into the creative synthesis of the Eternal Now, and the past-present-future time is now a trace left by the Creative Now.

Furthermore, time, as a linear trace of Eternity, has two contrary directions. In the direction from the past through the present to the future, there develops a world of cause and effect. It is the physical world, where the past determines with necessity the future. In the biological world, where the individual living being obtains significance, time moves in the reverse direction: from the future through the present into the past. This is the teleological mode of time in contrast to the causal one. The Eternal Now itself, however, as the synthesis of those opposite directions, runs from the present. There the time-stream from the past and the time-stream from the future meet with each other so as to make an infinite circle. Of course this is only another shadow of the Creative Now, just as linear time is only a trace of it.

The Creative Now is a synthesis not only in time but also in *space*. So let us now consider its temporal synthesis in space. As we have seen, every present moment is the present of an individual life. But the present in its proper sense must be considered as the present of world history. So the present of the world, refracting itself into the myriads of individual lifetimes (present moments), gathers these, at the same time, into the original unity of time, the present of world history.

For according to Nishida, the world is in itself the self-reflecting living being in which all the individuals are comprehended. The world is the body of the Eternal Self, or rather, Non-Self, as the individual existence in the body is the manifestation or embodiment of the individual self.

Now, every present moment is a monad of time. It re-collects (re-assembles) as the present instant all the instants of "past-present-future" into the "topological" field. And every instant, as a reflection of Eternity, is unique and independent. So apart from the linear time order, there must also be a temporal synthesis in *space* at every present moment. Joining the ends of the past and the future, time forms an infinite circle in the locus of Nothingness, where all the instants are situated in the center, because the circle is infinitely large. Therefore, every present has the character of a temporal synthesis in space. And the present of world history, refracting itself into the myriads of present moments of individual lives in the world, shows exactly the same structure, whether as the present of the whole or as that of the individual. The world and the individual, the present of world history and the present correspond to each other as macrocosm to microcosm.

Thus time is determined in two ways, linear and circular (spatial). These two different dimensions of time are interwoven at every moment, whether of individual life or of the world.

Nishida's consideration of this problem is many-sided but his central idea in this regard is the "disjunctional conjunction" between Eternity and the present. He often quotes the verse by Daitō Kokushi (1282-1337), a famous Zen master in Japan:

> From eternity to eternity Buddha (the Absolute) and I (the relative) are separated from each other, yet, at the same time he and I do not fall apart even for a single moment.
> All day long Buddha and I live facing each other, yet he and I have never a chance to meet each other.

To Nishida God is *deus absconditus* and *deus revelatus* at the same time. Here is the same dialectical relation as obtaining between Eternity and the present. The present, while representing in its essence the character of Eternity, yet is, as momentary moment, set free from the Eternal. In its momentariness it acts creatively at every instant, and in the creative act of every independent instant is the revelation of Eternity itself.

(B) *Action-intuition*

According to Nishida, not only the memory of the whole past but also of the whole future is stored in the Eternal Now. Does this not, even against his will, mean fatalism?

By asking this question one is duly introduced to the idea of "action-intuition." The past-present-future line of time is found in the world of cause and effect. The cause is that which determines the result unconditionally, and the law of causality prevails in the whole physical world. Strictly speaking, modern physics has begun to reveal another aspect of this problem which comes near to Nishida's consideration of the historical world.[12] But here only the classical theory of physics is to be considered. The universal validity of the law of causality is established by reason. It is the rational belief of man that nothing in the world occurs without sufficient causal ground. A teleological worldview will not change the matter completely. Teleologically, time runs from the future through the present into the past. It is also through reason that this scheme of time-order is established in the world. Praising the work of human reason, Hegel spoke to the following effect: By reason it is known that in nature the law of gravity prevails. Things are forced to go down. But by this force also, a heavy stone can be raised. For instance, the pillars of a gate sustain a stone-beam aloft against the force of gravity. Thus reason can convert the force of nature by obeying nature's own law.

The teleological world with its future-present-past scheme of time reverses the order of the physical world with its past-present-future scheme of time. Nevertheless, the causal and teleological points of view have this in common, that they consider the world objectively, i.e., from outside the world and time, as if the observer himself did not belong to it. This is natural, because reason itself does not belong in the world of time, contemplating its objects *sub specie aeternitatis*. It undergoes neither birth nor death. From eternity to eternity, reason remains the same, while human beings are transient always existing under the contradiction between Eternity and the present.

In the inanimate world, understood in the above sense, freedom and necessity are combined in such a way that the *telos* presides over the physical nature only in a formal way. The future-present-past scheme of time does not yet truly meet with the past-present-future scheme. But in the biological world teleology in the proper sense of the term may be more fully recognized. There teleological time becomes the living principle working from within the biological process. There, according to Nishida, time breaks through physical space at many points, forming, so to speak, curvature in various ways, and thus producing multifarious species. As Rilke reported in a letter to a friend of his that bulbs in his garden had pierced the surface of the globe on that day, so for Nishida the shooting of buds is a symbol of teleological time crossing the physical world per-pendicularly and forming itself into species. By the resistance of space, time is obliged to take various winding roads so as to make special visible forms (*species*) appear. The curvature of time into species may be compared to swellings in a body of water contingent on disturbances on the water's surface.

Thus in the biological world time is encased in space and refracts itself into a myriad of individual life-forms. There individuals are the ultimate; they do not come to be from species or genus or uni-versal concepts. As Aristotle said, "a man from a man"—an individ-ual comes to be only from another individual of the same species. In this creative relation of "from individual to individual," one may presage Nishida's existential category of the historical world: "from the created to the creative." But in the biological world the Creative Now is still treading the ground without marching. Only in a truly creative Synthesis will it be able to go forward.

Nishida insists that the world, whether biological or historical, should be seen from within itself, so that the very act of seeing may be a happening in the world. Thus a historical consideration *belongs in* history; it must be a consideration undertaken from within histo-ry. What a historian can do for his part, in this consideration, is to contribute a bucket of water into the tide of time (Toynbee). Here a viewpoint is taken which is qualitatively different from both the causal and the teleological. In the historical world necessity also pre-vails, but it is neither the necessity of causality nor that of teleology but the necessity of destiny and death. And here the self-conscious-ness of destiny, death, sin, fundamental ignorance (*avidyā*), etc. has a dialectic character, so that the present, afflicted with its fragile transiency and with the consciousness of man's bottomless nothingness, is converted into the blessing of participation in the Absolute (Nothingness), or into the Absolute in disjunctional conjunction.

A fact in the world is, according to Nishida, always an event in the sense of *Tat-sache*. It is at once an act and a happening in the world. "We are creative elements in the creative world," says Nishida. Notwithstanding destiny, death, sin, and ignorance; notwithstanding human struggles, social evils, injustices, wars, and catastrophes; with all its darkness, the world is still, in its true reality, the creative Synthesis and also the sacred result of this Synthesis. Time runs infinitely from eternity to eternity. But at every moment (instant) time is confronted with its beginning and with its end. It would be justifiable to say that time is redeemed by the incarnation of the Eternity in the instant, which is a point of time and yet, in its true nature, stands outside of time. All events, present, past, and future, are results of the creative Synthesis of the Eternal Now. As such they are recorded in the memory of it.

Now we have virtually treated the problem of action-intuition according to the pattern which we discussed in connection with archery and *haiku*. As the bull's-eye and the archer, or rather, his act of shooting and his seeing the bull's-eye, become one, the event of arrow-shooting takes place as a self-determination of the animated field of intense "magnetic" direction (i.e., the self-determination of the distance). Therefore, the event itself may be said to be the self-concentrated expression of this field—the shooter, himself a part of the event, being nothing but a self-conscious focus of it. The event as a self-reflection of the world attains self-consciousness in the disciplined mind of the archer. Bashō's *haiku*, his making the poem and being moved to it by the scene itself, will perhaps provide a better example of seeing and acting in dialectical unity (action-intuition). Here, the frog becomes one with the poet, and in this frog-poet event the Stillness of the whole scene expresses itself. So pregnant and suggestive is his *haiku*: it not only communicates to others the innermost heart of the poet; it also communicates the heart of the author to the author himself. And the Stillness here expressed acquires its depth as the poem resonates within itself. For it includes both the act of seeing and that of composing in their reciprocity so that their meaning is more and more deepened.

Through this reciprocal process of seeing ←→ acting (composing),
the heart of the author becomes transparent and lets a poem crys-
tallize itself. To the one who with concentration examines a sap-
phire, a moment suddenly comes when the inner world of the small
gem reveals itself. The admirer's sight now penetrates deep through
its surface, therein to find the blue sky in its infinite depth and
breadth. In the same way, the very compact expression of a *haiku*,
will introduce one to the depth of the poet's heart. The poet is the
focus of the field wherein the whole Stillness of a landscape is completely concentrated. Therefore he may be called "a creative element of the creative world."

According to Nishida, action-intuition is the structure and
dynamics of all creative activity. When a sculptor carves a statue, he
sees its form anew at each attack of his chisel. The seeing of the
form thus induces him to further chiselling. This reciprocal process
of acting ←→ seeing, in the dynamic unity of action-intuition, is repeated to the end of his work. Further, when it is completed, it may
inspire him and even urge him to undertake another piece. A work
of art, especially a masterpiece, acquires existence and dignity of its
own so that it may be admired even by the artist himself. As soon as
it leaves his hand, its own career in the world is started. Thus it is
from his seeing that the artist receives his urge to creation. It determines his work and thereby in a new way carves out his career as
well. Here again the same reciprocal relation of seeing ←→ making
may be noted. Nishida in his later years often used the phrase "from
the created to the creative," to express the character of the creative
function of intuition-action. This reverses the ordinary conception
of artistic work, which moves from the creative to the created, but
Nishida's formula seems to explain creative activity in a far more
adequate way. For any creation through human action becomes possible only if the self-reflecting world expresses itself in a human
being, and he on his part expresses himself as he sees his own reflection in the mirror of the world, both of them together performing
their creative Synthesis in the historical world. Nishida thinks that
his formula is near to T. S. Eliot's conception of "tradition" as the
historical force transmitting and creating civilization for the coming
age.

A way of thinking akin to Nishida's is found in the recent development of Heidegger's philosophy, although there was no direct
influence either way. In his essays on "Things" (*Das Ding*) and

"Building, Dwelling, and Thinking" (*Bauen, Wohnen, Denken*), Heidegger uses the pregnant symbol of the "four-together." This is a square in which *earth, heaven, divinities,* and *mortals* are gathered together. The present age has forgotten this original unity of the four and has, accordingly, become "materialized." The present age is called "atomic," but this name is ominous, because it is for the first time in history that an age has been named by those who belong to it after a phenomenon of physical nature. Due to the remarkable progress of science, the present world has practically overcome distance in time and space. Far-away occurrences may be seen and heard as if they were taking place here. Things in the remote past and in the remote future may be controlled by the human brain and action; and, of course, the stars and their orbits are being exactly observed and measured. But do the things really become so much nearer to us? Removal of physical distance does not necessarily result in the nearness of things. On the contrary, things are becoming more and more remote through their very proximity to man of the present age.

How does this uncanny problem arise? Solely by forgetting the Truth of beings and by treating beings merely as objects. Here Heidegger's philosophy of Being meets with a philosophy of Nothingness—because Being and Nothingness are identical in their contradiction.

A bridge across a river joins the parts of land on both sides of the river. But their respective landscapes may still retain their characteristics in spite of their union by means of the bridge. Thus the two landscapes (the earth) as well as the people (the mortals) who dwell there are joined together at the bridge, as a point of their concentration. But, not only the earth and people come together in the building of the bridge. The heavens also participate in the work. For the climate and weather of the locality have much to do with the construction. If due consideration is not given to these factors, the bridge might be washed away by the swelling waters. In fact, the bridge lets flow not only the stream of water under it, but also the meteorological streams across it. Thus earth, people, and heaven come together in concentration for the building of the bridge. Further, the grace of divinities is also at work there, and this to the extent that the enterprise is a human undertaking. From ancient times a bridge has been a sacred thing, symbolizing in its structure the being of man as a bridge from this side over to the Other-side, to be fulfilled through the grace of the Beyond.

Therefore, a bridge is a "thing" in which the four parties of heaven, earth, mortals, and divinities join together. As to the location of the bridge, of course, one particular point of the river is chosen, out of the many possibilities, for the concentration of the four factors. It is through human decision that the choice is to be made, with due consideration of the advantages and disadvantages of the place. Only then is the task of construction to be accomplished. Seeing and acting are thus a matter of human responsibility. And a bridge actually built in this way is a "thing" in its proper sense. As in the cases of the "poet-frog," or the "bull's-eye-archer," the "thing" here is an event, or a ring into which the whole world is concentrated and reflected. The "thing" is, according to Heidegger, the interplay of these four factors mirroring each other, and the unity of this interplay is the world as it turns around historically. The "thing" can exist only through human participation in it. And this human participation is man's "dwelling" in so far as he actually realizes and builds it. *Bauen* ("to build") is in its original meaning (Old High German, *buan*) the same as *wohnen* ("to dwell") and, furthermore, *bauen* (*buan*) comes from the root common to *buan*, *bhu*, *beo*, which means "to be," as it is still clear in the forms of *ich bin, du bist.*

This suggests that originally man's being is his dwelling, and his dwelling is his building a "thing" in his nearness to the truth of the thing, insofar as man is a mortal living on earth, under heaven, and by the grace of divinities. But man has lost his dwelling, and is estranged from divine grace. He now finds himself in the night of the world. The Truth of beings is now concealed from him, and it is for this very reason that beings in their sheer objectivity alone are so clear and self-evident to his consciousness. Seeing is now seeing an object in its objectivity, and even one's own self is thought of in an objective way.

Heidegger says that it was through intuition accomplishing a work of art that Plato realized the pure essence (*eidos*) of a thing. Here the subject and object are still yoked together, in contrast to the modern objectivization of thinking and seeing. Nonetheless Plato's *eidos* is objective in the sense that it is conceived after the pattern of making a thing by technical means.[13] Therefore, in order to recollect the nearness of the "thing," one must search further back in earlier Greek philosophy.

Now it is necessary to define carefully the terms "seeing" and "intuition." (a) To "see" a thing means usually to see a thing in a particular space-time locus: one sees a thing somewhere and sometime. Seeing in this sense is the first stage of discerning an object. (b) "Intuition" is immediate perception of an object. It is neither *cognition* nor *recognition*, and is reached neither by inference nor by recollection. In this sense, it may not be very different from "seeing." (c) But more technically, "intuition" is direct knowledge of the truth, or of the whole of the thing in question. For the sake of clarity, let us use the term "intuition" here in the latter sense only. Thus, it is not through seeing these roses in the garden, but by judging that they are white that one is concerned with the problem of truth. On the other hand, intuition belongs to the realm of truth from the very start, although it is also a direct perception.

However, Nishida uses the word "seeing" in the sense of "intuition" as defined under (c). According to him, it is related to "acting" and "making." Although it is immediate, "seeing" presupposes training and comes to perfection only after adequate training. The beginner sees the bull's-eye in a way qualitatively different from that of the master. Likewise, the same roses in a garden may be seen quite differently by various people. If an artist sees them, his "seeing" will soon develop into a painting. In making the painting he is so absorbed in seeing and acting that he forgets himself completely. He sees and acts as if it were not himself, but the roses themselves manifesting their true being. In his essays Nishida often speaks about "seeing without an observer," "acting without an agent," or "seeing and acting on a thing by losing oneself in its being." Referring to Dōgen (1200-1253), a Japanese Zen master, Nishida explains the quintessence of action-intuition as follows:

> To learn the way to Buddha is to learn the true Self. To learn the true Self is to forget it. To forget the Self is to bear witness to the Truth of all things in the world insofar as they reveal themselves. To do so, we must learn to loose the fetters of "mind-body" of ourselves as well as of others. It is illusion to think that we can learn and confirm the Truth through our effort of transporting our selves to things. In the Buddhist Enlightenment, all things of their own accord testify as self-evident (in the mirror of the Non-Self) that they themselves are the way and the truth of Buddha.

Here assuredly, is the whole of the situation,—seeing-acting, object, and its environment—subsisting all at once. To see a "thing" is to participate in the ring of these elements in the locus of Nothingness. Seeing is within the interplay of these elements' mirroring of each other. Therefore, seeing, at every stage of making, is in itself an intuition of the whole.[14]

NOTES

1. In preparing this article I myself owe much to those interpreters of Nishida's philosophy.

2. Shimomura Toratarō, *Nishida Kitarō and Some Aspects of His Philosophical Thought*, as quoted by V. H. Viglielmo in his translation of Nishida's *A Study of Good* (Tokyo, 1960), p. 199.

3. There is no relation between the following words, pronounced the same way but written with different characters: *zen*, the good; *zen* of Zen Buddhism; and *zen* meaning gradual.

4. Nishida, *A Study of Good*, p. 1.

5. Noda, "East-West Synthesis in Kitarō Nishida," *Philosophy East and West* IV/4 (1955): 347.

6. Nishida himself, even in his old age, maintained that the concept of pure experience remained basic throughout his works, although the expression of it had undergone revision and remolding.

7. Personally I would prefer "non-being" as an equivalent for *mu*. But "nothingness" is more commonly used in this sense. Wherever I use the latter term, I do so simply following current usage in English.

8. With Aristotle, Nishida defines the individual as the substance which is always the logical subject and can never be reduced to the predicate. He maintains that if we try to determine the individual substance by a universal concept, we shall never arrive at the goal even by an *ad infinitum* repetition of specifying the universal by successive delimitations of the general concept. Therefore, the individual is rather to be defined as something which determines itself by itself. In the very concept of "Caesar" his crossing the Rubicon may be said to be predestined (cf. Leibnitz, *Discourse on Metaphysics*). Thus in the concept of the individual all of its predicates, i.e., all of the universal concepts that can be predicated of it, are to be considered as included. In this sense, then, *the individual determines the universal.* On the other hand, however, the universal must be considered independent from the singular or the individual (Plato). There is indeed a qualitative difference between the universal and the individual. From this angle, it may be said that the truth of a judgment depends upon the predicated universal. The universal cannot be determined by anything else, therefore it should be considered as determining itself by itself. The individual is, in this sense, a specimen of the general concept. In other words, *the individual is subsumed to the universal.*

9. Cf. Komiya, *A Study of Bashō*; chap. II, "On *Sabi* and *Shiori.*"

10. Cf. *Identität und Differenz,* p. 38.

11. Otherwise, it would be impossible to explain our daily experience of recollection, according to Nishida.

12. Nishida interprets the operationism of Bridgman in the following way: "Bridgman says that the basic concepts of physics have hitherto been defined, apart from the physical operation, as some qualities of things, as in the case of Newtonian absolute time. In line with Bridgman, I (Nishida) think that philosophy has hitherto conceived the structure of the objective world in an abstract manner, apart from our formative activity (*poēsis*) in the historical world. . . . The content of the philosophical principle that is truly concrete should be given from the operational standpoint. In respect to all abstraction and analysis it should be specified from what standpoint and in what way they are performed," translated by Prof. Noda in his "East-West Synthesis in Kitarō Nishida," p. 356.

13. Heidegger, *Vorträge und Aufsätze,* pp. 11ff.

14. The article breaks off here rather abruptly, without developing the third theme of the historical world as an identity of contradictories which had been announced at the outset of section III. Professor Takeuchi had intended to write a sequel to this essay, but his plans were never realized. [Ed.]

14

ABE MASAO

Emptiness is Suchness[*]

The apparent simplicity and lightness of tone of this piece should not keep the reader from reflecting on the clarity of Professor Abe's pointing at fundamental differences between the Christian and Buddhist world views.

Buddhists emphasize "emptiness" and say that everything is empty. While this is a very important point for Buddhism in general and for Zen in particular, I am afraid that it is quite misleading, or at least very difficult to understand, particularly for the Western mind. I think that "Everything is empty" may be more adequately rendered in this way: "Everything is just as it is." A pine tree is a pine tree, a bamboo is a bamboo, a dog is a dog, a cat is a cat, you are you, I am I, she is she. Everything is different from everything else. And yet, so long as one and everything retain their uniqueness and particularity, they are free from conflict among themselves. This is the meaning of the saying that everything is empty.

A pine tree has no sense of superiority over bamboo; bamboo has no sense of inferiority to a pine tree. A dog has no sense of superiority over a cat, a cat no sense of inferiority to a dog. We human beings may think that plants and animals entertain such thoughts, but this is merely a projection of human capacities onto the non-human dimension. In fact, plants and animals do not have such a mode of consciousness; they just live naturally, without any sense of evaluation. But human beings are different: we often think of ourselves in comparison to others. Why is he so intelligent? Why am I not as gifted? Why is she so beautiful? Why am I not as beautiful? Some feel superior to others while some feel inferior.

This is because, unlike plants and animals, we human beings possess self-consciousness, and because we are self-conscious we look at ourselves from the outside, through comparison with others.

* "Emptiness Is Suchness," *The Eastern Buddhist* XI/2 (1978): 32-36.

Although we are "self," we are not really "self," because it is from the outside that we look at ourselves. In our daily life, there are moments when we are "here" with ourselves—moments in which we feel a vague sense of unity. But at other moments we find ourselves "there"—looking at ourselves from the outside.

We fluctuate between here and there from moment to moment: homeless, without any place to settle. Within ourselves there is always a breach. On the other hand, plants and animals are just as they are because they have no self-consciousness; they cannot look at themselves from the outside. This is the essential difference between human beings and other living beings.

This characteristic of human beings has a positive aspect. Since we have self-consciousness and are always thinking of something, we can plan, reflect, conceive ideals, and can thus create human culture, science, art, and so forth. As we live, we are all the while thinking how to live, how to develop our lives. This positive aspect, however, is at the same time somewhat problematic, because, as I mentioned above, by means of self-consciousness we look at ourselves from the outside. We are thus separated from ourselves. We are here and there, there and here. We are constantly moving between here and there, between inside and outside. This is the reason for our basic restlessness, or fundamental anxiety, which plants and animals do not have. Only human beings are not "just as they are."

D. T. Suzuki often spoke of "suchness" or "as-it-is-ness." Plants and animals are living in their "suchness." But we human beings are separated from our suchness, are never "just-as-we-are." So far as we are moving between here and there, between inside and outside, looking at ourselves in comparison with others, and looking at ourselves from the outside, we are always restless. This restlessness or anxiety is not something accidental to man, peculiar to certain individuals and not to others. It is not that some have this inner restlessness while others do not. Insofar as one is a human being, one cannot escape this basic anxiety. In fact, strictly speaking it is not that one *has* this anxiety, but rather that one *is* this anxiety.

How can we overcome this fundamental restlessness and return to suchness? To do so is the *raison d'être* and essential task of religion.

According to Genesis, whenever God created something, he "saw that it was good." When God created Adam and Eve, he blessed them and saw that they too were good. Are we to suppose that the term *good* in this context is meant in the merely ethical sense? I think not. When God saw that his creation was good, he was not referring to the merely ethical dimension. Rather he was indicating that all of creation was ontologically good, or, to use D. T. Suzuki's term, that all of creation is in "suchness."

God created a tree just as a tree, and saw that it was good: it is in "suchness" as a tree. He created a bird: it is really a bird, not a fish. When he created a fish, it is really a fish—very different from a bird. Everything is in its own "suchness." It was the same when he created Adam and Eve as it had been with plants and animals and other beings, Adam is really Adam, Eve is really Eve. Adam is good. Eve is good. They are just as they are, respectively and equally. They thus symbolize the original (true) nature of man.

But according to Genesis, Adam and Eve ate the fruit of knowledge—of the knowledge of good and evil. Does this indicate good and evil only in the ethical sense? In my view, the story illustrates far more than that. The eating of the fruit suggests the making of value judgments. You may say, for instance "Today we have good weather, but yesterday we had bad weather," or "This is a good road, but that one is bad." Here, the terms *good* and *bad* can be made to apply to the weather, the road conditions, etc. It is in this broader sense of knowing good and evil that the fruit of knowledge symbolizes the ability to make value judgments.

The ability to make value judgments is a quality unique to self-consciousness. With self-consciousness one can judge "This is good" or "That is bad," and so forth. In this way we make distinctions between this and that. We love this and hate that, pursue this and avoid that. Through this capacity for making distinctions, people come to be involved in attachments. Love is a positive attachment. Hate is a negative attachment. By making distinctions, we come to like some things and dislike others. And in this way we become attached to some things and reject others—rejection being the negative form of attachment. We are involved in and confined by our attachments. This is the result of having self-consciousness.

By means of self-consciousness we also make a distinction between ourself and others. As a consequence of this distinction, we become attached to the self, making ourselves the center of the world. We become involved in and limited by the distinction between self and others, the duality between love and hate, and so forth. Distinction turns into opposition, conflict and struggle as soon as the distinction becomes an object of attachment.

But this is not the state of man's original nature. As God saw, Adam is good and Eve is good, just as plants and animals in their original states are good. Fundamentally everything in the order of original creation is good.

Thus the question is: How can we return to that original goodness, our original suchness? Christianity, I think, has its own answer to this question. In Christianity self-consciousness—the result of eating the fruit of knowledge—is regarded as "sin," inasmuch as eating the fruit constitutes rebellion against the word of God, who said, "Thou shalt not eat." It is through the reunion of man and God by virtue of Jesus Christ's redemptive love that man can return to his original suchness. In Buddhism self-consciousness is regarded as "ignorance," inasmuch as in self-consciousness we lose the reality of "suchness," and are limited by our viewing of things in the universe from the outside. As such we even view ourselves from the outside. This outside view of ourselves constitutes the fundamental ignorance inherent in human existence.

Trying to grasp one's self by one's self from the outside may be likened metaphorically to a snake trying to swallow its own tail. When the snake bites its tail, it makes a circle. And the more it tries to swallow its tail, the smaller that circle becomes. When the snake carries this effort to swallow its own tail to its final conclusion, the circle turns into a small dot, until finally it must disappear into emptiness. In more concrete terms, the snake must die through its effort. As long as the human self *tries* to take hold of itself through self-consciousness (out of which feelings of inferiority, superiority, etc. develop), the human ego-self falls into an ever-deepening dilemma. At the extreme point of this dilemma, the ego can no longer support itself and must collapse into emptiness. When the attempt of self-consciousness to grasp itself is pressed to its ultimate conclusion, the human ego must die. The realization of no-self is a necessity for the human ego. Some individuals only come to realize the necessity of confronting this dilemma on their deathbed. Others may existentially intuit the need for resolving this dilemma while still quite young, and thus embark on a religious quest. In any event, the realization of no-self is a "must" for the human ego. We must realize that there is no unchanging, eternal ego-self.

In order to realize emptiness or suchness it is essential to face this dilemma and to break through it. This realization of emptiness is a liberation from that dilemma which is existentially rooted in human consciousness. Awakening to emptiness, which is disclosed through the death of the ego, one realizes one's "suchness." This is because the realization of suchness is the positive aspect of the realization of emptiness.

In this realization you are no longer separated from yourself, but are just yourself. No more, no less. There is no gap between you and yourself: you become you. When you realize your own suchness, you realize the suchness of everything at once. A pine tree appears in its suchness. Bamboo manifests itself in its suchness. Dogs and cats appear in their suchness as well. A dog is really a dog. No more, no less. A cat is really a cat. No more, no less. Everything is realized in its distinctiveness.

Then for the first time you come to understand the familiar Zen phrases: "Willows are green, flowers are red," or "The eyes are horizontal, the nose is vertical." Trees, birds, fish, dogs or cats—from the beginning they always enjoy their suchness. Only man has lost that suchness. He is in ignorance. Therefore he does not know the reality of human life and becomes attached to his life and fears his death. But when ignorance is realized for what it is through the realization of no-self, one may waken to "suchness," in which everything is realized in its uniqueness and particularity.

This is, however, not just a goal to be reached. It is rather the point of departure for life, for real activity, for "suchness" is the *ground* of both our being and the world. Not sometime in the future, but here and now we can immediately realize "suchness," because we are never separated from "suchness," not even for a moment. It is the ground to which we must return and from which we must start. Without the realization of suchness as our ground or point of departure, our life is restless and groundless. Once we return to that point of suchness, everything is realized in its distinctiveness. The distinctions between self and other, good and evil, life and death are *regrasped* in the new light of "suchness." It becomes then the real point of departure for our lives and our activity. However rich or poor in ability we may be, we display that ability in its fullness just as it is, without getting entangled in any feelings of inferiority or superiority. It does not matter whether your ability is grade three, grade five, or eight. You display your own power just as it is, at any given moment and according to any given situation, and can create something new. You can live your life really and fully, without creating conflict with others, so that every day becomes a good day. This is what is meant by the saying "Everything is empty."

III

What is Shin Buddhism?

15

SUZUKI TEITARŌ DAISETZ

Apropos of Shin*

When Bernard Leach, the great English ceramist, asked D. T. Suzuki to explain, in the context of his lifelong concentration on Zen, his later interest in Jōdo-Shinshū Buddhism, "the Road of the one, as contrasted to the Road of the many," Suzuki said, "If you think there is a division, you have not begun to understand—there is no dualism in Buddhism."

Indeed, during most of his life D. T. Suzuki pursued a scholarly interest in Shin Buddhism, stimulated by his teaching at a Shin institution, Otani University. In 1956 Higashi Honganji, one of the chief temples of Shin Buddhism, commissioned him to translate Shinran's monumental *Kyōgyōshinshō* ("Doctrine, practice, faith, and realization") for publication on the eight hundredth anniversary of Shinran's birth.

Throughout his career Dr. Suzuki stressed the essential oneness of Mahāyāna Buddhism as integrating Shin, surveying its development in the Mahāyāna tradition as it originated in India and developed after having been introduced into China, to reach its summit in medieval Japan. The symbols and concepts of Amida Buddha, the Buddha of Infinite Light (Amitābha) and of Infinite Life (Amitāyus), the forms of devotion and prayer (the "Vows") of the Pure Land, the distinction between self-power (*jiriki*) and other-power (*tariki*), the Nembutsu (invocation of Amida's name), the interpretation of the transfer of merit which distinguishes Shinran from Hōnen, all these arise for Suzuki from the universal religious awareness of the human race as such. This universally human intuition of the higher dimensions and potentialities of existence reflects the profundity, the essential mystery of human existence. He stresses the fundamental identity between Zen and Shin in basic thought patterns as well as in their ultimate goal.

In this posthumously published article D. T. Suzuki's lifelong concern with the problem of the self reappears, and is given a new angle in relation to Shin spirituality.

---

* "What Is Shin Buddhism?" *The Eastern Buddhist* V/2 (1972): 1-11.

Perhaps for us ordinary people the best approach to an understanding of Shin Buddhism is the psychological one, for the problem of consciousness is the one closest to us, and we all have a keen desire to know what constitutes this "self."

We talk of the self constantly; none of us know exactly what it is, and yet we seem to understand each other. We talk so much about individuality and individual responsibility, legal as well as moral.

Here is a dish broken on the floor. Unless it fell from the table by itself, there must have been somebody or something that caused it to fall and break. If it was not swept away by the wind or some inanimate agency, a human hand must have touched it accidentally or intentionally. If it were a mere accident, there would be no one responsible for the breakage of the dish.

If a cat or a dog happened to jump onto the table, it would not be held responsible for the event. Even if it were a human being, we would not blame him if he were a mere baby or a little child. We might scold the child for its carelessness, but would not hold it responsible for the broken dish. Only if the human agent were fully grown and acted out of ill will would he have to bear reproach as a moral being fully conscious of what he had done.

What is this moral responsibility? Who is the moral being? Unless this question is fully settled, the very existence of our society may fall into ruin.

To be a moral being one must first of all have consciousness, without which one cannot be held responsible for anything one may do. To have consciousness means that one can stand away from oneself and be a critic of oneself, pass a judgment over what one thinks or does. This means further that the self divides itself into two in order to be conscious of itself: it divides itself into a doer and an onlooker.

To be moral, therefore, means that there must be a self, an individual agent who performs certain acts in full awareness of what he is doing. Because of this consciousness he is a moral individual and differs from the animal as well as from the child.

Now, psychologically speaking, what is this individual, this self, who does all these things?

The idea of self is closely associated with the idea of a substance. A substance is something that remains unchanged under changing appearances. Buddhism takes up this question: Is there really such an unchanging substance behind appearances? Is there really what we call a "self"—a self unchanging, permanent, eternally holding itself behind the kaleidoscopic shifting of events?

According to Buddhism, the existence of this kind of self substantially conceived is to be denied. In a Pali text entitled, "Questions of King Milinda," which records the dialogue taking place between King Milinda and Nāgasena, the Buddhist sage, we read of the king asking the sage what his name is, to which the sage answers: "Your majesty, I am called Nāgasena; my fellow priests address me as Nāgasena: but whether parents give one the name Nāgasena, or Sūrasena, or Vīrasena, or Sīhasena, it is nevertheless, your majesty, but a way of counting, a term, an appellation, a convenient designation, a mere name, this Nāgasena; for there is no ego here to be found."

Hearing this, the king is surprised and makes this declaration to those who are assembled: "Listen to me, my lords, ye five hundred Yonakas, and ye eighty thousand priests! Nāgasena here says thus: 'There is no ego here to be found.' Is it possible, pray, for me to assent to what he says?"

After this, he directly addressed Nāgasena: *"Bhante* Nāgasena, if there is no ego to be found, who is it then who furnishes you priests with the priestly requisites—robes, food, bedding, and medicine for the sick? Who is it who makes use of the same? Who is it who keeps the precepts? Who is it who applies himself to meditation? Who is it who realizes the paths, the fruits and *nirvāna?* Who is it who destroys life? Who is it who takes what is not given him? Who is it who commits immorality, who is it who tells lies? Who is it who drinks intoxicating liquor? Who is it who commits the five crimes that constitute 'proximate karma'?

"In that case there is no merit; there is no demerit; there is no one who does or causes to be done meritorious or demeritorious deeds; neither good nor evil deeds can have any fruit or result. *Bhante* Nāgasena, neither is he a murderer who kills a priest, nor can you priests, *bhante* Nāgasena, have any teacher, preceptor, or ordination."

He then continues, facing the question of non-ego directly: "When you say, 'My fellow priests, Your Majesty, address me as Nāgasena,' what then is this Nāgasena?"

The king then asks if his hair is Nāgasena, if his skin is Nāgasena, his flesh, his "sinews, bones . . . sensation, perception, predispositions, consciousness? . . ."

To all these questions Nāgasena gives a negative answer, whereupon the king expresses his utter bewilderment: *"Bhante,* although I question you very closely, I fail to discover any Nāgasena. Verily, now, *bhante,* Nāgasena is a mere empty sound. What Nāgasena is there here? *Bhante,* you speak a falsehood, a lie: there is no Nāgasena."

It is now Nāgasena's turn to bombard the king with questions; he asks him how he came here, by foot or by carriage. When the king answers a carriage, Nāgasena asks what a cart is, whether it is axle, pole, wheels, chariot body, banner staff, the reins, goading stick, and so on, until every part of the carriage has been mentioned. The king gives a negative answer to every question Nāgasena asks.

Nāgasena then concludes: the king is just as much a liar as he says Nāgasena is; for when the king is asked what is the carriage in which he came, he answers that there is after all no carriage.

> Even as the word "chariot" means
> That members join to frame a whole;
> So when the Groups [*skandha*] appear to view,
> We use the phrase, "A living being [a living entity]."[1]

What is known as the body, the fleshy body, is analyzable into so many elements, and these elements are reducible to atoms or electrons, and electrons can be expressed in a kind of mathematical formula. The body is after all a composite and the composition is likely to undergo all possible combinations. There is nothing permanent in this combination. The world is therefore said to be in a constant flux.

Now, turning to what is designated as the mind: Is there anything permanently remaining as such that might be called mind-substance or ego-substratum? The mind, which is sometimes called soul or spirit, and said to be something enduring even after the decomposition of the body, is nothing but a combination of sensations, feelings, images, ideas, and so on. When it is dissected into so many consciousness units, there is nothing in it that remains as mind or soul or ego. It is just like "Nāgasena" or "the cart": it is but a name, a concept that hides nothing behind it.

Thus all things are declared to be transient, impermanent, in a state of constant flux, subject to birth and death, and this statement is generally understood to be the Buddhist doctrine of non-ego, *anattā* or *anātman*; there is, however, a deeper notion of *ātman* to be found in Buddhism which does not require the denial of *ātman*.

What is then this self, the integrating principle of human consciousness? All we can affirm about it is that it cannot be made an object of thought, that it cannot be brought out into the ordinary field of consciousness. For if we tried to do that, the self would have to divide itself into a "self" and a "not-self," which means that the self would no more be the self. The self is somehow to be grasped by the self and yet not to bifurcate itself. How do we do that?

The reason why Buddhists deny the *ātman* and establish the so-called doctrine of non-ego is that the ordinary self as it is conceived is not the real self but a divided self, a postulated self, a concept presented to the relative field of consciousness. This is negated by Buddhism, for such a concept is just a name, a convenient way of fixing our attention to something. There is no substance corresponding to it, and therefore it is absurd to cling to it as such. The doctrine of non-ego, of *anattā*, is not just psychological, but aims at morally fortifying us against undue attachments to things not really worth clinging to.

What then is it, that which makes us so tenaciously cling to the notion of the self, to the reality of an individual existence, to the dignity of human personality? There must be something in us which really constitutes selfhood. While this cannot be brought out in the relative field of consciousness, there must be some way to take hold of it, to explain the reason for our tenacious clinging to it, and, more than that, to give satisfaction to our never-tiring search after the true "substance" which holds not only this relative self together but in fact moves the whole universe.

What is this self? How do we "interview" it? How do we come to know that it really constitutes the basis of our being? All religious quests converge on the solution of this most fundamental problem. Each religion has its own method of realization whereby the ultimate reality, the final self, the integrating principle is reached. Shin has its apparatus whereby the final goal is attained: on the one hand, *Amida*, his Original Vow, his Enlightenment, his Pure Land; and on the other, we sentient beings called *bompu* (*bāla* or *prithag-jana*), our limited existence which invites us to commit all kinds of evil deeds, to cherish all manner of delusory thoughts and desires.

The former is called *hō* and the latter *ki*. To revert to an earlier terminology, the *hō* is the absolute self while the *ki* is the relative, conceptual self. Shin teaches then that the *hō* and the *ki* are one and that when this is realized you know what the absolute self is, what Amida is, what his Pure Land is, what the destiny of human existence is, what the significance of life is. But there is one most important thing in this connection which ought not to be missed by any means. It is this: the oneness of *hō* and *ki* does not interfere with their duality; they are one and yet two, they are two and yet one. This doctrine is known as the doctrine of non-hindrance, or of interpenetration.

This doctrine may be better illustrated by practical examples. I quote some of the free verses composed by Asahara Saichi, one of the most remarkable Shin devotees of modern time. He died in 1933 and was a quite illiterate person who had somehow managed to write his thoughts in the *kana* style of writing as he meditated on his wonderful spiritual experience with all its richness and exuberance.

To him, as he is to all Shin followers, Amida was *oya-sama*. *Oya-sama* means both father and mother and represents their combined qualities, a very expressive term in Japanese.

> O Saichi, who is Nyorai-san?
> He is none other than myself.
> Who is the founder of Shin Buddhism?
> He is none other than myself.
> What is the canonical text?
> It is none other than myself.

> Saichi exchanges work with Amida:
> When Saichi worships Amida,
> Amida in turn deigns to worship Saichi.
> This is the way we exchange our work.
> How happy I am for the favor!

> I am lying,
> Amida deigns to worship me,
> I too in turn worship him.
> Namu Amida Butsu!
> What are you saying to *oya-sama*, O Saichi?
> I am saying "Amida-bu, Amida-bu."
> What is *oya-sama* saying? He is saying,

"O Namu, O Namu."
Thus thee to me, and I to thee:
This is the oneness of *ki* and *hō*.
Namu Amida Butsu!

This reminds one of the seventeenth-century Christian German mystical poet Angelus Silesius:

I know that without me
God can no moment live;
Were I to die, then he
No longer could survive.

I am as great as God,
And he is small like me;
He cannot be above,
Nor I below him be.

This feeling of oneness, however, does not prevent Saichi from cherishing another feeling, which is that of wretchedness and misery of his sinfulness. The oneness does not wipe out the separateness of Saichi from Amida, who is great and infinitely beyond him.

How miserable!
Saichi's heart, how miserable!
All kinds of delusion thickly arise all at once!
A hateful fire mixed with evils is burning.
The waves mixed with evils are rising,
How miserable! A fire mixed with follies is burning.

This heretic, how miserable!
Cannot you call a halt? Saichi's heart, worrying,
A heart in utter confusion,
Saichi's heart rising as high as the sky!

The Shin philosophy rationalizing this experience so as to satisfy our logical cravings is, as we can well see, full of subtleties and abstractions and is not at all easy for ordinary minds to comprehend.

From the practical and experiential point of view, we might say that the *ki* is what we earlier called the conceptually postulated ego occupying the relative field of consciousness. This ego or self has no substantial existence, nor do all the other things we see about us: a table, a cup, a house, a mountain. They may seem to be existing forever, retaining selfhood. But as we all know from experience, they have no permanency, they are subject to constant change. Those we saw yesterday are gone today, those we see today will be gone tomorrow. Besides, we are such frail things, just one flash of an atomic bomb and thousands of human souls vanish into nothingness. The earth is in fact filled everywhere with the dead. There is not a spot of ground where life has not once thrived. The proud kings and wise philosophers are equally subject to the dictates of *Yāma-rāja*, the King of Death, they are all annihilated as are the humble creatures we carelessly crush under our feet. The "ego" so arrogantly asserting itself and carrying its "head" and "body" so defiantly is laid low when anything goes wrong with it. These limbs considered "mine" no longer obey "my" commands and the corpse is left as feed for worms. The psychological or logical ego is destined to undergo an ignominious death.

Where is now that which symbolized the dignity of human personality, that which embodied moral responsibility, that which enjoyed all sensuous pleasures, that which stood so magnificently or so gracefully among its fellow beings?

There is nothing permanent in this world, all is transient. *Sarvam anityam.*

As far as our conscious ego, the conceptually posited ego, is concerned, there is nothing substantial in us. This ego is called by Shin philosophers *ki*, and is the product of *hakarai*, human reasoning.

Hō can never be reached by *hakarai*, by the process of reasoning, and unless *hō* is grasped, there is no cessation of pain (*duhkha*), no attainment of peace; we have to go on worrying, fearing, trembling.

The *hō* is the *ātman* itself, not the *ātman* reflected in the relative field of consciousness, but that which activates consciousness itself, making it seek after its own foundation in something beyond itself.

Our consciousnesses are like so many reflections of the moon in the sky, which casts its images wherever there is even a drop of water; the reflected image is in the wave-disturbed ocean, in the mountain lake serenely tracing its well-defined outline; it is also in the little puddle of water on the road after rain. Whatever their size and quality, they are no doubt all reflections of the same moon illuminating the three million universes. A Japanese poet sings:

> Each mirrors the moon in its own way,
> Each paddy field in every possible shape;

But lift your head and look up at the sky,
And see one eternal moon serenely shining!

This externally serenely shining moon is Amida, here termed *hō*.
He casts his shadow or likeness or image in every one of us, and we
are to take hold of the real one through the shadowy one in us. It is
indeed because of this shadowy one, or *hakarai*, that we feel an
urgent desire to come to the real one. The desire will never be
appeased until this is accomplished. The desire takes the form of
anxiety, worry, fear, vexation, *Angst*.

Psychotherapy with all its varieties of psychic treatment will never
be effective until the real moon is taken hold of, for no amount of
psychic maneuver will enable one to break through the relative field
of consciousness. The fact that there are so many schools of psychotherapy—all well patronized by present-day Americans—shows
the desperate need for the Buddhist treatment, which, disregarding
all unnecessary paraphernalia and superficialities, reaches directly
to the root of the trouble.

The integrating principle of consciousness that takes it to its
deepest bedrock is "namu Amida Butsu"—in this the oneness of *ki*
and *hō* is embodied: *namu* is *ki* and Amida Butsu is *hō*.

If we call it a mystery, the mystery of namu Amida Butsu is utterly beyond human reasoning; however much *hakarai* we may bring to
bear on it, we can never analyze this mystery, for what we can reach
by *hakarai* does not go any deeper than the outer shell of things.
The mystery is to be experienced, and like every experience of really fundamental value, it eludes rationalistic analysis.

In namu Amida Butsu, we experience the oneness of *ki* and *hō*,
the oneness of the relative self and the absolute self.

Let us go back to Saichi again and listen to his personal experience of "namu Amida Butsu," which might help save us from
indulging in *hakarai*, ratiocination. Saichi uses here the word *taste*,
which is quite expressive, and it is interesting to find that a Jewish
mystic also uses this word. In this poem Saichi, as is common among
Shin devotees, uses *Nembutsu* and *namu Amida Butsu* interchangeably.

"O Saichi, tell us what kind of taste is namu Amida Butsu,
Tell us what kind of taste is the taste of namu Amida Butsu."
    "The taste of namu Amida Butsu is:
A joy filling up the bosom,
A joy filling up the liver,

Like the rolling swell of the sea—
No words—just the utterance: Oh, Oh!"
Namu Amida Butsu is not just one undifferentiated oneness, it
moves in two directions: the *ki* way and the *hō* way. Saichi is fully conscious of this:

"How wretched!
The Nembutsu of wretchedness
And the Nembutsu of gratitude.
O Saichi, are there two kinds of Nembutsu?
No, not necessarily two;
Only, one Nembutsu working in two ways."

"O Saichi, let me have what your understanding is."
"Yes, yes, I will:
How miserable, how miserable!
Namu Amida Butsu, namu Amida Butsu!"
"Is that all, O Saichi?"
"It will never do."
"Yes, yes, it will do, it will do.
According to Saichi's understanding
Ki and *hō* are one:
Namu Amida Butsu is none other than Saichi himself.
This is indeed Saichi's understanding:
He has flowers in both hands,
Taken away in one way and given as gift in another way."

This passage is somewhat mixed with reasoning and is not as
good as the one that follows:

Namu Amida Butsu
Is like the sun god,
Is like the world,
Is like the great earth,
Is like the ocean!
Whatever Saichi's heart may be,
He is enveloped in emptiness of space,
And emptiness of space is enveloped in namu Amida Butsu.
O my friends, be pleased to hear namu Amida Butsu—
Namu Amida Butsu that will liberate you from *jigoku* [your private
hell].

NOTES

1. *Buddhism in Translation*, trans. Henry Clarke Warren, Harvard Oriental Series, vol. 3 (Cambridge, Mass.: Harvard University Press, 1922), pp. 129-33.

16

SOGA RYŌJIN

Dharmākara Bodhisattva*

Soga Ryōjin (1875-1971) served for a number of years as president of Otani University, the foundation of which was laid by Kiyozawa Manshi, the great reformer of Shin Buddhism without whose work modern Pure Land Buddhism is unthinkable. The essay reprinted here appeared originally in *The Eastern Buddhist* as a reconstruction of Soga's writings in Japanese by professors Itō Emyō and Bandō Shōjun. Here, in order to make it more accessible to the general reader, it has been somewhat abridged and especially simplified by omitting some of the Sanskrit terminology.

Soga's essay convincingly places Pure Land Buddhism in the mainstream of the Mahāyāna tradition, elucidates its centrally important concept of *ālayavijñāna*, the Store Consciousness expounded by the Vijñānavādins of the Mind-Only school, and retelling the Dharmākara myth in relation to this all-important concept, to end with the extraordinarily noble and moving expression of Shin spirituality in the form of the author's personal credo which sustained him throughout his long life.

Particularly noteworthy in this essay is Soga's exposition of the nature of the Dharmākara concept and his clear distinction between the historical and transhistorical functions of respectively the Teacher and the Savior.

I

Since, in the sixth century, Buddhism came to Japan, it has undergone gradual modifications, adapting itself to changing historical and social situations, giving rise to a variety of schools and sects which embody characteristically Japanese expressions of faith. Some of these now belong to history and are past cultural assets of Japan, after fulfilling their respective missions as living religions. Other schools, however, survived and are still sources of religious

---

* "Dharmākara Bodhisattva," *The Eastern Buddhist* I/1 (1965): 64-78; reconstructed and adapted from Professor Soga's writings by Bandō Shōjun and Itō Emyō.

229

inspiration for our contemporaries. These include the Rinzai sect of Zen Buddhism, introduced in Japan by Eisai (1141-1215); the Sōtō sect of Zen Buddhism initiated by Dōgen (1200-1253); the Jōdo sect of Pure Land Buddhism founded by Hōnen (1133-1212); the Jōdo-Shinshū sect of Pure Land Buddhism of Shinran (1173-1262); and the Nichiren sect founded by Nichiren (1220-1282). All originated in the Kamakura period (1192-1333).

Whereas the term *Zen* is now known all over the world thanks mainly to the works of D. T. Suzuki, the Pure Land Buddhism of Hōnen and Shinran is undeservedly still almost a terra incognita.

Zen Buddhism teaches that we may work towards the realization of our potential Buddha-nature to attain, in a flash of enlightenment, the realization that all sentient beings are by nature Buddhas. According to Shingon Buddhism, on the other hand, we can become Buddhas with our earthly bodies through the practice of the three-fold mystical union of body, speech, and mind (*sammitsu kaji*). Tendai Buddhism teaches practices of concentration and contemplation; for Nichiren Buddhism the chanting of the formula "*namu Myō Hō Renge Kyō*" is an important spiritual discipline. But all these stress one's own efforts, one's self-effort (*jiriki*) as the way to attain *prajñā* (transcendental, undefiled wisdom), of realizing that Buddha-nature, that is the goal of all Buddhist disciplines. Jōdo or Pure Land Buddhism on the other hand teaches us to relinquish all self-effort and to place one's trust solely in the invocation of the name of "namu Amida Butsu" as the way to liberation by Amida, the Buddha of Infinite Light (Wisdom) and Eternal Life (Compassion), thereby stressing Other-Power (*tariki*).

Although the Pure Land faith has sometimes been criticized as being outside of the mainstream of Buddhism, its exponents, following Hōnen and Shinran, are deeply convinced that the Jōdo way is entirely faithful to the spirit of Mahāyāna Buddhism in its concern to enable all sentient beings to attain Buddhahood. It is their conviction that it is impossible for sentient beings to attain Buddhahood without realizing the depth of the Vow of Dharmākara Bodhisattva, designating the name given to Amida during his time of discipleship. All sentient beings equally endowed with a latent form of *prajñā*, and hence have the potentiality of becoming Buddhas, and it was Dharmākara's Vow to awaken all sentient beings to their innate *prajñā*. *Prajñā* itself becomes manifest as faith, and is active in the practice of the invocation of the Nembutsu.[1]

To be saved by Amida therefore means to be awakened to the depth of the Vow of Dharmākara Bodhisattva. It should be explained here that the Dharmākara Bodhisattva of Pure Land doctrine is synonymous with the "Storehouse Consciousness," the *ālayavijñāna* of traditional Mahāyāna, as taught by the Vijñānavādins in particular. If it has been suggested that Pure Land Buddhism is not authentic Mahāyāna, and that it is closer to Christianity in advocating salvation by Amida, it must be pointed out that Amida is not a transcendent Other standing opposed to, and independent of, sentient beings. Amida is inherent in all sentient beings in his Bodhisattva manifestation as Dharmākara. Amida therefore is at once innate and transcendent. If *ālayavijñāna* and Dharmākara Bodhisattva are really one and the same it implies that the fundamental principle of Mahāyāna is here actualized as the realization in this world of the Infinite in personified form, so that salvation by Amida is not a heteronomous one by some transcendent Other, but a salvation attained the moment man is awakened to the depth of the Original Vow of Dharmākara. To be awakened to the depth of the Original Vow then means to attain the enlightened wisdom to know who one really is. Once awakened to the depth of the Original Vow, one shares in the enlightenment of Amida in the Pure Land—the transcendent realm—while yet remaining in this world of relativity: one's eventual attainment of Buddhahood is a certainty, is assured.

The discussion of Dharmākara Bodhisattva which follows will, I hope, make it clear that Pure Land Buddhism is rooted in the self-same soil as all schools of Mahāyāna; that it is truly a way to actualize the principle of Mahāyāna Buddhism in this life by the individual's affirmation of the Buddha's infinite wisdom and eternal compassion, and, moreover, that Pure Land Buddhism and Christianity differ in essence.

II

It may be recalled that the two major schools of Mahāyāna Buddhism are the Mādhyamika School of Nāgārjuna (second century C.E.), which expounds *śūnyatā* ("emptiness"), and the Yogācāra or Mind-Only school of Asanga and Vasubandhu (fifth century C.E.). The Mind-Only school teaches that what we regard as existing outside of ourselves is nothing but the differentiated forms of our consciousness in its unbroken continuity of transformation. The sole reality therefore is consciousness. The *Avatamsaka Sutra* states that the triple world is illusory and only the product of One Mind. In order to expound this teaching, the Vijñānavādins postulate beyond the six forms of consciousness of Theravāda Buddhism—eye, ear, nose, tongue, body, mind—a seventh and an eighth form in order to explain the whole structure of consciousness, for we continue to live even if the original six forms of consciousness cease. It is assumed then, that there are some forms of consciousness that function uninterruptedly even during deep sleep. *Manas* is therefore postulated as a kind of supraconsciousness which sustains our particular identity or ego. *Manas* generates the instinctive impulse to appropriate external objects as "mine," it takes things from the standpoint of "I" and "mine"; but according to this teaching even *manas* by itself cannot have illusions like "I" and "mine" without a further basis, and this basis is called *ālayavijñāna*, which never ceases to receive and store stimuli, all "things as they come." This "storehouse-consciousness" is the I in its most authentic sense. It is the most basic subjectivity capable of creating human life *per se*. It is the seed of the realization of salvation in this life. It is grasped, appropriated as it were, by *manas*. Still, it is the self-realization in the act of self-realizing itself. It is at once the principle of *avidyā*, primal ignorance, and of enlightenment. The actual world of ignorance is brought about by *ālayavijñāna*, but once aware of, awakened to, the process by which *ālayavijñāna* comes to be defiled, we are already on the way toward enlightenment. Enlightenment involves the dynamic process in which ignorance, *avidyā*, itself is infinitely subjected to penetrating insight.

Most probably *ālayavijñāna*, the basic principle of the Vijñānavādins, is the same reality that various Mahāyāna sutras and commentaries have tried to explain. For example, in the *Nirvāna Sutra* there appears the phrase, "Buddha-nature is eternal"; in the *Saddharmapundarīka Sutra* Bodhisattvas are depicted as springing up from beneath the earth; and in Ashvaghosha's *Awakening of Faith in the Mahāyāna*, we find expositions on *ālayavijñāna* with reference to the *Lankāvatāra Sutra* and the *Avatamsaka Sutra*.

The history of Buddhism shows, however, that the teaching of the Vijñānavādins, which leads to the transcendental wisdom of enlightenment by the transformation of illusory consciousness, has been understood only by an elect few of superior intelligence. Even if the doctrine were understood, it would be extremely difficult for ordinary people to actually practice it as taught, since the teaching of *ālayavijñāna* involves a system of practices relying upon self-effort (*jiriki*).

Therefore let us turn to the exposition of the *Larger Sutra of Eternal Life* on which the Pure Land doctrine is based and in which *ālayavijñāna* is described in terms of the relationship between Dharmākara Bodhisattva (the causal name of Amida) and sentient beings. In this sutra the philosophical concept of *ālayavijñāna* is presented in the personal form of Dharmākara Bodhisattva, with the purpose of making it clear that the Way by which Dharmākara attained Buddhahood is open to each and every sentient being whose spiritual life is rooted deep in *ālayavijñāna*, the Buddha-nature.

III

Dharmākara Bodhisattva is presented by the *Larger Sutra of Eternal Life* in the following myth: Innumerable aeons ago, the story begins, a Buddha called Dipankara appeared. After he had enlightened numberless people, he left the world. Dipankara was followed by fifty-three Buddhas—among them Kō-on (Far-Light), Gakkō (Moon-Light), Sendankō (Shining Sandalwood), and so forth—who appeared and disappeared in successive aeons. The narrative then turns to the time of the appearance of the fifty-fourth Buddha, Lokesvararāja, and tells of a certain king who upon hearing the preaching of Lokesvararāja was so profoundly touched that there sprang up in his mind an eagerness to seek supreme enlightenment. Forsaking his country as well as his royalty, he renounced the world, became a *srāmana* ("way-seeker") and called himself Dharmākara ("storehouse of Dharma"). His wisdom was superior, his resolution steadfast, and he was in every respect without peer among mortal men.

The Bhiksu Dharmākara faced the Buddha Lokesvararāja, saluted him in reverence with his palms respectfully held together, and praised the sublime virtues of the Buddha in verse, expressing his aspiration: "I wish to become a Buddha so as to deliver suffering beings. In order to fulfill my purpose, I wish to establish a land, pure and peaceful."

Thereafter he meditated for five kalpas until he realized that there was no other way but the teaching of "namu Amida Butsu": "I take refuge in the Buddha of Infinite Light (Wisdom) and of Eternal Life (Compassion) for sentient beings one and all to be delivered." Thereupon he expressed in forty-eight articles his Vow to realize the teaching of "namu Amida Butsu" (which are also known as the Forty-eight Vows), and epitomized them in this verse:

> I have now made a vow transcending the world. First of all, I shall become a Buddha myself, then I shall deliver each and every sentient being. This vow of mine shall reverberate throughout all the worlds, being embodied in the invocation of "namu Amida Butsu," to be heard by all people in all conceivable worlds. It shall be heard and believed.

As soon as Bhiksu Dharmākara had uttered this verse, the earth shook in six ways, divine flower petals fluttered down, heavenly music filled the air, and a voice was heard to say: "O Bhiksu Dharmākara, you are sure to attain the supreme enlightenment." Bhiksu Dharmākara thus made his vows after having gone through the severe practices required over innumerable kalpas so that he might fulfill his Original Vow, and finally fulfilled his prodigious vow to become Amida Buddha, the Buddha of Infinite Wisdom and Compassion.

This, in brief is the myth of Dharmākara. Its narration points to the profundity of the background from which the historical Sakyamuni Buddha appeared in the world.

It is generally accepted that Buddhism as such started with Sakyamuni Buddha. Indeed, all the scriptures which convey the message of Buddhism have appeared after Sakyamuni Buddha. Yet all Mahāyāna scriptures reflect the Buddha-Dharma prior to the historical Buddha, as the principle which made the manifestation of Sakyamuni as a historical person possible. The background of Sakyamuni's appearance, testifying to his transhistorical aspect, is what we find in the mythical narrative of the fifty-four Buddhas preceding him, and which is worked out in the *Larger Sutra of Eternal Life*. The historical Sakyamuni's preaching in the *Larger Sutra of Eternal Life* enables us to conceive of the Buddha-Dharma as pre-dating Sakyamuni.

Contemplating the profound background of his own experience of enlightenment, Sakyamuni successively encountered innumerable centers of light in eternity. Penetrating deeper and deeper into his being, Sakyamuni finally encountered Dharmākara Bodhisattva, whom he recognized as none other than his own primordial being for which he had long been searching....

IV

The *Larger Sutra of Eternal Life* therefore presents, as it were, a record of the preaching in which the historical Buddha describes the Buddha-Dharma prior to his own existence in terms of the myth of Dharmākara Bodhisattva. The doctrine of *ālayavijñāna* in the teachings of the Mind-Only School attempts to explain this Buddha-Dharma prior to Sakyamuni in philosophical terms. When we read the *Larger Sutra of Eternal Life* and the *Vijñaptimātratāsiddhi-śāstra*, we become aware of the profound aspirations in our own mind—springing up from *ālayavijñāna*—to become denizens of a world of truth and purity. Or rather, we become aware of this innermost aspiration as belonging to us as our birthright, as our very origin.

Although it may be clouded in waking consciousness by momentary impulses, this deeper aspiration flows along far beneath the surface and is indestructible.

The *Trimśikā* says that the *ālayavijñāna* is never being transformed, like a rushing torrent. It will manifest itself amidst illusory thoughts, break through all the forms of ignorance of sentient beings, and someday must fulfill all of their innermost aspirations.

The dynamism of our momentary impulses is caused by *manas*, the all-ignorant self-consciousness which takes hold of the basic *ālayavijñāna* as its own ego. *Ālayavijñāna* accepts all manner of differentiation and limitation as they come, yet never loses its identity. For as the ultimate subjectivity, *ālayavijñāna* is the eternal Mind itself, communing in the depths with all sentient beings, submerged as they may be in the darkness of ignorance or *avidyā*. This innermost Mind is none other than the aspiration expressed by Dharmākara Bodhisattva in the presence of the Buddha Lokesvararāja. It is none other than his Original Vow that declared: "O sentient beings in the ten directions! I shall never attain the Supreme Enlightenment until you are all delivered."

The text of the *Larger Sutra of Eternal Life* says that prior to his pronouncing of the Vows, Dharmākara Bodhisattva meditated for five kalpas, and that the perspective revealed to him was the very origin of our spiritual world: The utter darkness of ignorance in which from the beginningless past Dharmākara sits in profound and silent meditation is broken through by the Buddha's light of wisdom, representing the innermost aspiration of man, integral to the *ālayavijñāna*.

Dharmākara Bodhisattva rose up from the seat of his agelong meditation and set out on his kalpa-long journey. In other words, in accordance with the instruction of the Buddha Lokeśvararāja, his teacher, Dharmākara Bodhisattva stepped out into the life of practice for the benefit of all sentient beings. Here the Bodhisattva, for so long submerged deep in the bowels of the earth, emerges to the earth's surface to become truly the Bodhisattva, the one who walks the Way. This shows that he, before and above all others, becomes the one who practices the Nembutsu, the invocation of "namu Amida Butsu." The passage in the sutra relating Dharmākara Bodhisattva's five kalpas of meditation and the austerities he practiced for innumerable kalpas presents him as the primordial proclaimant of the Nembutsu. The *ālayavijñāna* illuminates the mystery of the realization of Dharmākara Bodhisattva, as the primordial proclaimant of the Nembutsu.

Many years ago I called the *ālayavijñāna*, this supraconsciousness in which all *dharma*s are stored, this "storehouse-consciousness," "Dharmākara-consciousness." For in the *Vijñaptimātratāsiddhi-śāstra* we find three interpretations of the meaning of *ākara* (literally a "mine," a "storage"): in the sense that *ālayavijñāna* is grasped by man as the real self it is a treasure house tightly guarded by its owner, but also it is a storehouse in the sense that *ālayavijñāna* contains the seeds of all things within itself, and once again it is a storage in the sense that *ālayavijñāna* "stores" (gathers) *karma*s of all kinds.

Here I should call attention to the fact that our fleshly body as such is the embodiment of *ālayavijñāna*, for not only does it refer to the consciousness that stores infinite potentiality, but also to our actual fleshly body. Consciousness and body are totally identified in *ālayavijñāna*. In fact, one's salvific self-realization as a person can only take place in the unity of consciousness and body. Salvation takes place only when one realizes this unity personally according to the teachings of Dharmākara Bodhisattva and *ālayavijñāna*. We then become completely aware of the reality we are living.

V

Some forty years ago, I wrote an article on the meaning of this reality. As my conviction expressed there has undergone little change, let me quote from it at some length:[2]

> It is not as if we sentient beings suddenly fell from heaven upon this earth. We are rooted deep in the earth. We have all sprung up out of the earth with a beginningless history behind us. Looking up towards heaven we feel lonely, but once turning our eyes to earth, we see there, high and low, a great panorama of solid mountains and winding rivers, we see numberless sentient beings moving about. Each movement they make springs up, so to speak, from beneath the earth and then returns to the depths of the earth. The function of the earth always unfolds itself through sentient beings. When we dig into the earth, we shall find the spirit of sentient beings identical with those found upon earth; the earth with her mountains and rivers is none other than the actual body of my universal self. Undoubtedly, it was to this fact that the fabulous description in the *Larger Sutra of Eternal Life* alludes, namely, that as soon as Dharmākara Bodhisattva expressed his aspirations, the earth shook in six ways and flower petals fell from heaven. We need to penetrate into our own body in deep contemplation, to see the primordial man. There we must see the original man, and realize explicitly that this fleshly body is none other than the actual manifestation of our fundamental self.
>
> Indeed, various kinds of sinful deeds are committed because of this physical body. All defilements, such as ignorance, craving, anger, and so forth are rooted in this physical body. Therefore, if it were not for this fleshly body, all defilements would lose their foundation and no problem would arise in this life; nay, this life itself would have never existed. Where there is no physical body, there is no actual self. But in spite of the fact that it affords a foundation for all defilements, there is no reason, I believe, that we should curse this body. For the reason that all defilements arise is that this body, disturbed by the external world of senses, is unaware of the true subjectivity upon which the external depends. This physical body ever haunted by defilements is as it were the outward crust of that pure subjectivity. The actual body testified to by the heartfelt declaration of the fundamental subjectivity, "Here I am!"[3] is by nature pure and spotlessly undefiled.

In this undefiled body, within each sentient being, is stored up the ancestral heritage of the "teaching" from time immemorial. Each action and each movement we make is done on the command of this teaching, of which we are not conscious. The succession of sentient beings from time immemorial is for us a teaching of naturalness. The inner experiences of our ancestors all constitute a teaching of which we are usually not conscious. We are expected to go our respective ways, being ever urged on, encouraged by this implicit teaching. Is there anybody on earth who has learned from others how to beget a child? The preservation of life which is transmitted from parents to children is one of the teachings implicit in the world of the unconscious from time immemorial, prior to our birth. We are born with this mysterious sutra in our hand! Nay, our birth itself was brought about by this sutra.

Tathāgata, the eternal Buddha, wrote a living sutra on paper made of his skin, with a brush made of his bones, and with ink made of his blood. The sutra is this very physical body of mine. The *Larger Sutra of Eternal Life*, in which the eternal Buddha expressed his experiences through Sakyamuni, the incarnate, in terms of his life, is the sutra of this body. It is only through this teaching of Sakyamuni that we are made to acknowledge in faith the Original Vow of Bodhisattva Dharmākara, the causal figure of Amida. Accepting Sakyamuni as the revealer of the teaching, we are able to hear the inner voice of the sutra which is our physical body itself.

VI

The teaching of the *Larger Sutra of Eternal Life* is, I would venture to say, that we should hear in this pure and undefiled physical body of ours the voice of Dharmākara Bodhisattva, the self-declaration of the Original Vow. Thus Vasubandhu, who composed the verses expressing his aspiration for birth in the Pure Land (the *Gwanshō-ge*) in accordance with the teaching of the *Larger Sutra of Eternal Life*, confesses at the outset of these verses: "O world-honored one, single-mindedly I take refuge in the Buddha of unobstructed Light shining throughout the ten directions [Amida], and I wish to be born in the Land of Peace [Amida's Pure Land]." In calling Sakyamuni "world-honored one," he expresses his wish to be enlightened through the way of "namu Amida Butsu," that is, by taking refuge in the Buddha of unobstructed Light shining throughout the ten directions.

As the above passage makes evident, we must not be confused about the difference between a "teacher" and a "savior." Shinran taught us clearly to distinguish between the two, thereby correcting the grave mistake of taking a single historical person as a savior. Sakyamuni-centered Buddhism or Jesus-centered Christianity is religiosity of a servile kind. We must always remember the great primordial subjectivity, the fundamental subjectivity which underlies the reality which gave rise to Sakyamuni and Jesus Christ.

Those enlightened predecessors of ours to whom we look up as ideals are all historical characters. They are the projections of our respective ideals. They may indeed be our idealized teachers, but they are by no means our saviors, for the real savior is not some idealized historical character but the universal self—that fundamental self in which our true self is based. The real savior is Dharmākara Bodhisattva, who does not exist apart from this physical body of mine as the fundamental subjectivity. Manifesting himself in phenomenal bodies, Dharmākara Bodhisattva becomes the living witness to his own reality, thus depriving all futile arguments, illusions, dogmatisms, superstitions, doubts, controversies, and so forth, of their foundations. He can therefore be called a real savior, for he guides our life to its truth.

Sakyamuni is our teacher, master, father, and ideal. Dharmākara Bodhisattva, however, is the real person whom we can directly experience, for he is our own eternal actuality. The preaching of our teacher Sakyamuni urges us to hear the voice of Dharmākara Bodhisattva, that clarifies for us the way by which we are to return to the undefiled, pure self.

Consequently, my understanding of Shinran and the Jōdo-Shinshū School's doctrine is that it teaches us to realize the way to become a Buddha, and that it does so initially by pointing to the difference between "teacher" and "savior."

VII

To repeat, the Dharmākara Bodhisattva as he appears in the *Larger Sutra of Eternal Life* is the personification of *ālayavijñāna* as taught in the *Vijñaptimātratā* doctrine. This should make it evident that in the first place, Pure Land Buddhism is rooted in the soil shared by all other Mahāyāna schools. Secondly that Dharmākara Bodhisattva as a personal realization that is one with the fleshly body shows that salvation as taught by Pure Land Buddhism is a universal way, accessible to all, to realize the Mahāyāna ideal that each and every sentient being becomes a Buddha. In the third place, in spite of superficial resemblances between Pure Land Buddhism and Christianity, Dharmākara Bodhisattva clearly points to the qualitative distinction between them. For Dharmākara Bodhisattva is at once innate to and transcendent over all sentient beings, and fulfills his Original Vow, liberates all sentient beings through his becoming Amida. In other words, sentient beings are saved by accepting in faith the aspiration of Dharmākara Bodhisattva, at once transcendent and innate.

I should stress that I have confined myself to drawing attention to those points of doctrine regarding the nature of Dharmākara Buddha which, I believe, represent the basic theme which characterizes explicitly the nature of Pure Land Buddhism for those inside and outside of the Mahāyāna tradition.

NOTES

1. Namu Amida Butsu: "I take refuge in the Buddha of Infinite Light (Wisdom) and Eternal Life (Compassion) for sentient beings one and all to be delivered."

2. *Kyūsai to Jishō* ("Salvation and Self-realization"), pp. 163-74.

3. Self-declaration of the fundamental subjectivity as it is awakened to itself.

17

KIYOZAWA MANSHI
The Great Path of Absolute Other-Power*

It seems fitting to offer as a coda for this book the short but powerful document taken from Manshi's personal journal, *Rōsenki*, slightly edited by his disciple Tada Kanae. It is a statement many Shin Buddhists can still recite by heart as a profession of their faith.

Kiyozawa Manshi, that great and tragic figure, was born in 1863 and died at the age of forty. During his short but extremely intensive lifetime he revealed Shin Buddhism—which in the beginning of the Meiji period (1868-1912) had been looked down upon as a primitive faith for ignorant country bumpkins and hence unworthy of serious philosophical interest— to be as profound a manifestation of the human spirit as any, and as fully integrated in the heritage of the authentic Mahāyāna tradition. Kiyozawa, who graduated in religious philosophy from Tokyo University, found in Shin a spiritual treasure house of universal significance, a significance far transcending Japan's territorial borders, provided it could be freed from limitations imposed on it by its rigidly feudal past.

At the outset his efforts caused such hostile reactions that he was excommunicated from the Higashi Honganji branch of the Shin sect. He withdrew from academic life, immersed himself in the meditation of the Āgama Sutras, subjected himself to extraordinary austerities, and found in the Greek Stoic thinker Epictetus' "Do not be affected by anything" the stimulus he needed to find the detachment, the peace of mind he had searched for. His extreme asceticism, however, had ruined his health and made him the victim of the tuberculosis which would cause his early death. Meanwhile, in 1899, three years before he was to die, he was not only fully rehabilitated by Higashi Honganji but entrusted with the organization of the college which was to develop into the distinguished Otani University, Kyoto.

---

* "The Great Path of Absolute Other-Power," trans. James W. Heisig, from Kiyozawa's collected works.

With the group of disciples that gradually had gathered around him, he founded *Seishin Kai* ("Spiritual World"), a monthly which exerted considerable influence on Japanese Buddhism. By 1902 his health had deteriorated to such an extent that he had to withdraw from all his functions and return to his home temple in Aichi Prefecture, where he died in 1903.

He was revered as a teacher, and the austere character of his teaching sheds light on the man, as his great disciple Haya Akegarasu describes it in *Shout of Buddha* (Chicago: Orchid Press, 1977): "What did I learn from my teacher? Nothing! He took everything away from me. When I became attached to what he was saying, he took it away from me. By meeting him I had taken everything away from me.... He crushed and crushed and completely crushed me.... He never let one hang on to anything. And that was his theory of teaching Buddhism.... After he died, people called me a heretic, but I am not good enough to have a heresy, because I have nothing. There is no Pure Land or Zen or Buddhism or philosophy. Nothing to hang on to. Nothing controls me. I was raised as a real, free man. And I am deeply grateful...."

I

The self. Resting its trust in the wondrous works of the Absolute and Infinite, it takes things just as they are and lets go. It makes a place for itself in whatever surroundings it happens to be. That is what the self is. Merely that and nothing more.

It simply rests its trust in the Absolute and Infinite. So it has no need to be worried about the matter of life and death. And with that worry behind it, how much easier it gets for matters of lesser moment! Exile? Imprisonment? They can be put up with. Slander, contempt, insults of every sort—why let them get to us? Better to enjoy what the Absolute and Infinite has allotted us.

II

The countless myriads of events that make up the cosmos all belong to the wondrous doing of the one Great Miracle. And yet we take the whole spectacle as if it were quite ordinary and matter of course. The reverence and esteem it ought to inspire in us is stillborn. As if we had no thoughts, no feelings, we let things stop there. But here we are, endowed with thoughts and feelings and we just cut them short. If we keep doing that sort of thing, what is to prevent us from falling into perversion?

The glow of a color, the fragrance of a scent, these things can never come to be of their own power. They cannot exist without relying on the power of the one Great Miracle. And not only color and fragrance, but what of this self of ours? Wherever that self might have come from, and wherever it might be finally headed, it is not within the power of our will to sway it the slightest bit from its course. What *was* before life and what *will be* after death are not ours to control. We cannot even control the coming to be and passing away of a fleeting thought that passes through our mind. The hand of the Other-Power has us absolutely in its palm.

III

One day we shall die. But even in dying we do not simply pass away. For we are more than just life—death, too, is ours. Life and death have their being together in us, yet life and death do not hold sway over us. We exist in spirit apart from life and death.

This does not mean that we are free to fix life and death as we will. Our life and death depend on the wondrous workings of an Other-Power that is Miracle through and through. So it is not for us to grieve or to rejoice in the face of life and death. And if this is so for life and death, how much more so for all the other things that come and go. Better we should simply stand in awe of the works of this wondrous Other-Power among all the myriad events of the cosmos.

IV

Neither to ask nor to seek. Is there something you lack? If you think something is lacking to you, why would not that be due to your unbelief?

Has not the Tathāgata allotted you everything you need? And, supposing even that something be lacking in these gifts, could something else ever possibly satisfy you?

Perhaps you suffer because you imagine that something is wanting in you. If so, you have to learn to go on cultivating yourself and to find repose in the Great Life of the Tathāgata. To ask others for it or to seek it from others is disgraceful and beneath you. It is an insult to the Great Life of the Tathāgata. The Tathāgata may be beyond insults, but what of the suffering it brings on you?

V

Where is it, this Infinite Other-Power? You may see it in what you yourself have received. Everything you have received is an apparition of the Infinite Other-Power. Honor it. Treasure it. And be grateful for the Great Blessing of the Tathāgata.

In order to fill up what is wanting, a man chases after things outside of himself and follows the way of other men when he should be trying to be sufficient to himself. Isn't this getting things backward?

Chasing after outer things is the wellspring of greed. Following the way of other men is the wellspring of wrath.

VI

How does one cultivate oneself? It is said one must reflect on the self and gain insight into the Great Path. Once you have seen into the Great Path, you shall never know want among the things the self possesses. And once you feel no want among the things of the self, you will not seek anything from others. Once you no longer seek what belongs to others, you will have no cause for strife with others. Fulfilled in the self, seeking nothing, and contending with no one. Is there anything anywhere under heaven mightier than that? Is there anything anywhere more encompassing? In this way alone the Great Cause of independent freedom will be lifted up for the world of men to see.

A self like that is beyond harm from other things and other people. To be obsessed with getting hurt is to stray into delusion. Let all such fantasies be swept away!

VII

The independent man stands ever firm atop the boulder of life and death. From the start he is always ready for death by slaying or starvation.

From the first he is ready for being slayed or being starved. He takes food and clothing, if there is any to be had. If there is none he goes on to his death with calm.

Should he be the head of a household, however, he should first see to the food and clothing of his wife and children. He should lay aside concern for himself and first provide them with what he has. What is left over he can then use to feed and clothe himself. But one thing he should not trouble himself over: how they are to be fed and clothed in case he dies. In such matters, it is enough to have confidence in the Great Path of Absolute Other-Power. That Great Path will see that they are never abandoned. Somehow or other they will find a way to care for their food and clothing. And if not, it is because the Great Path wills for them to die. Let them submit to their lot. As Socrates said: "When I was in Thessaly, away from home, Heaven was gracious enough to sustain my family through the magnanimity of others. Even if I were to go to a faraway land now, how could Heaven fail to look after them?"

Biographical Notes

FREDERICK FRANCK was born in the Netherlands in 1909 and began his career as an oral surgeon before moving more seriously to his artistic pursuits in the 1930s. Between 1958 and 1961 he served as a doctor on the staff of the renowned missionary and humanitarian Albert Schweitzer in Africa. In 1962 Franck was the only artist invited to draw at all four sessions of the Second Vatican Council in Rome, and for his efforts was awarded a medal by Pope John XXIII shortly before the pontiff's death.

Frederick Franck's sculpture and artwork are amongst the permanent collections of the Museum of Modern Art, the Whitney Museum, the Tokyo National Museum, and other public and private collections. He is the author of over thirty books, including *The Zen of Seeing* (1973), and the award-winning *Pacem in Terris: A Love Story* (2000). He is the editor of *What Does it Mean to be Human* (2001), also translated into Spanish and Chinese. He was recently honored with the World Citizenship Award by the Nuclear Age Peace Foundation. Queen Beatrix of the Netherlands knighted him Officer of Orange-Nassau in 1994.

Franck, now age 94, lives with his wife Claske at their estate, Pacem in Terris, located in Warwick, NY. Pacem in Terris is equally dedicated to Angelo Roncalli (Pope John XXIII), Albert Schweitzer, and Daisetz T. Suzuki. Franck says of his home: "Pacem in Terris is not tied to any particular religion, but to all ... and to none. For I hope that it may speak also to those who, while shunning religious labels, share fully in the specifically human quest for meaning and for values to live by. For to be human or not to be, that is the question!"

JOAN STAMBAUGH is Professor of Philosophy at the City University of New York. She is the author of several works dealing with Buddhist and Existentialist topics, including *Impermanence is Buddha-Nature: Dogen's Understanding of Temporality* (1990), *The Other Nietzsche* (1994), and *The Formless Self* (1999). Dr. Stambaugh is in the process of translating the major works of the renowned German Existentialist philosopher Martin Heidegger into English. Her translations of Heidegger's *Being and Time* (1996), *Identity and Difference* (2002), *On Time and Being* (2002), and *The End of Philosophy* (2003) have all been received with critical acclaim.

Index

For a glossary of all key foreign words used in books published by World Wisdom, including metaphysical terms in English, consult:
www.DictionaryofSpiritualTerms.org.
This on-line Dictionary of Spiritual Terms provides extensive definitions, examples and related terms in other languages.

Titles in the Spiritual Classics Series by World Wisdom

Titles on Buddhism by World Wisdom

The Buddha Eye: An Anthology of the Kyoto School and Its Contemporaries,
edited by Frederick Franck, 2004

A Buddhist Spectrum, by Marco Pallis, 2003

The Essential Shinran: A Buddhist Path of True Entrusting,
edited by Alfred Bloom, 2007

The Golden Age of Zen: Zen Masters of the T'ang Dynasty, by John C.H. Wu, 2003

Honen the Buddhist Saint: Essential Writings and Official Biography,
edited by Joseph A. Fitzgerald

An Illustrated Outline of Buddhism: The Essentials of Buddhist Spirituality,
by William Stoddart, 2013

The Laughing Buddha of Tofukuji: The Life of Zen Master Keido Fukushima,
by Ishwar C. Harris, 2004

Living in Amida's Universal Vow: Essays in Shin Buddhism,
edited by Alfred Bloom, 2004

Naturalness: A Classic of Shin Buddhism, by Kenryo Kanamatsu, 2002

*Samdhong Rinpoche, Uncompromising Truth for a Compromised World:
Tibetan Buddhism and Today's World,* edited by Donovan Roebert, 2006

The Shin Buddhist Classical Tradition: A Reader in Pure Land Teaching, Volume 1,
edited by Alfred Bloom

The Shin Buddhist Classical Tradition: A Reader in Pure Land Teaching, Volume 2,
edited by Alfred Bloom

Treasures of Buddhism, by Frithjof Schuon, 1993

The Way and the Mountain: Tibet, Buddhism, and Tradition, by Marco Pallis, 2008

Zen Buddhism: A History, Volume 1: India and China,
by Heinrich Dumoulin, 2005

Zen Buddhism: A History, Volume 2: Japan,
by Heinrich Dumoulin, 2005